Wacky America Before the Internet:
Join the Club!

*Hundreds of Crazy Clubs from
the Church of Beaver Cleaver to
the Vampire Studies Society*

Todd Greenwood
and
Ruth Greenwood

Wacky America Before the Internet:
Join the Club!

Copyright 2020, Todd Greenwood

Authors can be contacted at:
Todd_author@yahoo.com

To all the dreamy procrastinators
who found their perfect pragmatic doers

TABLE OF CONTENTS

PREFACE

In 1987 I set out to write a book called *Join the Club!* The idea (to write something interesting about the oddest clubs in America) was spawned after perusing the *Encyclopedia of Associations,* an amazing compendium. Although I had never written or published anything before, I found a publisher, received a fairly nice advance, and then went ahead sending out letters to the clubs. We received piles of mail. Fascinating mail.

After about six months of typing on our brand new Macintosh 512K, with editing and rewriting from my wife, the book was complete. I sent it off to the publisher in Chicago. They sent back the cover art for my approval. The title was entered in the ISBN database and appeared in *Books in Print.* We waited! And then we heard the news: the publisher had gone belly-up. No book.

"Someone else will want it," my mother said.

"Find another publisher," my wife said.

But I didn't.

Printouts from the book got put into a box, and that box was moved to Santa Rosa, San Francisco, Indiana, Michigan, and then New Jersey. It lay on the top shelf of my office in a place far beyond human hands until Christmas 2019. Then I opened it up to show my son (who is nearly as old as I was when I wrote *Join the Club!*) The pages were incomplete. Chapters were missing. But at the bottom of the box were three floppy disks: Disk 1, Disk 2, and Disk 3. I sent them away to a service found on the internet and a few days later I was reunited with my book, now 33 years old.

A lot has happened in 33 years, a third of a century. Fair to say that this book wouldn't be written today. That Mac 512K that we bought with our wedding money was the beginning of something quite extraordinary that has changed the world. Personal computing was an essential ingredient in the birth of the internet.

But there is no internet in this book. It is a snapshot of a time when people connected with each other in a corner bar, in a meeting room, or they felt connected because a monthly newsletter slipped through their mail slot.

The internet has changed the very nature of "joining." Our expectations are very different. Instead of sending an envelope containing a check for five dollars in return for a welcome letter and a monthly newsletter, we no longer expect to wait a month to hear from our club. Online bulletin boards, then communities, then Yahoo Groups and Facebook Groups have eliminated the barriers to entry. They are free. All you need to do is declare your honest interest and you have joined. Our club members are on our smartphones. In 1987, you wrote, or you telephoned, and most of the time you waited patiently.

Of the more than 1000 clubs and associations in this book, about 250 are still active as traditional dues paying organizations, as of January 2020. Many more still exist somewhere online. Others have simply disappeared. Most fan clubs have gone online, as have quirky special-interest groups. However, for those who find pride and meaning in the rare and exotic (be it cars, pets, or collectables), traditional clubs for their interests are often still alive and kicking. No doubt this because the desire to belong to something exclusive and to come together with others who share your passion is an unquenchable human desire.

This book reflects a time and a place: America in 1987, when might and dominance of the United States were intact and untarnished. The Soviet Union was on life support. China was an infant in its transformation from a rural economy to a global economic steamroller. Although some of the clubs in this book, such as the International Stop Continental Drift Society and the International Jugglers Association, say "International," they are squarely located in US territory. The very idea of internationalism that is so much part of our 24-hour, never-off, connected world was just emerging. CNN was only a few years old. The first trans-Atlantic fiber-optic cable hadn't yet been laid. There were perhaps fewer than 12 communications satellites in orbit in 1987. Thirty-three years later, the skies are filled with more than 2,000, each able to carry hundreds of thousands of times more data.

Looking at this book, with its collection of weird and wonderful associations, feels nostalgic. It may suggest a simpler time when joining something was a simple declaration of interest and curiosity. The overlays of political affiliation, race, sex, and political correctness seem to only whisper up from the pages.

But perhaps it wasn't so innocent. My wife and I lived in NYC's West Village then, only a few blocks from Christopher Street. Each day in the mid-'80s we saw signs of how the world around us was reeling. Stores were closing. We lost good friends. Went to funerals of people barely out of their teens. And we were outraged that then-President Reagan didn't acknowledge the AIDS crisis or the existence of the gay and lesbian community.

Yes. In 33 years many things have changed, but what hasn't is our need to belong and, in a complicated world, to find others who share our interests. With that in mind, there is a sweetness in publishing this book myself. Screw the publishing house, it's DONE! Let the world learn the truth about the Dicks of America and the National Chimney Sweep Guild (whose motto is "Don't make an ash of yourself.")

On a personal note, I want to say that I'm happy to still be here to publish this book. To have my family to share it with. To be able to give a copy to my parents, who have stood by me every day

of my life. To my sister, who always brings laughter and intellect, my
children, who make me proud of their fierce independence and
creative might. But most of all, the person who went on this
adventure, and so many others over the last 35 years of marriage. I
love you, Ruth.

Todd Greenwood
January 2020

INTRODUCTION

So, you're a redheaded tuba player? A flying funeral director? A S.O.B. with a Th.D.? Good news...you're not alone...JOIN THE CLUB! No matter how wacky your hobby is, how offbeat your occupation, how strange your politics are, somewhere in America there's a club president ready to sign your new I.D. cards, making you an official "Friend of Calamari" or "Hatpin Collector." Americans do funny and unusual things, and love to invite a whole group to share in their consuming passions.

We've been asked how this book came into being...Todd was skimming down a list of associations, while researching a business project and came across "The Fred Society" and "The California Depopulation Society." Two wonderfully silly clubs. He came home wondering, "Why doesn't somebody write about all these odd groups?" As a dutiful inventor's wife, Ruth said, "It's a great idea-- why don't you do it?" And, lo, thousands of letters, postcards, and phone calls later, it was done. We've worn out two mailmen, tested our marriage, and nearly melted our Macintosh...but rounding up this cast of 1000+ has been fun.

Yes, Virginia, there *are* a lot of wackos out there (Todd gets letters from a rabid anti-circumcisionist who fills all the margins of his densely-written missives with rubber stamp messages. We decided that the sanity of the sender is in inverse proportion to the amount of type they can cram onto a page.) But, there are many more goodhearted club presidents who xeroxed their file cabinets for us, sent irreplaceable books and photos, and gave great interviews on the phone. (Ruth got to talk to the #1 Jim Smith!)

Know of any unusual clubs we may have missed? Write to us at todd_author@yahoo.com, and we'll include them in future editions. (Note: while we can't guarantee the response you'll get from the groups listed here, we'd love to hear about your favorites.)

We send a big thank you to all of the club presidents and secretaries who responded so warmly to our inquiries. Thanks also to everyone who sent in club information after reading the newspaper articles about the book.

Todd Greenwood & Ruth Rosen
June 1, 1987

WHO WE ARE!

People like people who are like them--be they tall, short, lefthanded or just named Fred. Birds of a feather flock happily below.

Absent-Minded Club

112 S. Woodward Ave., Birmingham, MI 48011   (313) 644-7060
Founded: 1982   Members: 38
Dues: $15.00 lifetime membership   Contact: Bob Gwynn

Never be embarrassed for forgetting someone's name again-- just say, the club's standard greeting "Hello Colleague" and that person with "the familiar face" upon hearing the word "Colleague" will be tipped-off to your dilemma.

The Absent-Minded Club Lament starts:

"I know your face but there it ends,
And still I know we're more than friends.
Your name is one I should recall
If I remembered names at all."

Abundantly Yours

PO Box 151134, San Diego, CA 92115
Founded: 1978   Members: 2200
Dues: Write for details   Contact: Joyce L. Rue

"The time has come to lighten up on ourselves." Abundantly Yours is "not about losing weight and it's not about *not* losing weight"; its members strive to accept themselves and strive to feel proud of who they are, regardless of how others see them. The group also tries to dispel the myths that people are fat because they are undisciplined, self-hating and compulsive. There are meetings, recreational activities, and workshops to help lonely, isolated people participate more fully in life. Their motto is "Be the best you are regardless of size."

Ancient and Honorable Order of Small Castle Owners of Great Britain

900 McKay Tower, Grand Rapids, MI 49503   (616) 458-1464
Members: 8   Contact: Hollis M. Baker

The logo of this American club depicts a wine bottle, wine glass and a radiator surrounding a castle--any castle owners will tell you the biggest headache is the heating bills.

Their Motto: "Tax Vobiscum" (Tax be with you)

Bald-Headed Men of America

Morehead Plaza, Morehead City, NC 28557   (919) 726-1855
Founded: 1973   Members: 15,000
Dues: $5.00   Contact: John T. Capps, III

"You'll have a Bald! " promises John Capps, III. The fourth generation of men to go bald in his family, he started the club to "instill pride in having bald heads" and to "put a smile on people's faces." Scorning "drugs, plugs, and rugs, " Capps has given out over 500 certificates to women in Morehead City who have rubbed bald heads for good luck. (The club's slogan? "Morehead - Less Hair.") The initial membership pack consists of a membership card, certificate, Bald is Beautiful poem, bumper sticker, large combs, hairbrush for bald heads. Members include former President Ford, actor Telly Savalas, Joe Garagiola, Willard Scott, and Phil Silvers. all of whom experienced what Mark Twain called "premature balditude." BHMA believes, "If you don't have it, flaunt it!" and "We know the Lord only made a few perfect heads, the rest He covered with hair." Capps says that there are three basic types of bald heads: the chrome-dome, the balding pate and the bald spot.

At the well-publicized annual convention, four women judges picked the sexiest bald head, the most kissable head, smoothest, prettiest and best all-round head. John T. Capps, III said "It's all done in fun--we think it's a topless event." The convention is held yearly on the second weekend in September, ending "Rub a Bald Head Week." *Chrome Dome* newsletter is published at least once a year. Demonstrating that baldness has no boundaries, members hail from all 50 states and 28 foreign countries.

Boston Beanstalks Tall Club

1135 Front Street, S. Weymouth, MA 02190   (617) 331-0444
Founded: 1982   Members: 271
Dues: $18.00 per year   Contact: Mary Ellen LaBonte´

"How's the weather up there?," "Jolly Green Giant" and "You're as tall as a beanstalk" are some of the remarks fellow members have endured. To qualify, men must be at least 6' 2" tall and women, 5' 10". Most of the members are single, and women outnumber men (even though it's statistically more difficult for women to qualify--3.6% of men in the country measure up as opposed to only .08% of women.) To become a member, an officer must measure you (no shoes and no cheating.) The tallest male member is 6' 9" and the tallest female is 6' 7". "People notice you. Being tall opens doors," says one member. Another member said other members were surprised when they learned that she played basketball...she has yet to find another member who did. Boston Beanstalks Tall Club is a member of Tall Clubs International (see separate entry.)

The club is mainly a social club, though members help fellow members with the never-ending problems of where to buy shoes and clothes. Members commiserate about the problems of needing to get an aisle seat on an airplane for their legs and riding the subway or Amtrak without hitting their heads. One member has a permanent sore spot on the crown of her head from hitting low-clearance doorways: "It was sad not being accepted as '12 and under' at the matinee because even though you were 8, you were tall enough for 14." Member Lynn Stinson said "When you grow up being tall, everyone expects you to behave like a grown-up, even if you're still a kid. "Big girls don't cry" was something I heard very often." Of course, there were plenty of positive aspects of towering over everyone: being able to see the parade over everyone's head, changing the light bulb without standing on a chair, killing an annoying fly that defiantly sat on the ceiling, easily reaching books on the top shelves and quickly being spotted in a crowd. The club T-shirt bears the club logo, the beanstalk and bean pot, and the club saying, "Tall People Have Higher Standards." Member John Donovan jokes that now whenever someone asks, "How's the weather up there?" he spits on them and says, "It's raining."

Caterpillar Club
PO Box 1325, 1325 E. State St., Trenton, NJ 08607   (609) 587-3300
Founded: 1922   Members: 17,000
                                                   Contact: Richard Switlik, Jr

Members have saved their own life by parachuting out of an aircraft. They are awarded a caterpillar pin.

Dicks of America!
PO Box 20782, San Diego, CA 92120   (619) 286-5448
Dues: $12.00 lifetime membership   Contact: Dick Monaco

Question: Are you or do you know a nice guy named Richard?
Question: Do you know a not-so-nice guy, regardless of his name, who's a REAL DICK?

Members receive a wall certificate and an *I'M A DICK* badge plus a wallet-sized membership card. There's a *Dickin Around* newsletter, too. Founders Dick Fruzzetti and Dick Monaco say "We've decided to search the U.S.A. for the biggest Dick! We've already had several Dicks entered that weigh over 250 pounds. Now that's a BIG DICK!"

Fred Society
PO Box 4092, Palm Desert, CA 92261-4092
Founded: 1983   Members: 3500
Dues: $2.50   Contact: Fred Daniels

The Fred Society envelope read: "Making the World a Better Place for all Freds," "Do Not Bend, Contains Fredrobilia" and "Confredential." "Think of the most commonly known Freds in the last 30 years," says Fred Daniel. "Fred Flintstone, Fred Mertz from the old "I Love Lucy" show, Red Skelton's Freddy the Freeloader. They're all boob-like guys." Mr. Daniel, a freelance designer, decided that Freds have been portrayed as fools for long enough, and formed the "Fred Society," to "combat the negative images of Freds in the media and promote the positive aspects of life as a Fred."

Fed up with the lack of respect shown to Freds, Fred Daniel wrote an invitation to every Fred he could find in the Los Angeles phone book. He received 125 responses to whom he sent membership cards and offered what he calls "Fredrobilia." T-Shirts, bumper stickers and buttons that say, "Fred and Proud," "Better Fred than Dead," "I Brake for Freds," "Put a Fred in Your Bed," and "Have You Hugged Your Fred Today?" There are "Have a Fred Letter Day" mugs, and brown, stuffed "Freddy Bears." The society even sells those ubiquitous yellow diamonds that have invaded the rear windows of America's cars...theirs say "Fred in Car," "Fast Freddy at the Wheel," or "Fat Fred on Board." Today, member Freds hail from as far away as Ethiopia.

But the dreaded "Fred-a-phobia" still exists in this country. It seems that professional and semi-pro bicyclists accuse Freds of clogging bikeways and highway, wearing oversized helmets with mirrors and getting in the "true cyclist's" way. These complainers have militantly donned T-shirts that say "NO FREDS" Daniels says, "Whomever dreamed up the "No Fred" concept, must have thought they were attacking a pretty docile and unconcerned group of people. They couldn't have been more incorrect. Fred will persevere, and one day the roadways, and airways will be free of negative Fred references."

Fred Society members receive *The Fred Connection* newsletter. The current issue points out that some Fred wear skirts-- (Winnifred is sometimes shortened to Fred.) A "Fredfest" in Southern California is planned. Daniel's also working on a campaign to have people name their next child Fred, since the name is threatening "to go the way of the California Condor. When you think of someone exciting or popular these days, you don't think of Fred. Imagine Fred Rambo, or that great rock star, Fred Springsteen." Not yet, that is.

Fruitarian Network
Box 5333, Takoma Park, MD 20912   (301) 270-3444
Founded: 1976   Members: 7000
Dues: Write for details   Contact: Sai Om

Fruitarians wouldn't harm a flea! They are vegetarians who eat only fruits and vegetables that naturally fall off a vine, stem or tree without harming the plant in the process. A typical diet consists of apples, beans, squash, cucumbers, berries, corn, nuts, peas and tomatoes. Fruitarians believe that their practice of eating "fruit foods" is good because by not killing the plants, erosion is prevented, and a stable environment for wildlife is created. Furthermore, the group disapproves of lawn mowing, citing that an unmowed lawn encourages the growth of trees, saves gasoline and oil (that powers the lawnmowers) and helps to end deterioration of current weather patterns by protecting water tables.

Girth and Mirth

PO Box 14384, Chicago, IL 60614   (312) 871-7158
Founded: 1980   Members: 500
Dues: Write for details   Contact: Hal Wand

A social club for overweight gay men over the age of 21. With Girth and Mirth groups in a half dozen US cities, they publish the monthly *Girth and Mirth's Meet Rack* and *Girth Shaking News*.

Golden Gate Tip Toppers

793 B Clayton, San Leandro, CA   (415) 441-3889
Founded: 1940

One of the 48 tall clubs around the US and Canada (78 worldwide) that are members of Tall Clubs International (see separate entry.) Some of the other tall clubs are the Kansas City Skyliners, the Skyscraper Club of Cleveland, The Towering Texans of Houston, the Seattle Timberliners, The Central Arizona Tall Singles (CATS) and the Tower Club of Philadelphia.

Intertel: The International Legion of Intelligence

PO Box 15580, Lakewood, CO 80215   (303) 980-1521
Founded: 1966   Members: 2000
Dues: $21.00 per year ($15.00 initial fee)   Contact: Laura Diskin

"Bright people need each other, bright people like each other." Intertel requires for membership a score at or above the 99th percentile on a test of intelligence. No cheating is allowed, and the test must be supervised! ILIans (as they call themselves) keep in touch with *Integra*.

International Society for Philosophical Enquiry

304 Lexington Blvd., Carmel, IN 46032-2250
Founded: 1974   Members: 443
Dues: $20.00 per year   Contact: Robert D. "Russ"
Russell

A virtual Who's Who of people with high IQs (99.9 percentile), members come from 23 countries around the world. Almost anything is discussed at meetings and in the monthly journal. "Sports and weather are seldom mentioned," says Robert Russell, "unless it's the effect of barometric pressure on the liveliness of a basketball."

International Twins Association

PO Box 28611, Providence, RI 02908   (401) 751-4949
Founded: 1934   Members: 800
Dues: $15.00 per twin   Contact: Kay Cassill

"Twins are like Rosetta stones," said founder Kay Cassill, "They are ideal control groups." The group holds annual convention every Labor Day where twins compete in the "Twin Judging Contest." Trophies are awarded to the most alike and most unalike twins in different age categories.

Jim Smith Society

2016 Milltown Rd., Camp Hill, PA 17011   (717) 737-7406
Founded: 1969   Members: 1450
Dues: $10.00 lifetime   Contact: James H. Smith, Jr.

Imagine a softball game where everyone on the winning team is named Jim Smith---for that matter, everyone on the losing team, plus the announcer **and** the umpires are named Jim Smith, too. The annual Jim Smith Fun Festival is attended by 70 Jim Smiths and their families. Founder James H. Smith of Camp Hill, Pennsylvania says that the convention is ideal for people who have trouble remembering names. Hotel owners all vie to have Fun Festival participants stay in their hotel, though there *have* been problems--imagine 75 Jim Smiths at the registration counter saying, "I'm Jim Smith, I believe you have a room for me." The society has solved the sticky problem of telling members apart--everyone just uses their hometown name--there's Kansas City Jim, Dillsburg Jim, Dayton Jim who's never missed a Fun Festival in 17 years, and of course Camp Hill Jim. (He's the kind of guy who will go up to a member and say, "Hi, I remember your face, but the name escapes me.")

Camp Hill Jim, former police beat reporter and PR man for the telephone company founded the Society after being tired of years of good-natured kidding about having a name that sounded as authentic as John Doe. "People said--and still say--to me, 'You can do better than that, can't you?' I often thought when I got this response that it would fun to pull out a membership card showing I was a member of some sort of Jim Smith Society." So, Camp Hill Jim finally did just that. He started by pouring over the local phone books, sending invitations to all the Jim Smiths he could find. After that he made up a newsletter (each quarterly edition starts out, "Hello, Jim), a membership card, certificate and 1000 genuine

Jim Smith wooden nickels to give out. He says that while Jim Smith is probably the first or second most popular name in the English world, he's not quite sure how many Jim Smiths there are--probably upwards of 2.5 million.

Members include 8 female Jims (Jim can be Jim Ann or Jimmie Lou), but all members spell their last name "Smith" (not Smythe.) Members hail from as far away as Australia and New Zealand...Israel Jim is a Baptist minister who's been working with Jew and Arabs for 30 years. While famous Jims have included the current attorney general of Florida and heavyweight champ James "Bonecrusher" Smith, the *most* famous one was James Smith of York, Pennsylvania, one of the 56 signers of the Declaration of Independence. Current projects include a book about Jim Smiths throughout history, called *Jim Smith: Greats of the Common Names* and a composite survey of the "perfect" Jim Smith.

Their motto? "We Don't Shun Fun."

Johnson's Only
PO Box 20722, Columbus Circle Station, New York, NY, 10023
Founded: 1986   Members: 480
Dues: $16.95 lifetime   Contact: Richard M. Johnson

"Johnsons Only, a somewhat exclusive club" unites all with that popular last name. Johnsons are in good company. There have been two Johnson presidents, plus famous Johnsons such as Davey in baseball, Magic in basketball, Don on television and Betsey in fashion. "And only a Johnson can get that thrill of kinship from using a Band-Aid, waxing a floor or running an outboard motor." Johnsons Only is planning a Johnson Family Reunion, a tour to Johnson homelands, and a line of Johnsons Only jeans. Lifetime membership includes a Johnson Only T-Shirt, and membership card.

League of Lefthanders
PO Box 89, New Milford, NJ 07646   (201) 265-9110
Founded; 1975   Members: Currently inactive
Contact: Robert P. Geden

Equality for lefthanders!! Equality for students and equality on the job. Equality in price of lefthanded tools and goods. The League sponsors the annual "Lefty Awareness Week," and publishes the quarterly newsletter, *What's Left?*

Lefthanders International
PO Box 8249, Topeka, KS 66608   (913) 234-2177
Founded: 1975   Members: 23, 000
Dues: $15.00 per year   Contact: Dean R. Campbell

With 10-15 percent of the world's population lefthanded, Lefthanders International decided it was their job to write the "Bill of Lefts," designating August 13th of each year as International Lefthanders Day. They're working to remove the stigma of left-handedness from the culture and language (left in Latin is "sinister," in German "linkisch" means unhandy and in Spanish "zurdas" mean the wrong way.) Parents are encouraged to work with school boards to make sure the needs of lefthanders are met (lefthanded desks, scissors and notebooks), and that the preferences of lefthanded children are never interfered with. *Lefthander* magazine is published bimonthly offering everything from lefthanded steam irons to lefthanded rulers.

Little People of America

PO Box 633, San Bruno, CA 94066   (415) 589-0695
Founded: 1957   Members: 4000
Dues: Write for details   Contact: Harriet Stickney

Members are dwarfs shorter than four feet, ten inches high. Little People of America provides practical information on where to buy shoes and clothes, and other problem items.

Motto: Think Big!

Losers Anonymous

Miami Springs, FL
Founded: 1984   Members: 250
Dues: $10.00 lifetime membership   Contact: Al Stubblefield

"We try to tell people to maintain a sense of balance, make light of a bad situation and keep our sense of humor." Membership card and newsletter.

Mega Society

439 W. 50th St., New York, NY 100 19
Founded: 1982   Members: 26
Dues: Write for details   Contact: Ronald K. Hoeflin

The second most selective high-intelligence society of all, even the founder Ronald Hoeflin felt he had to drop out because he wasn't qualified! The Mega Society with its large membership of 26 accepts those with I.Q. scores of 177 and over. That translates into one individual in one million. Of course, many people who could qualify *don't* join. The membership includes a state governor, a person who works with brain-damaged children, a cancer researcher and Marilyn Mach vos Savant who, according to the *Guinness Book of World Records*, is the "smartest person in the world," having an IQ score of 230!! One-quarter of the members have doctorates and another quarter dropped out of college. Income varies between zero and $250,000 per year. Vos Savant says that members tend to be entrepreneurial, not salaried employees.

Mensa

2626 East 14th Street, Brooklyn, NY 11235   (718) 934-3700
Founded: 1960   Members: 53,000
Dues: $33.00 per year   Contact: Margot Seitelman

It's certainly the largest "high-intelligence" club, with 150 local chapters. Membership is limited to those who score over the 98th percentile on a standardized score of intelligence (or have an IQ of 132.) Members need not worry about finding someone that shares their interests, since Mensa has over 200 special interest groups on everything from body language to astronomy to allergies. There's the SoulSIG (a special interest group for black Mensans), SWIG (Special Winemakers Interest Group) and then there's the DAMSIG (Dirty Adult Movie Special Interest Group.) One Mensan described the typical member as "arrogant": "They assume their mental superiority and their social inferiority." One absolute no-no is discussing test scores with other members at get-togethers. The organization administers intelligence tests to prospective members ($9.00 for the home practice test, then $20.00 to take the supervised test and $15.00 to have it evaluated.) There is an annual Mensa convention and Mensa has a couple of regular publications including the *Mensa Bulletin*, ten times a year.

Messies Anonymous

5025 S.W. 114th Ave., Miami, FL 33165
Founded: 1980   Members: 6,000
Dues: $10.00/$1 for an introductory packet   Contact: Sandra Felton

Are you a 'messie', perhaps married to a nagging 'cleanie'? Just seek out ex-messie Sandra Felton, who teaches chronically disorganized people to neaten up. A math teacher, minister's wife and mom to three, Felton had been a long-term messie who thought that if clothes and dishes were clean, it didn't matter if you put them away. Even having her son scrape his knee and being unable to locate any of the three containers of Bactine or the Band-Aids wasn't enough to reform her. But when those newspapers she'd been saving under the sink ("in case we ever got a puppy") covered up a leaking sink pipe--which ultimately necessitated getting the whole kitchen remodeled because water had rotted through the floors under the sink--Felton knew it was time for drastic action. She asked clean friends for advice. Finally, a friend who'd visited George Washington's home, and had been so impressed with the site's spotlessness she'd spoken to the custodians, revealed the **Mt. Vernon method**: work in one corner of the house and continue to the left or right until you come back to where you began. Felton tried it out, with success, and formed a small self-help group in her community. A Miami newspaper wrote an article about the group, which was published nationally and resulted in 12,000 letters from messies across America.

Felton has developed many other aids as well: her unique Flipper system is a series of color-coded cards with chores, schedulers, menus and shopping needs. She says that repairmen are wonderful for messies, because they force you to clean up before they come -- too bad they're so expensive, she muses. Members receive the *Messies Anonymous Newsletter* quarterly for two years and can also peruse the MA book selection for such titles as *Is There Life after Housework?*, *File...Don't Pile!*, *It's Here...Somewhere!*, *The Procrastinators Guide to Good Housekeeping* and Felton's *The Messies Manual* (*and Messies 2, The Sequel*. "Don't wait for the movie!" she counsels.) Members can come out of the closet (after organizing it), proudly displaying their colors with the "Happiness is an Organized House" T-Shirt. Also available are seminars on housekeeping techniques. (Author's note: Wonder why Todd insisted *I* work on this entry?...RR.)

Mikes of America

PO Box 676, Minneapolis, MN 55440   (715) 549-6871
Founded: 1987   Members: 13,000
Dues: $15.00 lifetime   Contact: Michael D. Nelson

Calling all Michaels, Mickeys, Mitchells, Miguels, Mikkels, Miskas, Mikes and all variations thereof--Mikes of America has a twofold objective of making Mikes aware of (1) the great and glorious heritage of their name and (2) just how many others share the same great and glorious heritage. And the ranks have been swelling with such illustrious members as Mike Wallace and David Letterman (David Michael Letterman.) Members receive a Mikes T-shirt, a plastic membership card, a membership certificate suitable for framing and all future copies of *Mikes World*. This newsletter features "Open Mike" (a letters to the editor page), the Mike of the Year Award, plus lots of statistics about Mikes...did you know that since 1970, hospital records have shown Michael to be the most popular name for boys in the United States, as well as a popular one for girls (e.g., Michael Learned, who played the mother on the Waltons)? Mike was relatively uncommon in the US during the 1800s. It didn't become popular until after World War I. But Mikes' heritage dates back to the time of archangels and derives from Hebrew means "one who is like God."

National Federation of Grandmother Clubs of America

201 N. Wabash Ave., Chicago, IL 60601   (312) 372-5437
Founded: 1938   Members: 20,000
Dues: Write for details   Contact: Jeanne Martin

With 450 local groups, National Federation of Grandmother Clubs of America sponsors National Grandmother's Day on the second Sunday in October and raises money for charity.

National Organization of Mothers of Twins Clubs

12404 Princess Jeanne NE, Albuquerque, NM 87112 (505) 275-0955
Founded: 1960   Members: 9,000
Dues: vary from club to club   Contact: Lois Gallmeyer

Representing 300 clubs all over the US, the National Organization of Mothers of Twins Clubs refers mothers to the nearest club. Each mom is sent a copy of *Your Twins and You*, with interesting facts and information on twins: Twins occur once in 90 births (triplets once in 9,300 births) and only one-third of all twins are identical. They hold an annual convention.

Motto: Where God Chooses the Members.

The Old Grand-Dad Club

99 Park Ave., New York, NY 10016   (212) 551-0264
Members: 130,000   Contact: Julia M. Branan

The club selects "Grand-Dad of the Year." Former winners include Danny Thomas, Lawrence Welk, President Eisenhower and Bob Hope. There are no dues or obligations, and anyone can sponsor up to two grandfathers of their choice, who will receive a keychain, certificate and wallet card.

Procrastinators Club of America, Inc.

111 Broad-Locust Bldg., Philadelphia, PA 19102 (215) 546-3861
Founded: 1956   Members: 4800
Dues: $16.00   Contact: Les Waas

September 5
(Be Late for Something Day)

Dear Fellow Procrastinator:

Since you put off joining for so long it sounds like you'll make an ideal member. When you get around to it, can you fill out the application including a reference who might be called upon to attest to your procrastination? We'll eventually rush back your recent membership card, official "License to Procrastinate," copy of *LAST MONTH'S NEWSLETTER*, and a bumper sticker. Remember: "If it's worth doing, it's worth putting off."

Belatedly,
Les Waas, President

P.S. Since time is of the utmost unimportance, no applications will be accepted until tomorrow.

Prometheus Society

13 Speer Street, Somerville, NJ 08876	(201) 722-6949
Founded: 1983	Members: 73
Dues: $12.00 per year	Contact: Robert Dick

Presenting a high-intelligence society for those with IQ's of 164 or better--the top one out of thirty thousand of the population. *Gift of Fire*, its newsletter, is edited by 28-year-old Romero Anton XIV Montalban-Anderssen, who speaks 26 languages including Antonese (a language he invented himself), works for Chrysler in quality assurance, plays a couple of musical instruments and writes a local newspaper column called "Ask the Genius."

Pygmy International...or...Respect the Rights of All

Rainbow Productions

2322 S. 64th Avenue, Omaha, NE 68106	(402) 554-0123
Founded: 1970	Contact: Nils Anders Erickson

Limited to people under five feet two inches tall, the group was "formed to triumph the rights of shorter people and to the wrongs created by taller people." The group name Respect the Rights of All was adopted when group members spent too much time and energy thinking of tall people as "villains" and the "enemy."

Redheads International

3519-A East Coast Hwy. #119,

Corona Delmar, CA 92625	(714) 859-7537
Founded: 1982	Members: 18,000
Dues: $10.00	Contact: Stephen Douglas

After dating a fiery redhead, redhaired Stephen Douglas fantasized of being in the midst of a whole roomful of gorgeous red-tressed women. With $15,000 made by selling his recording and musical equipment, he formed Redheads International--for the 12 million redheads in the United States--with an office in *Orange* County, California. Walls of his office have pictures of famous redheads such as Little Orphan Annie, Red Buttons and Lucille Ball, even George Washington and Thomas Jefferson! (Surprised? Don't forget they wore white wigs.)

The main objective of Redheads International is to improve the image of redheads. Lucky Mr. Douglas sponsors Redhead Beauty Pageants and runs the Redhead Singles Referral Service, for those who'd like to meet redheads or correspond with them. Douglas also wrote *The Redhead Dynasty*, an encyclopedia of redhead history with listings of redhead leaders and innovators, redhead folklore, and anecdotes and stories about red hair (such as "What some ancient civilizations used to do to redheads...What a redhaired Irish queen did to her unwanted husbands" and more.)

Membership includes a newsletter, bumper sticker, window decal and membership card. And for the over-18 group, there's Douglas' steamy autobiography, *The Fire Still Burns*, with "behind-the-scenes scandals of the Redhead Beauty pageants." We're warned it has "mature themes"--after all, "people of the redheaded persuasion can get into trouble very easily, but you love them anyway for making life exciting."

Sinistral Sig

200 Emmett Ave., Derby, CT 06418	(203) 735-1759
Founded: 1977	Membership: 100
Dues: $3.50 per year	Contact: Sharlene McEvoy

Why are some people left-handed? Are left-handers more likely to have a high I.Q.? Sinistral Sig is a special interest group of Mensa that keeps members up to date on the scientific and medical findings in the area of left-handedness. *Sinistralian* appears bi-monthly. (Non-Mensans are welcome.)

Southpaws International

PO Box 31170, Birmingham, AL 35222	(205) 324-2596
Founded: 1967	Members: 2500
Dues: Write for details	Contact: Herman Moore

Sponsors the Lefthanders Hall of Fame, as well as presenting Southpaw of the Year Award to an outstanding left-handed personality. Members receive *Lefties Unite!*

Tall Clubs International

2750 South Las Flores, Mesa, AZ 85202	(602) 838-6502
Founded: 1938	Members: 3,000
Dues: Varies by local club	Contact: Ken Obenshain

The first tall club was started by Kae Sumner Einfeldt, a 6' 2" woman who illustrated dwarfs for Walt Disney, working on Snow White and the seven little ones. (Her friends remember her complaining about her knees knocking on the inside of her school desk, seeking leg room in cafeteria and on buses.) Thinking "It's wonderful that Disney is doing something for little people, but what about tall people?" she wrote an article in the *Los Angeles Sunday Magazine* about the problems of towering over everyone. In 1938, she and nine other tall people founded the first tall club ever, the California Tip Topper Club. Publicity was a natural for the group and new clubs formed quickly. By 1945, there were 60 tall clubs in the U.S. and Canada. The first convention was held in 1947 where the first club beauty queen was selected. In 1966, the various clubs officially joined to form Tall Clubs International and to pick "Miss Tall International." Today there are 48 tall clubs in the US and Canada. The minimum height requirement for all clubs is set at 5'10" for females and 6'2" for males.

The Titan Society
PO Box 7430, New York, NY 10116   (212) 582-2326
Members: 10   Contact: Ronald K. Hoeflin

Titan is by far the most selective high-intelligence organization. Originally, it was called the Savant Society after Marilyn Mach vos Savant, the person with the highest I.Q. ever recorded. *Insight*, its four-page journal considers the possibility that the admission standards are too lenient. Members must rate in the 99.99997 percentile of intelligence to rate for this one.

Triple Nine Society
PO Box 1111, Madisonville, KY 42431   (502) 821-3677
Founded: 1978   Members: 400
Dues: $15.00 per year   Contact: Barry Kington

Achieving the 99.9 percentile on a test of intelligence or general aptitude or having an I.Q. of 148 qualifies you for this one. Statistically, only one in a thousand would be eligible for Triple Nine. The astounding diversity of members ranges from a ditchdigger to a diversified investor, from a muscle-bound lumberjack to a bookish chain-smoker. One member was featured on "That's Incredible!" for solving Rubik's Cube in one minute and forty-eight seconds. Members test each other's intellectual prowess through logic and math problems printed in the monthly newsletter, *Vidya* (Sanskrit for "divine knowledge".)

Triplet Connection
2618 Lucile Avenue, PO Box 99571, Stockton, CA 95209   (209) 474-0885
Founded: 1983   Members: 2000
Dues: $12.00 per year   Contact: Janet L. Bleyl

Even breastfeeding takes on a special degree of seriousness with three mouths to feed. The Triplet Connection was started by Janet Bleyl after going through it alone with her three sons. Advice and warm support are given on high-risk multiple pregnancies. Parents having or expecting triplets or larger multiples, or those who are members of triplets or larger multiples themselves are welcome to join.

Triton College Active Retired Citizens Club

Triton College, River Grove, IL 60171   (312) 456-0300
Founded: 1971   Members: 600
Dues: Write for details   Contact: Leon A. Muller

"Living in retirement is not retirement from living." The club offers courses through Triton College, dedicated "to living with Spirit of Youth zest beyond retirement."

The Twins Foundation

PO Box 9487, Providence, RI 02940   (401) 274-TWIN
Founded: 1983
Dues: $15.00 per person (if a twin)   Contact: Anne Richards
   $20.00 per person (individual)

The organization is now building a hall of fame of twin achievers and a research library on the subject of twins and multiples, in order to learn more about the twin phenomenon. Members receive *The Twins Letter* and other services.

Uglies Unlimited

1714 Merrimac, Garland, TX 75043   (214) 271-5705
Founded: 1973   Members: 250
Dues: Write for details   Contact: Danny McCoy

McCoy claims he's ugly...at least by Madison Avenue and Hollywood standards, noting, "There are more ugly people in the United States than there are blacks, Chicanos, Indians and Jews." But Uglies Unlimited, as the self-proclaimed "guardian of ugly people," believes "uglies can sell products too!" To this end, UU works to end job discrimination against ugly people. In 1973, American Airlines gave stewardesses an application form which disdained moles, active pimples, scars, large pores and excessive facial hair. In response, Uglies Unlimited picketed American Airlines' offices at Dallas-Ft. Worth, succeeding in removing the offending language. Says McCoy: "Sean Connery could not play James Bond without a toupee. That's a sick commentary on our world." Uglies Unlimited also holds the 'Ugly Stick'

WHAT'S MY LINE?

Reindeer herder or ex-Rockette, you'll find a club to celebrate your chosen field. (And look quick, or the Flying Funeral Directors will get you!)

Air Mail Pioneers
468-D Calle Cadiz, Laguna Hills, CA 92653   (714) 581-6246
Founded: 1943   Members: 50
Dues: Write for details   Contact: Jerome Lederer

The last of the truly brave pilots who flew the mail for the U.S. Air Mail Service between 1918 and 1927 are gathered here. The average age of the surviving members is 85+. 84-year-old Jerome Lederer tells us that of the first 40 pilots hired to fly the mail, 31 were killed on duty. (Pilot life expectancy was three years.) There was no radio communication, no weather reports, no lighted airstrips and no instruments of any kind on board. Ground personnel worked against fatigue, weather and numerous technical problems too. Mr. Lederer recommends *Aerial Pioneers* by William Leary for those who want to know more. The group is too old and frail to meet in person now, but they do still publish *Air Mail Pioneer News* every four months or so.

American Association of Railway Surgeons
PO Box 4232, Rockford, IL 61110   (815) 398-0641
Founded: 1888   Members: 1200
Dues: Write for details   Contact: Elayne Bilka

American Handwriting Analysis Foundation
Box 6201, San Jose, CA 95150   (408) 377-6775
Founded: 1967   Members: 300
Contact: Dr. Patricia Wellingham-Jones   Dues: $25 initiation, $30 dues

"Handwriting is not really handwriting, it's *brain*writing" says AHAF Vice President, Rose Matousek. Handwriting is behavior frozen on paper, as individual as your fingerprints, as specific as your dental charts. "It's been calculated that (the chances of) two people writing alike is something like one in 68 trillion," Mrs. Matousek said. People like AHAF president Dr. Patricia Wellingham-Jones say that handwriting analysis is still considered trivial or invalid by some. "My goal is to make people aware of the professional value of it...we are not a kooky organization." Today handwriting analysis is used for child development work, compatibility analyses, counseling, criminology, jury screening, and vocational

appraisal. They hold an annual convention--last year, a four-day cruise and are
also working on an educational exchange trip for graphologists to China. AHAF
also publishes a newsletter.

American Society of Golf Course Architects

221 N. LaSalle St., Chicago, IL 60601   (312) 372-7090

Members: 86

Dues: Write for details   Contact: Paul Fullmer

American Society of Questioned Document Examiners

1432 Experson Bldg., Houston, TX 77002   (713) 227-4451
Founded: 1942   Members: 50

Contact: Maureen Casey-

Owens

These people can prove guilt or innocence by examining handwriting, typewriter
ribbon ink or anything else on a document which might reveal authenticity.

Anonymous Society of Second Bananas

Office of Management and Budget
Old Executive Office Building, Room 252, Washington, DC 20503
Founded: 1983   Contact: Joseph R. Wright, Jr.

This group of deputy-secretaries of Federal cabinet-level departments meet
monthly for dinner.

Association of Former Agents of the US Secret Service

PO Box 31073, Temple Hills, MD 20748   (301) 894-2115
Founded: 1971   Contact: Floyd M. Boring

Association of Former Intelligence Officers

6723 Whittier Ave., Suite 303A, McLean, VA 22101   (703) 790-0320
Founded: 1975   Members: 3000

Contact: John K. Greaney

When these secret agents meet, the stories sound like they were taken right out of
spy novels. "My claim to fame is that I was sentenced to death by the Russians,"
ex-agent Frank Binder said, "but I refused to show up for my execution." Binder
also helped organized the surrender of Nazi forces in Czechoslovakia during

World War II while working for the forerunner of the CIA--the U.S. Office of Strategic Services. Members say that the NSA accounts for more than 85% of all the intelligence gathered by the United States government.

Association of Former Senate Aides...or...Ex SOBs

1140 19th St. NW, Washington, DC 20036

Founded: 1960

Members: 150

Contact: Murray Zweben

Who said there's no honesty in government? Actually, calling themselves Ex-S.O.B.'s is not as derogatory as it sounds...they all worked in the *Senate Office Buildings*.

Association of Space Explorers

3278 Sacramento St., San Francisco, CA 94115   (415) 931-0585

Founded: 1985

Members: 40

Dues: Write for details

Contact: Ted Everts

If you're one of the astronauts from 16 of the 18 countries (including the USSR, Mongolia, Poland, and Saudi Arabia) who have flown in space, making at least one orbit around the earth, we've got a club for you. The purposes of the association are to encourage world cooperation, plus to work to educate young space explorers about the importance of international cooperation. Other goals: to communicate to the world the historic significance of humans reaching to space and to try and communicate how deeply moving and transforming the experience of seeing the planet earth from outer space was.

Callerlab-International Association of Square Dance Callers

Box 679, Pocono Pines, PA 18350   (717) 646-8411

Founded: 1971

Members: 1,400

Dues: $50.00 per year

Contact: John Kaltenthaler

"Your caller is the quarterback of the square dance team," says the American Square Dance Society. "Square dancing is constantly changing and your caller is a person who keeps current with all that is going on in the world of square dancing." Callerlab keeps professional callers current on new "calls" and how to "stack" them. Callerlab even has developed a caller training curriculum and a caller school run by outstanding leaders in the square dancing field. Though square dancing is a true American invention, Callerlab has members around the world. Remember, the American Square Dance Society says, "Don't be afraid of your caller--he's your friend."

Central Intelligence Retirees Association

PO Box 1150, Ft. Myer, VA 22211
Founded: 1975

Members: 2000
Contact: Eugene H. Haas

Flying Chiropractors Association

7301 Hasbrook Ave., Philadelphia, PA 19111
Founded: 1968
Dues: $12.00 per year

(215) 722-7200
Members: 300
Contact: Dr. W. J. Quinlan

Flying Dentists Association

4100 McEwen Suite 101, Dallas, TX 75234
Founded: 1960

(214) 386-9403
Members: 500
Contact: Linda Hill

Flying Funeral Directors of America

PO Box 608, Shawnee, OK 74802
Founded: 1960
Dues: $20.00 per year

(405) 275-2200
Members: 140
Contact: Betty F. Wiley

"To create and further a common interest in flying and funeral service; to join together in case of mass disaster, and to improve flying safety" is their pledge. Some members use their aircraft as flying hearses.

Flying Veterinarians Association

101 Bingham Rd., Columbia, MO 65203
Founded: 1977
Dues: $10.00 per year
McClure

(314) 449-4497
Members: 200
Contact: Dr. Robert C.

Hebrew Master Bakers Association

Sylvan Law Bldg.
14401 Sylvan St., Suite 200, Van Nuys, CA 91401
Found: 1923

(818) 989-0887
Members: 50
Contact: Max Gewirtz

Matzo makers unite!

Helicopter Loggers Association
PO Box 206, Wilsonville, OR 97070   (503) 678-1222
Founded: 1980   Contact: Steve Martin

These modern lumberjacks use helicopters to carefully prune trees from difficult
terrain. They can pluck a tree off a mountainside, eliminating the need for
destructive roads, or large clear-cut areas that ruin forest environments and
increase soil erosion.

2020 Update:
ACTIVE

Independent Association of Questioned Document Examiners
518 Guaranty Bank Bldg., Cedar Rapids, IA 52401   (319) 363-5121
Founded: 1969   Members: 175
                                           Contact: Robert P. Larson

Promoting justice through the discovery and proof of the facts relating to
questioned documents.

2020 Update:
ACTIVE

International Association for Identification
PO Box 90259, Columbia, SC 29290   (803) 776-2001
Founded: 1915   Members: 2500
                                           Contact: Kay J. McClanahan

Police officials and doctors engaged in forensic sciences(legal-oriented medicine.)
Innovative ways of identifying people, like voice print and acoustic analysis, are
studied. (TV's "Quincy" might've joined.)

International Association of Professional Bureaucrats
National Press Building, Washington, DC 20045   (202) 347-2490
Founded: 1968   Members: 2000
Dues: $25.00 lifetime membership   Contact: Dr. James H. Boren

Promoting the principle of "dynamic interaction"--doing nothing, but doing it in
style. The International Association of Professional Bureaucrats believe in orbital
dialoguing, decision postponement, communicative fuzzification, and procedural
abstractions--as a way of keeping things from happening and keeping mistakes
from occurring. IAPB has staged pony express races with the US postal system
from Philadelphia to Washington. Most of the time the horse got the mail to
Washington faster...no surprise...but a couple of times winning by eight days!

The highest IAPB award is the Order of the Bird for sustained bureaucratic
excellence. The award, a two foot high, 20 pound sculpture of a featherless,
potbellied bird has been given to such bureaucratic overachievers as Vice

President Spiro Agnew, The U.S. Department of Housing and Urban Development, the US Postal Service and Senator William Proxmire. One fat bird was given to Reagan, but he has yet to accept it. Members meet on September 30th, the last day of the federal government's fiscal year. The professional bureaucrat members receive *Mumblepeg: The Voice of the Bureaucrat*, monthly, plus a choice of fine publications entitled "Have Your Way with Bureaucrats; Fuzzify!" and "The Bureaucratic Zoo Book Series."

Motto: When in charge, ponder. When in trouble, delegate. When in doubt, mumble."

International Flying Farmers

Mid-Continent Airport, PO Box 9124, Wichita, KS 67277   (316) 943-4234
Founded: 1944   Members: 5,000+
Dues: $35.00 per year (plus chapter dues)   Contact: Kyle Ann Stream

Although hard times for farmers have decreased their membership from 11,000 in 1977 to 5,000, this association of farmers who fly is still going strong. Members use the planes to sow and dust crops, to haul supplies into areas not accessible by road, to feed livestock marooned by blizzards, to check fences and shoot trouble-making coyotes, as well as to enjoy regional and national fly-ins. Oklahoma was the first region to organize, and expansion quickly followed with Canadian regions joining in 1955, making the organization international. Programs for teens makes the club a family affair, as women are encouraged to fly by awarding a Teledyne Motors "Landit" certificate of achievement on the first time each lands a plane without assistance. Flying Farmers members own over 2000 aircraft and 2000 landing strips (mostly on their own land)! At the annual convention, 500 planes converge upon the convention site. *The International Flying Farmer* is published monthly.

International Graphoanalysis Society

2020 Update:
ACTIVE

111 N. Canal St., Chicago, IL 60606   (312) 930-9446
Founded: 1929   Members: 39,000
Dues: Write for details   Contact: V. Peter Ferrara

Handwriting experts.

International Order of the Golden Rule

2020 Update:
ACTIVE

Iles Park Pl., Suite 315, Springfield, IL 62718

A public relations group of funeral directors.

Their motto: "Service measured not by gold but by the Golden Rule"

International Society of Copier Artists
800 West End Avenue, New York, NY 10025   (212) 662-5533
Founded: 1982   Members: 150
Dues: $25.00 per year   Contact: Louise Neaderland

As the price of photocopying machines has dropped, they have become accessible for personal use. The ISCA brings together artists who use photocopiers in their art. Their purpose is to establish electrostatic prints and bookworms as legitimate and collectible works of art.

Johns & Call Girls United Against Repression
PO Box 1011, Brooklyn, NY 11202
Founded: 1978   Contact: Hugh Montgomery

Seeking to dispel "the notion that there is anything reprehensible or immoral in being a prostitute whose customers are adults, or in being the customer of an adult prostitute." Johns and Call Girls United Against Repression is trying to instill a sense of self-respect in adult prostitutes and their customers .

Librarians United to Fight Costly, Silly, Unnecessary Serial Title Changes
University of North Carolina Library, Chapel Hill, NC

Founded: 1973   Contact: David Taylor

When the *Journal of Gynecology and Obstetrics* changed its name to the *Journal of Obstetrics and Gynecology*, librarian David Taylor became angry. Asked to make a speech to a group of librarians at the U. of Michigan, he named it "Librarians United Fight Costly, Silly, Unnecessary, Serial Title Changes." He wrote a constitution for the group and designed a flag and a symbol. The response was tremendous. The librarians took the flag and marched through the halls, handing out copies of the constitution. Soon there was a newsletter, then awards were given for the worst serial title change at the American Library Association meetings.

Taylor says that group is trying to make uncaring publishers aware of the work and money that goes into cataloguing and identifying library materials. He remembers one government serial called "Human Needs" that creatively hid its title on the cover each month. One month the name appeared on a wall of graffiti behind a gang of motorcyclists and another time it appeared stitched into a sampler that a granny was working on. Though creative, the treasure hunt approach wasn't appreciated. *Title Varies* is the newsletter that keeps track of these most ridiculous title changes--but don't fall in love with it, the title varies.

Melvil Dui Marching Band and Chowder Association

CW Post Center, Graduate Library School
Long Island University, Greenvale, NY, 11548   (516) 299-2866
Founded: 1947   Contact: Dr. Joseph N. Whitten

New York metropolitan area librarians need not spend lonely evenings lost in a
book anymore. The Melvil Dui Marching Band and Chowder Association, is a
librarians' social club named after Mr. Dewey Decimal System...Melville Dewey.
Dewey was a proponent of spelling reform and simplification---thus the spelling
of the club title.

The Moles

PO Box 1389, Southampton, NY 11968   (516) 283-6322
Founded: 1937   Contact: Mrs. A. Gallagher

These men dug the auto tunnels, the subway systems, the water tunnels and sewer
systems of this country. They bore out Cheyenne Mountain to make way for
NORAD and they dynamited the valley for projects like the Hoover and Grand
Cooley Dams. Named for the mole, a furry, almost-blind creature that can rapidly
dig tunnels, these men meet regularly at dinners recognizing the best among
them. Though recently opened to women, the club has been noted for its
exclusively male membership. Club officers don't expect many women moles to
climb out and join in the near future.

Motorcycling Doctors Association

495 Carriage Way, Deerfield, IL 60015   (312) 945-9096
Founded: 1976   Members: 100+
Contact: Arnold A. Gutman, M.D.

Not only doctors, but dentists, veterinarians and podiatrists.

National Chimney Sweep Guild

PO Box 563
18115 Georgia Avenue, Olney, MD 20832
Founded: 1977   Members: 1000
Dues: Per company   Contact: Mary Ann Beaufait

You're driving down the road, and the bumper of the car in front reads, "Don't
Make an Ash of Yourself"--he's probably a chimney sweep off to clean someone's
flue. It all started with a handful of sweeps who joined together to help boost their
businesses. The first ten years have been a period of rapid growth in the National
Chimney Sweep Guild, with woodburning stoves becoming popular again. It's

been an exciting time--celebrating one member's wedding on top of the Sears Tower and establishing a chimney-climbing race with racers donning the traditional top hat. Today, like everything else, chimney sweeping has gone high-tech, with computerized sweeping and special suits and masks. But still today, sweeps have to deal some of the eternal problems of their dusty, dirty forebears? Many have been chased down a chimney, even bitten, by the vicious, rabid raccoon who likes the warmth of a chimney. Affiliated with the "Chimney Safety Institute of America," members receive *Sweeping*.

National Porkettes (now National Pork Council Women)
c/o National Pork Producers Council
PO Box 10383, Des Moines, IA 50306   (515) 223-2600
Founded: 1962   Members: 18,000
Dues: Write for details   Contact: Marjorie Ocheltree

These are the wives of the members of the National Pork Producers Council, helping their husbands sell swine and protecting and improving the image of pork. Each year they work with school dieticians and home economics teachers to push pork to the young homemakers of the future. (You might spot a Porkette in your local supermarket distributing pamphlets on summertime pork cook-outs.) Each year they pick the "Pork Industry Queen." (Editor's note: Followed by the "Shake-n-Bake" dance?)

National Taxidermists Association

18626 St. Clair Ave., Cleveland, OH 44110   (216) 531-1971
Founded: 1972   Members: 2500
Dues: $30.00 per year   Contact: William Lee Birch

Seminars at the annual convention include "Painting a Rainbow Trout" and "Mounting Bass for Profit."

Navajo Code Talkers Association

Box 1182, Window Rock, AZ 86515   (602) 729-2728
Founded: 1971   Members: 90
Dues: Write for details   Contact: Albert Smith

Considered to be the only unbreakable, foolproof code ever devised, the intricacies of the Navajo language were used by Native Americans for secret Marine Corps communications during the Second World War. The "code talkers" meet at the annual convention each August.

New Amsterdam Antiquarian Chowder & Marching Society

New York, NY
Members: 12

(212) 286-0320
Contact: Peter Salwen

A group of Big Apple walking-tour guides who meet for monthly dinners.

New York Corset Club, Inc.

309 Fifth Ave., New York, NY 10016
Founded: 1910

(212) 679-6677
Contact: Ray J. McInerney

Nine Lives Associates

North Mountain Pines Training Center
Founded: 1978
Dues: $25.00
Kobetz

(703) 955-1128
Members: 500
Contact: Dr. Richard W.

Bodyguards of elected officials, executives and the rich and famous, members must pass a very stressful and strenuous training program (held only in December.) At the annual conferences, spouses and friends can participate in "practical protective movements."

Old Old Timers Club

1417 Stoneybrook Ave., Mamaroneck, NY10543
Founded: 1947
Dues: Write for details

(914) 698-4384
Members: 2450
Contact: A. J. Gironda

These pioneers of early wireless history now meet on the ham radio bands. They've had many distinguished members, including Charles Ellsworth, a man who handled the radio traffic for Canadian Marconi Company in Newfoundland during the Titanic sinking. The Old Old Timers Club is for those old timers who have been in radio for at least forty years while the Old Timers Club is for twenty-year veterans.

Old Time Radio Club

56 Christen Ct., Lancaster, NY 14086
Founded: 1975
Dues: $17.50 per year

Members: 150
Contact: Jerome F. Collins

Starting as a local club outside of Buffalo, the membership is now international (though monthly meetings are still held in the town of Cheektowaga, NY.) Most members were involved in the radio industry 20 or more years ago. Over 1000 tapes of old radio shows are in the lending library. Its purpose is to make people aware that "old radio is still alive." and "there is an alternative to television."

Members receive a tape listing, library lists, the monthly *Illustrated Press* and the yearly magazine, *Memories*.

Pan Hellenic Society Inventors of Greece in USA

2053 Narwood Ave., South Merrick, NY 11566   (516) 223-5958
Founded: 1969   Members: 150
Contact: Dr. Kimon M. Louvaris

Finally, an organization to help inventors who are of Greek descent get their inventions patented and on the market.

Professional Golf Club Repairmen's Association

2053 Harvard Avenue, Dunedin, FL 33528   (813) 733-4348
Contact: Thelma E. Schloss

Reindeer Herders Association

PO Box 172, Nome, AK 99762
Contact: Mary Davis

Rockette Alumnae Association

908 North Broadway, Yonkers, NY 10701   (914) 423-3636
Founded: 1955   Members: 350
                                              Contact: Mrs. Fern Weizner

Former kickers who meet and raise money for charitable causes.

Society of Medical Friends of Wine

Box 218, Sausalito, CA 94965   (415) 332-0366
Founded: 1939   Members: 325+
Dues: Write for details   Contact: William J. Siegel, MD

Inspired by a German proverb, "There are more old wine-drinkers than old doctors, " this group conducts research as serious as "The Impact of Wine on Diabetes Mellitus" or as whimsical as "The Warfarin-Wine Interaction and the Dino Concept of Drinking." (A "dino" is someone who drinks wine only with meals...as opposed to a "wino," who drinks wine *instead* of meals.) Members, who are physicians and surgeons, can choose a seat on the Tastings Committee or Wine Aging Committee.

Society of Polish-American Travel Agents

9018 N. Milwaukee, Niles, IL 60648

Founded: 1959

(312) 298-0550

Members: 110

Contact: Elizabeth Zbyszewski

Encourages tourism to Poland.

Sommelier Society of America

35 West 36th Street, New York, NY 10016

Founded: 1954

(212) 686-7435

Members: 600

Contact: Richard J. Gaffney

The difference between a Beaujolais and a Bordeaux is a piece of cake here. Wine stewards together with wine merchants, connoisseurs and importers attend seminars and tastings of fine wines and liqueurs.

United States Dental Tennis Association

7324 SE 34th Avenue, Portland, OR 97202

Founded: 1967

Dues: $35.00 per year

Members: 500

Contact: Sue Ballantyne

Picturing Martinia N. with a racket in her teeth? Forget it....this is a club of tooth doctors who love the sport and volley the ball at twice-yearly meetings.

World Association of Detectives

PO Box 5068, San Mateo, CA 94402

Founded: 1950

(415) 341-0060

Members: 600

Contact: Vance I. Morris, Jr.

Seeks to eliminate "unreliable, incompetent and irresponsible" members of the profession.

A SAMPLING OF SOME OF THE MORE UNUSUAL INDUSTRY ORGANIZATIONS

American Institute of Nail & Tack Manufacturers
25 N. Broadway, Tarrytown, NY 10591   (914) 332-0040

American Catfish Marketing Association
Box 34, Jackson, MS 39205   (601) 353-7916
Founded: 1971   Members: 9

Affiliated with the Catfish Farmers of America.

American Mosquito Control Association
PO Box 5416, Lake Charles, LA 70606   (318) 474-2723
Founded: 1935   Members: 2500
Dues: $25.00 per year   Contact: Thomas D. Mulhern

2020 Update: ACTIVE

Members receive *Mosquito Control Quarterly*.

Bow Tie Manufacturers Association
75 Livingston St., Brooklyn, NY 11201   (718) 875-2300
Founded: 1952   Contact: Leonard Brodsky

Covered Button Association of New York
225 W. 34th St., New York, NY 10001   (212) 564-2500
Founded: 1941   Contact: Sheldon M. Edelman

Dome Committee of the Home Manufacturers
15th and M Sts., NW, Washington, DC 20005   (202) 822-0576
Founded: 1976   Members: 51
    Contact: Ray Howard

Promoting the efficiency of dome living.

Golf Ball Manufacturers Association
200 Castlewood Dr., North Palm Beach, FL 33408   (305) 842-4100
Founded: 1921   Members: 14
    Contact: Sebastian DiCasoli

Their convention is always in Florida.

Insect Screening Weavers Association
2000 Maple Hill St., Yorktown Heights, NY 10598   (914) 962-9052
Founded: 1941   Members: 15
                                                   Contact: Peter M. Miranda

International Technical Caramel Association
1575 I. Street, NW, Washington, DC 20005   (202) 789-7589
Founded: 1976   Members: 10
                                            Contact: Roger D. Middlekauff

Caramel coloring producers---after all, without caramel coloring, how could we make imitation maple syrup and other important goodies?

Kosher Wine Institute
175 Fifth Ave, New York, NY 10010   (212) 254-5170
Contact: David Herzog

Log Homes Council
15th and M Sts., NW, Washington, DC 20005   (202) 822-0576
Founded: 1977   Members: 21
                                             Contact: Ella R. Hubbard

Makers of log homes.

National Association of Insect Electrocuter Manufacturers
80 Telegraph Road, Middleport, NY 14105   (716) 735-7768
Founded: 1954   Contact: D. R. Coe

Sponsors *National Insect Electrocuter Week*, the first week of May and *Fight the Filthy Fly Month* in June, promoting the science of "insectocution"

National Association of Name Plate Manufacturers
1133 15th Street, NW, Washington, DC 20005   (202) 429-9440
Founded: 1950   Members: 105

                                              Contact: Penn L. Hoyt

National Church Goods Association

1114 Greenfield Ln., Mt. Prospect, IL 60056

Founded: 1908

(312) 253-5513

Members: 300

Contact: Don Latendresse

Bible makers.

National Hot Dog and Sausage Council

1211 W. 22nd St., Oakbrook, IL 60521

Contact: Frances Altman

(312) 986-6224

Sponsors of "National Hot Dog Month" in July and publishes the *Hot Dog Fact Sheet*.

Northern Nut Growers

PO Box 247, Chetopa, KA 67336-0247

Founded: 1910

Dues: $15.00 per year

(316) 236-4254

Members: 2,000

Contact: William Redo

This is an international group that advocates growing nuts in cold northern climates. It was founded in an effort to turn Canada into a profitable nut growing region. Now nut growing members come from all over North America. Quarterly newsletter called *The Nutshell*.

Pickle Packers International

PO Box 606, Charles, IL 60174

Founded: 1893

(312) 584-8950

Members: 188

Contact: William R. Moore

Gives an award to the person who has done the most for the pickle industry.

Pin, Clip, and Fastener Services

179 Allyn St., Suite 304, Hartford, CT 06103

Founded: 1933

(203) 246-6566

Contact: Lee Isenberg

Straight pin, safety pin, and paper clip makers.

Popcorn Institute

111 E. Wacker Dr., Chicago, IL 60601

Founded: 1943

(312) 644-6610

Members: 35

Contact: William E. Smith

Popcorn processors.

Sunglass Association of America

PO Box 1333, Stamford, CT 06904
Founded: 1970

(203) 323-3143
Members: 85
Contact: C. A. Greathouse

Vacuum Bag Manufacturers Association

380 N. Broadway, Jericho, NY 11753
Founded: 1974

(516) 822-8948
Members: 5
Contact: Robert W. McKellar

YOU COLLECT WHAT ?!

Buttons, bricks and barbed wire...these people collect two or more of just about anything...

Air Horn & Steam Whistle Enthusiasts
140 Forest Avenue, Glen Ridge, NJ 07028

American Bell Association International
Rt. 1 Box 286, Natrona Heights, PA 15065   (412) 295-9623
Founded: 1940   Members: 3000
Dues: $12.00 per year   Contact: Louise Collins

Collectors of sleigh bells, school bells and dinner bells. *Bell Tower* is published 8 times a year.

American Blade Collectors
PO Box 22007
2835 Hickory Valley Rd., Chattanooga, TN 37422   (615) 894-0339
Founded: 1981   Members: 12,500+
Dues: $15.99 per year   Contact: J. Bruce Voyles

If you love cutlery, and I don't just mean steak knives, then the annual American Blade Collectors Convention is for you. Learn how to make an axe, how to repair a pocketknife or maybe trade your sword for a good switchblade. Publish *Blade Magazine* (bimonthly) and *Edges* (quarterly.)

American Carousel Society
470 S. Pleasant Avenue, Ridgewood, NJ 07450
Founded: 1978   Members: 750
Dues: Write for details   Contact: Mary Fritsch

Restoring the wooden carousels of yesterday.

American Collectors of Infant Feeders
5161 W. 59th St., Indianapolis, IN 46254   (317) 291-5850
Founded: 1973   Members: 109
Dues: $20.00 per year   Contact: Jo Ann Todd

Keeping Abreast is really the name of their quarterly newsletter. Members, 25% of them doctors and nurses, are interested in the history of infant nutrition, and collect bottles, feeding cups and other baby items, like rattles.

American-International Matchbox

522 Chestnut Street, Lynn, MA 01904

(617) 595-4135

Founded: 1970

Dues: $18.00 per year

Matchbox car collectors.

American Lock Collectors Association

14010 Cardwell, Livonia, MI 48154

Founded: 1970

Members: 250

Dues: $9.00 per year

Contact: Charles W. Chandler

Shaped like a heart and made from tin by the Pennsylvania Dutch, the earliest padlocks in the U.S. date from 1685. ALCS members have catalogs from all the major lock companies, going back 100 years.

American Paper Exchange Club

Rt. 12 Box 485, Gray, TN 37615

(615) 477-3053

Founded: 1979

Members: 800

Dues: Write for details

Contact: Page Rea

Comic books, newspapers, books and other paper goods.

American Pencil Collectors Society

Wilmore, KS

Founded: 1958

Members: 250

Dues: $7.00 per year

Contact: Florence Booth

The wonder of it--Verner Hensel, pencil collector of Ohio, IL, met his namesake, Verner Hensel, pencil collector of New Port Richey, FL, through the American Pencil Collectors Society. (Apparently not related, they now are pencil pals.) Pencil collectors, many of whom are retired people, may enjoy collecting clean, unsharpened pencils. Others collect mechanical pencils, fountain pens, ball point pens...some even collect anything that has to do with writing. A folksy newsletter, *The Pencil Collector* is published each month, with stories and pictures of notable collections, personal news about members, and a classified section. A three-day convention is held every two years.

American Political Items Collectors

PO Box 340339, San Antonio, TX 78234   (512) 655-5213
Founded: 1945   Members: 2700
Dues: $20.00 per year   Contact: Joseph D. Hayes, Sec'y.

The 1940 presidential campaign of Wendell Willkie, to unseat FDR for a third term, produced several hundred different slogan buttons...more than any political campaign since. This proliferation of items led to the formation of the APIC. Today, collections come from local, regional, state and national campaigns. Some members are specialists in a particular campaign or area. With 30 regional groups, members have a national convention every two years (next one in 1989), a newsletter and a magazine called *The Keynoter*. The APIC alerts members to possible fakes and forgeries.

American Society of Bookplate Collectors & Designers

605 N. Stoneman Ave., No. F, Alhambra, CA 91801   (213) 283-1936
Founded: 1922   Members: 200
Dues: $35.00 per year   Contact: Audrey Arellanes

Bookplates are the labels you've seen pasted on the inside cover of clothbound books, bearing the owner's name and/or ex libris ("from the library of"), written on them, with artwork ranging from the humorous to the erotic to the profound. Society members are artists, librarians and historians worldwide who appreciate the engravings, calligraphy and etchings of these small designs. An ongoing project is to collect and catalogue the bookplates of The Library of Congress. Members receive copies of *Bookplates in the News*--some issues have included beautiful hand-pulled prints. Club motto: "Bookplates are a passport to friendship."

American Society of Military Insignia Collectors

1331 Bradley Avenue, Hummelstown, PA 17036
Founded: 1937   Members: 2800
Dues: Write for details   Contact: Donald Sexton

American Spoon Collectors

PO Box 260, Warrensburgh, MO 64093   (816) 429-2630
Founded: 1974   Members: 300+
Dues: $12.50 per year   Contact: Bill Boyd

American Transit Collectors' Association

8304 16th St. #208, Silver Spring, MD 20910   (301) 588-6579

Founded: 1976   Members: 45
Dues: $8.50   Contact: Bruce R. Gilson

Don't forget to ask for a transfer--these collectors always do. In fact, they collect
and trade "fare forms" or transfers. *The Collectors' Item* is published eight times a
year.

Angel Collectors Club of America

Four Whitewood Dr., Trenton, NJ 08628   (609) 883-5812
Founded: 1976   Members: 1000
Dues: $10.00 per year   Contact: Evelyn Jacobsen

If you're driving behind a car with a bumper sticker reading, "Make sure that
your last neighbors will be angels," the driver might be honorary Angel Collectors
of America member Michael Landon (of "Highway to Heaven") or "The Angel
Lady" herself, club president Evelyn Jacobsen. A thousand members, "from
newborn to 90," grace this international club, dedicated to collecting anything
"having wings and/or a halo."

Evelyn has over 3000 china, wood, plaster of Paris, and glass angels, many of
them acquired by her husband, a former pilot, in his global travels. Now retired,
Mr. Jacobsen obliges as an angel repairman and by piloting the family car on daily
trips to flea markets, antique shows and community fairs in search of new angels.

The club has published three cookbooks, including "Halo, What's Cookin'?" and
"Heavenly Hash," with profits benefitting "Angels, Inc.," a school for the
profoundly retarded in Dallas, TX. Many members are devoted correspondents,
too--there's a monthly poetry exchange, swapping of angelic-patterned gift wrap
and stickers, Secret Pals on both local and national levels, and Round Robin
letters. There are fourteen area chapters, which hold quarterly meetings.
Members receive the quarterly *Halo, Everybody!* and are invited to the biennial
national convention.

And there's the ACCA Anthem, with its final words:
> Gold, silver, metal, glass
> Paper, straw, wood, brass
> Food of thought and meditation
> Giving daily inspiration
> Angels! Angels! Angels!
> Angel Collectors of America, we are.

Antique Outboard Motor Club Inc.

1009 7th Avenue, Council Bluffs, IA 51501
Founded: 1965   Members: 1100

Dues: $20.00 per year   Contact: Allen Le Baugh

Members have outboard motors that are at least 20 years old (the first outboard
was invented and produced in 1866.)

Automatic Musical Instrument Collectors Association

PO Box 275, Cape Elizabeth, ME 04107   (207) 767-44~~
Founded: 1963   Members: 1500
Dues: $22.00 per year   Contact: Dorothy Bromage

Though the first automatic instruments were carillons set into church clocks as
early as the 15th century, it was the 1920s and 30's that were the era of the player
piano and orchestrions and nickelodeons. The music rolls are harder to come by
today, but these collectors trade and collect them at annual conventions.

Automobile License Plate Collectors Association (ALPCA, Inc.)

PO Box 712, Weston, WV 26452   (304) 842-3773
Founded: 1957   Members: 4758
Dues: $16.00 per year   Contact: Gary Brent Kincade

Where do you find a license plate made out of wood, porcelain, tin, copper,
brass...even leather? ALPCA members collect plates from around the world; some
have even *designed* plates. One member, Jim Fox, has practically every license plate
issued by every state in the United States, a collection of over 20,000 plates! His
greatest coup, though, was convincing the Sheik of the Arab emirate of Abu
Dhabi to give him a silver-on-red plate with "Abu Dhabi 4" on it that was lying in
the back seat of the sheik's Lamborghini. (The incident happened at a hotel in
London.) After spotting the plate, Fox had to find out who the car belonged to. He
then had to convince a half-dozen bodyguards that he wasn't a lunatic before the
sheik got on the hotel phone and said "This is the Sheik. Do you want that old
thing? I'll be happy to give it to you." He then came downstairs with 12
bodyguards and a blonde on each arm, opened the car and gave the astonished
Fox the plate. Members receive the *ALPCA Newsletter*, published every other
month. There is an annual meeting the last Thursday, Friday and Saturday of
June.

Barbie Collectors Club of California

1696 Valley Rd., Clarksville, TN 37040
Dues: Write for details   Contact: Sybil DeWein

Regional Barbie collectors' group.

Beer Can Collectors of America

747 Merus Ct., Fenton, MO 63026

Founded: 1969

Dues: $30.00 per year

(716) 681-2323

Members: 12,000

Contact: Bob Terray

Founder Denver M. Wright has 1,320 different full cans of beer in his house...and he has no intention of drinking even one. In fact, Wright doesn't believe beer cans should be bought or sold but should be traded among collectors. His most unusual brand is a can of "Soul" Beer, manufactured in the Watts ghetto of Los Angeles in the 1960s. Wright feels that any can is worth collecting as long as it is visibly different than another at a distance of six or eight feet. The BCCA sponsors an annual "can-vention"; at a recent one, a half-million cans were on display. The club offers a detailed listing of over 25,000 cans produced in the U.S., plus a newsletter with interesting articles, like one on generic beer and one on the invention of the pop-top.

Big Little Book Club of America

PO Box 732, Danville, CA 94526

Collecting miniature books.

Box Top Bonanza

PO Box 1039, Moline, IL 61265

I'll trade you a box top from Shredded Wheat for a box top from Rice Krispies.

California Barbed Wire Collectors' Association

1046 North San Carlos Street, Porterville, CA 93257

Candy Container Collectors of America

7500 Glenwood Rd., Conneaut, OH 44030

Founded: 1980

Dues: $18.00 per year

Members: 242

Contact: Shirley Stampels

Collectors of glass, plastic, or paper mache´ candy containers. Remember the plastic Pez dispensers sold in the candy store? Well, they rate as collectors' items today! Their newsletter's called *Candy Gram*.

Cartoon Collectors

5700 Sears Tower, 233 S. Wacker Drive, Chicago, IL 60606   (312) 876-6000

Contact: David Applegate

Cat Collectors

31311 Blair Drive, Warren, MI 48092   (313) 264-0285
Founded: 1982   Members: 800
Dues: $12.50 per year   Contact: Marilyn Dipboye

Members collect anything (short of kitty litter) that has to do with cats. *Cat Talk*, their bi-monthly newsletter, has a health column for your feline. One issue had info on dental care for your cat--anyone for a cat toothbrush?

Check Collectors Round Table

969 Park Circle, Boone, IA 50036
Founded: 1969   Members: 400
Dues: Write for details   Contact: Larry Adams

OK, you've heard of Bank of America and Citibank, but did you ever hear of The Bullfrog Bank & Trust, The Bimetalic Bank, The National Shoe and Leather Bank, or The First National Bank of Intercourse (of Intercourse, PA)? CCRT members know about these and thousands of others, and collect checks written against their meager deposits (there was a time when banks had about the same longevity as the corner lemonade stand.) Members receive *The Checklist*, about all phases of check collecting and bank history.

Cigarette Pack Collectors Association

61 Searle St., Georgetown, MA 01833   (617) 352-7377
Founded: 1976   Members: 200
Dues: $5.00 per year   Contact: Richard W. Elliott

Egyptian Heroes, White Rolls, Toppers, Turkish Trophies....are all American cigarette brands of different eras. For cigarette pack collectors, the graphics, the advertising and the names of brands provide rich clues to the times that produced them. At the turn of the century, Duke, in Durham, NC manufactured more than 80% of all cigarettes made! But the monopoly was broken up and R.J. Reynolds was spun off. Cigarette Pack Collectors are interested in preserving and collecting old tins, cardboard boxes, paper packs, as well as advertising material--primarily of American brands. A convention is held in North Carolina every five years, with visits to manufacturing plants and to the Tobacco Textile Museum (with its display of over 5000 brands of cigarettes.) The newsletter, *Brandstand*, is published bi-monthly.

Citrus Label Society

16633 Ventura Blvd., Encino, CA 91436   (818) 990-3220
Founded: 1980   Members: 250
Dues: Write for details   Contact: Harriet West

The labels affixed to the side of orange crates or lemon crates haven't missed
these collectors' eyes. The Citrus Label Society says they have "historic and
artistic" value. Each month the society publishes the *Citrus Peel* with stories about
early lithography houses that printed the labels.

The Cola Clan

2084 Continental Dr., NE, Atlanta, GA 30345   (404) 634-3552
Founded: 1974   Members: 2,500
Dues: $15.00 per year   Contact: Alice Fisher

Bob Buffaloe is a Coke addict. Not an abuser, mind you, but a collector of Coke
advertising items. It all started when he stumbled upon an old Coca-Cola
warehouse in Panama City, Florida. After getting permission, he pulled out a pile
of signs, calendars from the 1930s, napkins, even a 1910 advertising postcard
worth more than $200! Now Buffaloe's home is filled with thousands of Coke
items, including a five-foot-high model of a Coke bottle that stands next to the
television. The club was originally called "The Coke Club" but the company
made them change it, though the company has endorsed the club as the "official
collectors' organization for memorabilia relating to Coca-Cola." Unfortunately,
starting a collection today can be quite costly, as the price of some of the rare
pieces has been driven up by a few wealthy collectors. A 1906 syrup jug now
fetches $1,000 and a leaded-glass Tiffany-style lamp goes for over $3,000! Coke
quit shipping its syrup in red wooden barrels over 50 years ago. Most barrels were
broken up long ago, but survivors are worth hundreds of dollars now. The real
Cola Clansman lives just to spot a Coke collectible sitting in someone's garage
gathering dust waiting to be taken away. There is an annual convention and a
monthly newsletter, *The Cola Call.*

Collectors Record Club

3008 Wadsworth Place Hill, Decatur, GA 30032   (404) 288-1480
Founded: 1969   Members: 13,000
Dues: $5.00 one-time fee   Contact: George H. Buck

Provides members with the opportunity to purchase big band and authentic jazz
records at a discount. Club has own Jazzology label that makes obscure jazz
recordings available. Publishes newsletter and catalogs on jazz and unusual
recordings.

Cookie Cutter Collectors Club

5426 27th St., NW, Washington, DC 20015   (202) 966-1766
Founded: 1971   Members: 400+
Dues: $6.00 per year   Contact: Phyllis S. Wetherill

Conscientious cookie cooks commend cookers cutting cookies with carved cookie cutters. Wooden ones work well. Collectors keep up-to-date on new cookie recipes and new cookie-cutter companies and sources.

Corn Items Collectors
11825 S. Harding, Chicago, IL 60655

Collectors of corn cob pipes, Indian corn, etc.

Crown Point (Lightning Rods)
884 Lulu Avenue, Las Vegas, NV 89119

Lightning rod collectors.

Deltiologists of America
3709 Gradyville Road, Newton Square, PA 19073
Founded: 1966   Members: 1,800
Dues: $7.50   Contact: James Lowe

The window of opportunity for postcards slid open on May 25, 1901, when the production of commercial postcards became legal. Until World War I, picture postcards were the rage, with pictures of cities, scenic sights, greetings for holidays and even jokes. Deltiologists of America (deltiology is a new name for postcard collecting) will help new collectors start out. James Lowe suggests picking a particular subject or interest and building from there.

Dictionary Society of North America
Instructional Services
Indiana State U., Terre Haute, IN 47809   (812) 237-2330
Founded: 1975   Members: 500
Dues: $15.00 per year   Contact: Edward Gates

Members are interested in the use of dictionaries and also the collection, construction and history of them.

Doorknob Collector
4125 Colfax Avenue, South, Minneapolis, MN 55409

Unbelievable, eh?

Dr. Pepper Collectors Club

1614 Ashbury Drive, Austin, TX 78723

These collectors *definitely* are Peppers!

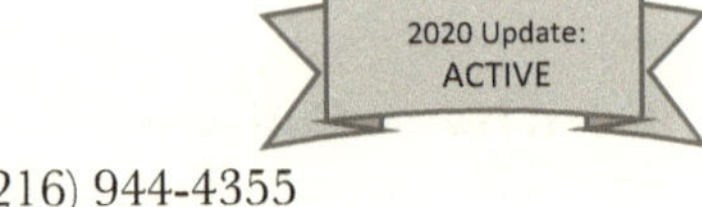

Eastern Coast Breweriana Association

30201 Royalview Dr., Willowick, OH 44094   (216) 944-4355
Founded: 1970   Members: 550
Dues: Write for details   Contact: Jeanette Bendula

Did you know that there have been 5 different brands of beer over the years called "Budweiser?" That's because "Budweiss" is a beer-making region of Czechoslovakia, where a particular type of brew was developed. The East Coast Breweriana Associations' members are interested in artifacts (beer bottles and cans, calendars, posters, etc.) of old beers and breweries...there are less than 50 breweries left today, out of 2,000 at the turn of the century in the United States. The group has a convention at a different East Coast brewery each year.

Eggcup Collectors Corner

Pastimes
67 Stevens Ave., Old Bridge, NJ 08857   (201) 679-8924
Founded: 1986   Members: 100
Dues: $10.00 per year   Contact: Dr. Joan M. George

Joan George has over 500 of these eggs-cellent "tiny treasures." A newsletter is published quarterly.

Electric Railroaders Association

89 East 42nd St., New York, NY 10017   (212) 986-4482
Founded: 1934   Write for details

Toy train collectors.

Electrical Horology Society

6 Stewart Place, Spring Valley, NY 10977
Founded: 1972   Members: 110
Dues: Write for details   Contact: Martin C. Feldman

Originally part of the National Association of Watch and Clock Collectors--these collectors have a special interest in early electric clocks--either battery or A.C. powered.

Ephemera Society of America

PO Box 943, Hillsboro, NH 03244
Founded: 1980
Dues: $25.00 per year

Members: 500+
Contact: Calvin P. Otto

They define ephemera as "the minor transient documents of everyday life"--it's a pretty loose definition for a collection of items that include menus, newspapers, letterheads, greeting cards, tickets--almost anything that is printed or handwritten.

Expo Collectors and Historians Organization (ECHO)

1436 Killarney Ave., Los Angeles, CA 90065   (213) 221-9789
Founded: 1976   Members: 1,600
Dues: $9.00 per year   Contact: Edward J. Orth

Collectors of World's Fair memorabilia. Mr. Orth who has published *Expo Info* continually since 1971 writes, "we wish to share world's fair collecting experiences with many, many people--collectors, dealers, historians, exhibitors and John Q. Public, too."

Famous Personalities' Business Card Collectors of America

PO Box 8028, Ann Arbor, MI 48107   (313) 761-9377
Founded: 1983   Members: 30
Dues: Write for details   Contact: Terry Robinson

Figural Bottle Openers Collectors Club

6 Shoshone Trail, Wayne, NJ 07470
Founded: 1978   Members: 80
Dues: $15.00 per year   Contact: Barbara Rosen

A figural bottle opener is a figurine designed solely for the purpose of lifting a bottle cap. The most common figures are drunks, donkeys, elephants and birds.

Flying Disc Collectors Association

225 Circle Dr., Las Vegas, NV 89101   (712) 384-1769
Founded: 1978   Members: 200
Dues: $5.00 per year   Contact: Donn Blake

A visit to the "wall of fame" at the flying disc museum will reveal that hundreds of Frisbees and other flying discs have been made. Yes-sir-ee, even one of the first Whamo Frisbees is on display here. Annual convention.

For Here Or to Go

PO Box 162281, Sacramento, CA 95816   (805) 252-8493
Contact: Patricia Craig

After a visit to Burger King, Wendy's or McDonald's, do you just casually throw the empty food containers away? Well, shame! For Here Or to Go is a club of fast-food container collectors. Sure, they collect napkins and paper bags, too-- anything with the name of their favorite burger joint.

Frog Pond

Box 193, Beech Grove, IN 46107
Founded: 1986   Members: 300
Dues: $15.00 per year   Contact: Merleaine Haskett

Yes, this is the frog collectors club you've been hearing about... and I'm afraid it's true that their newsletter is called *Ribbit, Ribbit*. Members collect anything,.*anything* having to do with frogs--frog puppets, a tadpole game, frog candy molds, and frog jokes. One member, Mabel Winters has collected over 5,000 frogs (sounds like a plague) and displays them in her Frog Fantasies Museum. There she runs the Frogs Only Gift Shop--with inspiring items like a full set of J.C. Penney frog dinnerware and frogs in every mood...from sad to lonely to mischievous to exultant. Club president Merleaine Haskett says that while most members' frogs are made of paper Mache´, plastic, leather, or soap, there are some that collect live frogs "and since this is a frog-collectors' club, I see no reason to exclude them." Merelaine said that the most favorite frogs in her own collection include one frog with a little zipper that when opened lets a little prince pops out. The bi-monthly *Ribbit, Ribbit* includes a section called "What's New in Frogs" and contests for the "Special Froggie Person" award.

Golf Collectors Society

J. R. Kuntz Co.
235 East Helena Street, Dayton, OH 45404
Founded: 1970   Members: 750+
Dues: Write for details   Contact: Robert Kuntz

Members collectively own between 150,000 and 200,000 old clubs, helping each other restore them. Co-founder Joseph Murdoch owns every book ever written on the subject of golf--that's over 2,500 books (he is actually missing one book, called *Golf in the Year 2000.*)

Hallmark Collectors Club

PO Box 110, Fenton, MI 48430
Dues: $18.00 per year   Contact: Jane Jarvis

Not only greeting cards, but little Hallmark figurines, Christmas tree ornaments, and party favors too!

Handle on the Teapot Enthusiast Association

882 South Mollison Avenue, El Cajon, CA 92020
Write for more information

Teapot and teacup collectors.

Hubcap Collector's Club

Box 54, Buckley, MI 49620   (616) 269-3555
Founded: 1976   Members: 50
Dues: Write for details   Contact: Dennis H. Kuhn

A founding member, Bruce Ledingham, tops the collector's list with over 1,600 threaded hubcaps, all from cars built before 1930. This figure is not difficult to believe when you consider that over 5,000 companies manufactured cars at one point or another in the early years of the automobile. Members receive *The Hubcapper*.

Ice Screamer

Box 5387, Lancaster, PA 17601
Founded: 1982   Members:
Dues: $12.00 per year   Contact: Edmund L. Marks

The history of the ice cream industry is represented in the IS collection of memorabilia. *The Ice Screamer* is their bi-monthly newsletter, with articles on the history of the ice cream scoop, the origin of the ice cream cone, the era of the Dixie cup lip, etc. Recent editions had reprints of the song "Come Have a Soda with Me" and the 1954 "True Mystery Puzzler" called "The Ice Cream Murder." The fifth annual Ice Screamer Convention was held concurrently with the Milk Bottle Collectors (their publication's *The Milk Route*.) The clubs thought that there were enough "ties-that-bind" to make the joint meeting worthwhile. Books are available through the club, including *Ice Scream Dippers*, a history of the dipper through the ages...including the unusual heart-shaped dipper of 1925.

International Association of Jazz Record Collectors

RR 1, Box 217A, Pittsboro, IN 46167   (317) 852-8528
Founded: 1964   Members: 1300
Dues: $20.00 per year   Contact: Duncan Scheidt

International Association of Jim Beam Bottle and Specialties Clubs

5120 Belmont Rd., Suite D, Downers Grove, IL 60515   (312) 963-8980
Founded: 1966   Members: 21,000+
Dues: $8.00 per year   Contact: Shirley Slimbles

Local clubs around the country meet at the annual Jim Beam Convention. Members say that the bottles are most valuable when everything including the tax stamp and original boxes are intact--(we say, what about the tasty contents of the bottle?) Members receive *Beam Around the World* monthly.

International Barbed Wire Collectors Association

c/o Jack Glover, Sunset Trading Post, Sunset, TX 76270   (817) 872-2027
Founded: 1969   Members: 6,000
Dues: $20.00 per year   Contact: Bill Marquis, Pres.

These are not just barbed wire collectors--no, they have fun hosting the "World Champion Greased Armadillo Races," the "Post Hole Digging Contest" and "World's Largest Barbed Wire Collection Contest." They tend the "Barbed Wire Hall of Fame" in Wichita, Kansas and publish the "Bobbed Wire Bible" replete with the thousands of barbed wire designs that have been patented over the years.

International Barbie Doll Collectors Club

PO Box 79, Bronx, NY 10464   (212) 885-2439
Founded: 1977   Members: 1000+
Dues: $15.00 per year   Contact: Ruth Cronk

The original 1959 Barbie doll in mint condition (in the box) is worth about $1,000. There have been over 50 different Barbie dolls produced over the years! There has been "Fashion Queen Barbie" (1964) and "Twist and Turn Barbie" (1967.) In 1966 Barbie's cousin "Francie" was white and in 1967, she was black. The kids just couldn't handle that and "Black Francie" was a flop. So, in 1968 Mattel offered "Christie," "Barbie's "black is beautiful friend" as the television ads proclaimed. Other Barbies followed: "Living Barbie" (1970), "Malibu Barbie" (1971.) There is even an unauthorized Barbie family doll put out called "Gay Bob," who comes with his own closet. The joke is that when you put "Gay Bob" on the shelf with "Barbie" and "Ken," he takes "Ken" away from "Barbie."

International Brick Collectors Association

10942 Montego Dr., San Diego, CA 92124   (619) 560-1035
Founded: 1983   Members: 400
Dues: $10.00 per year   Contact: Dr. Ronald P. Anjard, Sr.

Ronald Anjard says that even the rarest brick will never be as valuable as an old coin or stamp--but so what! A "Don't spit on the sidewalk" brick--(a warning from Kansas public health officials) is only worth about $10.00 and a brick with the profile of Abe Lincoln brings a staggering $75! "Most people think we're strange," he confesses, "but after a while, they start appreciating what's there, the history and all." Nebuchadnezzar, the ancient king of Babylon, had his name imprinted on bricks made for his construction projects. "I have a 15th Century brick from a temple in India," Anjard says, "but there's no marking on it." Anjard, who holds a Ph.D. in engineering doesn't just collect bricks, he lives bricks--sending them through the mail, writing articles about them and traveling thousands of miles to attend brick swap meets.

The typical brick collector loves rummaging around demolition sites. Bricks aren't as fragile as butterflies, and don't need to be polished like coins. Bricks fit in where painting never will--like in your rose garden for example--and if you get tired of your collection they can be retired to the fireplace.

International Chinese Snuff Bottle Society

2601 North Charles Street, Baltimore, MD 21218 (301) 467-9400
Founded: 1968   Members: 500
Dues: $50.00 per year   Contact: John Ford

Serious collectors are kept up-to-snuff at the annual meeting and through the slick journal.

International Correspondence of Corkscrew Addicts
RFD #1, Box 169, Hilsboro, NH 03244   (603) 464-3335
Founded: 1974   Members: 50
Dues: Write for details   Contact: Robert P. Nugent, Jr.

Limited to 50 members, these collectors of corkscrews, some with over 1,000 wine openers in their collection, write each and every one of the other members once a year--club rules! Plus, each letter must be accompanied by six photographs of corkscrews in their collection. That's a lot of pictures--which is why the membership is limited to 50.

International Doll Makers Association
3364 Pine Creek Drive, San Jose, CA 95132

International Hajji Baba Society
7404 Valley Crest Blvd., Annandale, VA 22003
Founded: 1962   Members: 500

Dues: $20.00 per year--residing less than 50 miles from Washington DC
($15.00 outside of D.C. area)   Contact: Jeff Boucher

"Hajji Baba is the 'patron saint' of the Oriental rug," explains Jeff Boucher. Jeff should know. He's been collecting rugs for years, traveling to the Middle East for the last 25 years through his work in the US Army. He says that there is a mystical quality in oriental rugs, especially those given as gifts, dowries or to an important person. These rugs are said to take on the soul of weavers from generations past. The society has hung major rug exhibitions in dozens of museums around the country and has helped produce catalogues for even more. The International Hajji Baba Society is a good place for the novice collector to start a new collection.

International Newspaper Collectors Club
Box 5090, Phoenix, AZ 85010   (602) 273-7288
Founded: 1950   Members: 100
Dues: No membership fee   Contact: Charles J. Smith

The club maintains a little newspaper museum with papers dating back as far as 1537.

International Pin Collectors
Box 227, Marcy, NY 13403   (315) 736-4019
Founded: 1980   Members: 600
Dues: $10.00 per year   Contact: Rowan Fay

No, not straight pins or safety pins, but Olympic pins from around the world. Formerly called the "Olympic Pin Club."

International Rose O'Neill Club
P. O. Box 668, Branson, MO 65616
Founded: 1967   Members: 1,000
Dues: $3.00 per year   Contact: Mrs. Pearl Hodges

Rose O'Neill was a Branson, Missouri advertising artist who created the Kewpie-- an elfin baby with a knot of hair and blue wings. It started with the "Kewpie Pages" drawings in *Good Housekeeping* and *Ladies Home Journal* but soon her character was turned into Kewpie dolls. Every April, Kewpiesta, a three-day celebration of the Kewpie doll, is held in Branson, Missouri, where Kewpie collectors and appreciators convene.

International Sand Collectors Society

43 Highveiw Ave., Old Greenwich, CT 06870   (203) 637-2801
Founded: 1969   Members: 200
Dues: None   Contact: William S. Diefenbach

When William Diefenbach asked a friend to bring back some sand from a trip to the Fiji Islands for his personal collection, his friend balked. "No way," he said, "I have to come back through some steamy parts of the world, and if you think I want to go through customs with a little packet of white granular material in my baggage, you are just plain nuts!" Diefenbach's response was to create the International Sand Collectors Society on the spot. He printed up membership cards with "official sand transportation authorization" and gave them out to his well-travelled friends. Initially a joke, the organization has grown, until today his collection...the society's collection has over 400 specimens, from 89 countries. The 40 dram containers contain sand from the Gaza pyramids, Orly Airport and Mt. St. Helens, to name a few. Members are encouraged to trade sand between themselves and in lieu of dues, members may be asked to contribute unusual specimens to the society's collection. Special divisions of the club include the "Golf Trap" division and the "Historic Locations" division.

International Seal, Label and Cigar Band Society

8915 E. Bellevue St., Tucson, AZ 85715   (602) 296-1048
Founded: 1957   Members: 200
Dues: Write for details   Contact: Myron H. Freedman

Myron Freedman has over 60,000 cigar bands covering 1890 to the present. Some members have over 300,000. The attraction here is the fine lithographed artwork that was used in decorating the bands, seals and boxes.

International Society of Animal License Collectors

4420 Wisconsin Avenue, Tampa, FL 33616
Founded: 1976   Members: 176
Dues: $8.00 per year   Contact: K.L. Rose

Members meet yearly to trade and discuss dog tags and the like. They hold competitions to find the oldest licenses from each state, and compile statistics on licensing laws from each town, city, country or state agency. *Paw Prints* is published quarterly.

International Society of Bible Collectors

PO Box 2485, El Cajon, CA 92021   (619) 440-5871
Founded: 1964   Members: 200
Dues: $6.00 per year   Contact: Dr. Arnold D. Ehlert

International Swizzle Stick Collectors Club
Greenwood Village
2150 Avenue A, #10, Yuba, Arizona 85364   (604) 525-3120
Founded: 1985   Members: 136
Dues: $7.50 per year   Contact: Polly Rusk

We've been wondering who's been hoarding all the swizzle sticks. Members
receive the monthly *Swizzle Stick News* spotlighting regional sticks (stirrers from
Montreal, Canada have been the center of attention recently.) A convention is
planned, where collectors can swap and sell their sticks. From time to time the
club offers "special sticks" to *all* members, free of charge. Co-founder Ray Hoare
has one stick from the Stork Club, that looks like a stork with a cane and top hat,
that he's been offered $7.50 for (quite stirring news, when you consider the stick
was free!!)

International Watch Fob Association
6613 Elmer Dr., Toledo, OH 43615   (419) 841-4023
Founded: 1965   Members: 900
Dues: $8.00 per year   Contact: Dan Anderzack

Before the wristwatch was popular, most men used a pocket watch tethered with a
strap and a fob. The fob was a metal shape stamped or cast with the names of
companies, images of machines, or a registration number. Many of the fobs were
given away as advertising by companies or political hopefuls. Some were given to
a man when he was qualified to use a piece of machinery, embossed with a
registration number of the back. Collectors estimate the number of fob designs in
the tens of thousands. The International Watch Fob Association has a semi-
annual newsletter and there is a yearly convention with an auction.

International Wood Collectors Society
2913 Third Street, Trenton, MI 48183
Founded: 1947   Members: 1500
Dues: $15.00 per year   Contact: Robert M. Bartlett

"Welcome to the Wonderful World of Wood"! The only requirement for
membership is an interest in "woody" things. The society's standard wood sample
measures 1/2" x 3" x 6," but many members are woodworkers and craftsmen
with useful things like wooden thimbles, cups and saucers and gavels in their
collections. Specimens from colorful, exotic trees or even from historic buildings
are encouraged. The monthly journal, called *World of Wood*, listing various rare
and exotic woods for sale or exchange, is printed regularly.

International Wristwatch and Cigarette Lighter Club
832 Lexington Avenue, New York, NY 10021

Japanese Sword Society of the United States
PO Box 4387, Grasso Plaza Branch, St. Louis   MO 63123 (314) 832-3477
Founded: 1965   Members: 1000
Dues: $15.00 per year   Contact: Ronald C. Hartmann

Membership benefits include a sword supply service and association with the
majority of sword collectors outside of Japan. Ron Hartmann, who constructed a
special samurai sword room in his basement for his collection, says that what he
likes about swords is that "you can collect them all of your life and still not be an
expert."

Jukebox Collectors
2545 SE 60th Court, Des Moines, IA 50317

Kansas Barbed Wire Collectors Association
La Crosse Chamber of Commerce, PO Box 716, LaCrosse, KS 67548
Founded: 1967   (913) 222-3116
Dues: $6.00 per year   Contact: Donna Schmidt

La Crosse, KS, is proud to be called the Barbed Wire Capital of the World, home
of the KBWCA headquarters and the Barbed Wire Museum, with over 500
varieties of barbed wire. Members swap and sell wire at the annual convention in
La Crosse the first weekend of May. The convention is also the site of the annual
splice-off and meeting, the first weekend in May. Ranchers and farmers, who
would have battled in fence-cutting wars during the late 1800s, now compete to tie
the strongest and fastest splices. Gloves are permitted but no tools are allowed.
(There's a ladies' contest, too.)

Kennedy Political Items Collectors
PO Box 922, Clark, NJ 07066   (201) 382-5429
Founded: 1976   Members: 250
Dues: $7.50 per year   Contact: Harvey Goldberg

Part of The American Political Items Collectors, they collect memorabilia of
John, Robert and Edward and publish the bi-monthly newsletter, *The
Hyannisporter*. Meetings every two years in conjunction with the American Political
Items Collectors. Twice a year, they hold an auction through the mail.

Key Chain Tag Collectors Club

888 Eighth Ave., New York, NY 10019   (212) 765-2660
Founded: 1984   Members: 100
Dues: $3.00 per year   Contact: Dr. Edward H. Miles

Collectors of mini license plates and key chain tags plus chauffeur's badges, metal license plates included in cereal boxes, etc. Newsletter and meetings twice a year.

Key Collectors International

Box 9397, Phoenix, AZ 85068
Founded: 1978   Members: 300
Dues: $18.00 initial membership   Contact: Don Stewart

Founded by Don Stewart, after he published the *Standard Guide to Key Collecting*, the club's goal is to advance the knowledge of lock and key collectors. Members may collect casket keys, railroad keys, skate keys, ancient keys, keys that shoot or fold-- even keys to the city. One of the most unusual keys in Don Stewart's collection, opened a safe in the assayer's office in an old mining town. The safe was rigged so that if you used to wrong key, it would explode the lock and the safe couldn't be opened. Stewart has managed to reprint over 120 old lock and key manufacturer catalogs, whose wares ranged from car keys to padlock, restraint and handcuff keys. The *Key Collectors Journal*, which comes out five times a year, has included floor plans and drawings of locks, keys and gates of old jails (including one in Chloride, Arizona) and safe deposit vaults. Regional collectors' shows held.

Lilliputian Bottle Club

5626 Corning Ave., Los Angeles, CA 90056
Founded: 1970   Members: 300+
Dues: $7.50 per year   Contact: Jay Love

You order a drink and the stewardess brings you one of those tiny little bottles. How many times did you think that those wee empties would be perfect to collect? The Lilliputians collect those miniature liquor and soda pop bottles and others (slightly larger) from around the world, aided by members in Europe, Africa, and Asia. One S. California member, rumored to be "giving his liver up for the club," reviews both the insides and outsides of new bottles for the bimonthly newsletter, *Gulliver's Gazette*. Meetings are every other month and a yearly miniature bottle show and sale is planned for each autumn.

Lionel Collectors Club

1425 Ruthbern Rd., Daytona Beach, FL 32014   (904) 258-9574
Founded: 1970   Members: 5000
Dues: $16.00 per year ($10.00 initiation)   Contact: Dienzel C. Dennis

Members meet each year at the annual convention--Lionel makes a special commemorative club car with the city name on it, for members. Convention highlights usually include a *real* train ride and the swap and sell sessions. Members receive the bi-monthly *Lion Roars*.

Lithophane Collectors Club
Box 4557, 2032 Robinwood Ave., Toledo, OH 43620 (419) 243-4115
Founded: 1965 Members: 200+
Dues: $15.00 per year Contact: Laurel G. Blair

Figures made with Lithophane--porcelain that is translucent.

Marble Collectors Society of America
PO Box 222, Trumbull, CT 06611 (203) 261-3223
Founded: 1975 Members: 1000
Dues: $12.00 per year Contact: Stanley A. Block

Aggies, cats' eyes and mibs are serious collectors' items for this society, which is gathering and placing collections of marbles in The Smithsonian and Corning Glass museums. They also publish the quarterly *Marble Mania* and are preparing photographs of marbles and articles about marble factories.

Marx Toy Collectors
916 West Armitage Avenue, Chicago, IL 60614

Pop quiz: Who remembers the "Knock-'em, Sock-'em Robots?" These collectors do.

Merchant Token Collectors Association
1416 Third Avenue, Seattle, WA 98101

Especially popular in the Midwest at the turn-of-the-century were the merchant and trade tokens, the advertising of the day. They were worth a penny or a nickel and were minted with the picture of a town or a store. Iowa alone issued over 10,000 tokens! METCA members will trade tokens, and many tokens can still be found at yard sales, etc.

Miniature Figure Collectors of America
813 Elliston Drive, Wynmore, PA 19118 (215) 649-4144
Founded: 1940 Contact: Brian Stonier

National Association of Breweriana Advertising

2343 Met-To-Wee Ln., Wauwatosa, WI 53226   (414) 257-0158
Founded: 1972   Members: 700
Dues: $15.00 per year   Contact: Robert E. Jaeger

These are *not* just collectors of coasters and neon signs, but "anything that has the name of a beer or brewery on it," including trays, bottles, clocks, glasses, labels, mugs, and more. Through the *Breweriana Collector*, published four times a year, members hear the latest about the health of the industry plus news items such as The Vancouver Lucky Larger Brewery being dismantled tank-by-tank to be resurrected in China, a book review on Victorian pubs and a review of the best beer for the slopes and the best brew for the beach. The yearly convention is held at the beginning of August.

National Association of Miniature Enthusiasts

PO Box 1178 Brea, CA 92622   (714) 529-0900
Founded: 1972   Members: 12,000
Dues: $15.00 per year   Contact: Joseph Hermes

Collectors and builders of miniatures enjoy the quarterly *Miniature Gazette*. The miniature convention, called their "National Houseparty," is held in a different region each year.

National Association of Paper and Advertising Collectors

PO Box 500, Columbia, PA 17552
Founded: 1979   Members: 3000
Dues: Write for details   Contact: Joel Sater

Collectors of antique advertising --- posters, calendars, etc.

National Association of Timetable Collectors

Five Offenbach Pl., Lake Oswego, OR 97034
Founded: 1964   Members: 500+
Dues: $20.00 per year   Contact: Jeff Asay

This club started with railroad timetables but has recently taken a bold expansion move into bus, airline, and steamship tables.

National Association of Watch and Clock Collectors

514 Poplar Street, Columbia, PA 17512   (717) 684-8261
Founded: 1943   Members: 32,000

Dues: $25.00 annual   Contact: Stacy B. C. Wood, Jr

Collectors, historians and others interested in horology--the science of measuring
time form over 130 active chapters of this association. The headquarters houses
an extensive museum of timepieces and a library with thousands of books,
records, slides, patents and manufacturers' catalogs. The *NAWCC Bulletin* is
published in even-numbered months, and *Mart* is published in odd-numbered
months. A convention is held annually.

National Autumn Leaf Collectors Club
6505 W. Cameron, Tulsa, OK 74127
Dues: Write for info.   Contact: Suzan Fausset

National Bit-Spur & Saddle Collectors Association
3370 West Bijou, Colorado Springs, CO 80904   (303) 632-2617
Founded: 1980   Members: 300
Dues: $10.00 per year   Contact: Lee Jacobs

Spur bits, saddles, chaps, bridles, quirts, wrist cuffs---the gear of the cowboy.
National Bit-Spur & Saddle Collectors meet at the yearly auction in Loveland,
Colorado. Equipment made between 1850 and 1950 is highly prized.

National Button Society
2733 Juno Place, Akron, OH 44313   (216) 864-3296
Founded: 1939   Members: 2060
Dues: $15.00 per year   Contact: Lois Pool

Interested in bartering your better buttons? This society is open to collectors,
libraries, museums and members of the button trade with an interest in antique
and unique buttons. Local groups can be found in almost every state. The *National
Button Bulletin* is published 5 times a year and members have the opportunity to
"exhibit your buttons" at the National Button Show.

National Elephant Collectors' Society
89 Massachusetts Ave., Box 7, Boston, MA 02115
Dues: Write for details   Contact: Richard Massiglia

Members are *NOT* zookeepers---they collect statues and other items that look like
Dumbo or Jumbo.

National Fishing Lure Collectors Club

PO Box 1791, Dearborn, MI 48121
Founded: 1976
Dues: $10.00 per year

(313) 842-2589
Members: 2100
Contact: Rich Tremi

The artificial lure was invented by accident when, in 1830, Julio Buel dropped a spoon overboard and noticed a fish excitedly snatching it. The thousands of beautiful and bizarre wooden, metal and plastic lures made over the years with names like "Luny Frog, Dowagiac Minnow, Dreadnaught" are now collected and traded. The club publishes a quarterly newsletter and holds an annual meeting.

National Geographic Collectors

Box 465, Wilmington, DE 19899
Dues: Write for details

Contact: Edwin C. Buxbaum

Keeping stacks of old *National Geographic* magazines in your garage? Then join.

National Insulator Association

3557 Nicklaus Drive, Titusville, FL 32780

The old ceramic insulators used atop telephone poles are the pride and joy of these collectors.

National Pop Can Collectors

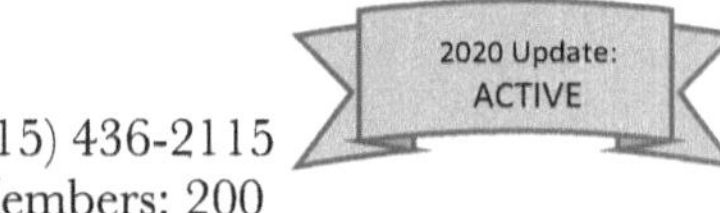

3014 September Dr., Joliet, IL 60435
Founded: 1976
Dues: $15.00 per year

(815) 436-2115
Members: 200
Contact: Fred Bogdam

To Fred Bogdam and others, picking up old soda cans can be worth more than just the nickel deposit. Old openers, trays and caps also find their way into the collections and the pages of the monthly *National Pop Can Collector*.

National Reamer Collectors Association

Rt. 1 Box 200, Grantsburg, WI 54840
Founded: 1980
Dues: $18.00

(715) 689-2563
Members: 100+
Contact: Larry Branstad

"Collecting of fruit juice extractors, which most collectors refer to as "reamers," must certainly rank close to number one in popularity among hobbies today," starts *Citrus Fruit Reamers, A Brief History* ...from the first hand-held lemon squeezer to the Cuisinart. This fact is as hard-to-believe as the fact that some reamer collectors have spent upwards of a quarter-of-a-million-dollars on their collection! Yet one member ignores her collection of 300 juicers each morning and heads straight for the refrigerator, opening a cold fresh can of V-8 Juice.

National Shaving Mug Collectors Association

RD #6, Box 176, Bedford, PA 15522

Founded: 1979

Dues: $15.00 per year

Members: 200

Contact: Deryl Clark

What's so interesting about a shaving mug? Could be the pictures on them--theme mugs, they're called. But members collect not only shaving mugs, but shaving equipment, straight and safety razors, barber bottles, basins, etc. Members get *Barber Shop Collectables* newsletter.

National Toothpick Holder Collectors' Society

PO Box 204, Eureka, IL 61530

Founded: 1973

Dues: $10.00 per year

(309) 467-2535

Members: 600

Contact: Audrey Trumbold

Members have donated their toothpick holders to the Neal Wendling Hospitality Fund--created to provide a bigger, better hospitality room at the National Toothpick Holders Annual Convention. And they also sponsored the book, *1000 Toothpick Holders*.

National Valentine Collector's Association

Box 1404, Santa Ana, CA 92702

Founded: 1977

Dues: $8.00 per year

(714) 547-1355

Members: 375

Contact: Evalene Pulati

Collectors of antique valentines can receive a quarterly bulletin and buy by auction through the mail.

New England Society of Open Salts Collectors

Pleasant Valley Road, PO Box 2007, Wolfeboro, NH 03894

Founded: 1978

Dues: $5.00 per year

Members: 300

Contact: Otto W. Olson, Jr.

New Mexico Barbed Wire Collectors' Association

2816 Camino Principe, Santa Fe, NM 87505

Founded: 1972

Dues: $6.00 per year

Members: 150

Contact: Dan Sowle

Yes, more barbed-wire collectors. The only membership requirement is an appreciation of barbed wire. There are over 800 different wire patents, and a full barbed-wire collection could have as many as 6000 different wires. It's hard to believe, but some of these rare wires are worth $50, even $500, in four-inch "shorty" segments! *Wire Barb & Nail* is the bi-monthly newsletter.

Nixon Political Item Collectors

PO Box 2354, Mission Viejo, CA 92690
Founded: 1975   Members: 100
Dues: $7.00 per year   Contact: Chris Crain

Buttons serve as a history lesson of the Nixon career: "Let's Clean House with Ike and Dick," "Khrushchev does not want Nixon & Lodge, I do." "Don't be a 'Jack' Ass, Vote Republican," "Lady Bird, Start Packing. the Nixons are coming." Chris Crain, who has been club president for 8 of its 12 years, grew up in San Clemente with parents who were staunch Republicans. He started his collection of Nixon memorabilia in 1968. Club members not only collect buttons but all other Nixon memorabilia including bumper stickers, jewelry, rubber elephants with the head of Nixon and long nose, books, and Nixon-Mao postage stamps. (The Nixon Catalog contains 100 pages of over 1,200 Nixon buttons.) *Checkers*, their quarterly newsletter, is named after the Nixon's dog and the 1952 speech in which he defended the use of an expense fund that supporters had raised for him by saying that the supporters had also given his daughters a dog called "Checkers" and regardless of the impropriety of that gift, he wasn't going to give the dog back.

Club members met with the former President at the "Western White House," San Clemente, in 1984. There they shared their collections with him. Chris Crain hopes his collection will end up in the Nixon Library. Nixon trivia: Nixon holds the record for the highest game bowled on the White House lanes: 233. Dick's favorite breakfast is corned beef hash and poached eggs. Nixon's 1968 campaign plane was called "The Tricia."

North American Vexillogical Association

Box 580, Winchester, MA 01890   (617) 729-9410
Founded: 1967   Members: 350
Dues: $12.00 per year   Contact: Dr. Whitney Smith

Interested in the design, manufacture, or history of flags? This group of individuals and corporations is. Vexillology is the study of flag history and symbolism.

Oil Products & Ephemera Collectors (OPEC)

2151 East Dublin-Granville Rd., Ste. G-292, Columbus, OH 43229
Founded: 1982   Members: 1000

Dues: $12.00 per year   Contact: Jerry Keyser

OPEC members have their own private "cartel" on oil company memorabilia.
Remember the Mobil Pegasus? How about the Humble tiger? Collections include
road maps, gas pumps, oil cans, bottles, matchbook covers---just about anything
from the gas stations of yesterday. The group was recently forced to change its
name to the International Petroliana Collectors Association (IPCA), (pressured by
some crabby oil sheiks??.) Members receive *Check the Oil!*

Old Sleepy Eye Collectors Club of America
PO Box 12, Monmouth, IL 61462
Founded: 1976   Members: 1200
Dues: Write for details   Contact: James Martin

Sleepy-eye pottery.

Olympic Collectors
PO Box 41630, Tucson, AZ 85717
Dues: $6.00 per year   Contact: Bill Nelson

Collectors of Olympic pins, medals and figurines.

On the Lighter Side
Route 3, 136 Circle Drive, Quitman, TX 75783
Dues: Write for details   Contact: Judith Sanders

Cigarette lighter collectors.

Orders and Medals Society of America
PO Box 484, Glassboro, NJ 08028
Founded: 1951   Members: 1000
Dues: $15.00 per year   Contact: John E. Lelle

The Medal Collector is published 10 times a year and a convention is held annually.

Organization for Collectors of Covered Bridge Postcards
P.O Box 68, Columbia City, OR 97018-0068   (503) 397-2999
Founded: 1976   Members: 299
Dues: $4.00 per year   Contact: Lorraine Hagen

"We are a group who go "nuts" over anything with a covered bridge on it, mostly postcards," says Lorraine Hagen, editor of *The Bridge Covered* newsletter. Their motto: "One by one, they disappear...the Covered Bridge of yesteryear."

Owl's Nest

PO Box 5491, Fresno, CA 93755   (209) 439-4845
Dues: $12.50 per year   Contact: Donna Howard

Owl collectors...not live birds, but lots of "tchotchkes."

Paileontologist's Retort

3608 Chelwood NE, Albuquerque, NM 87111

Believe it or not, this is a club for **lunch pail** collectors!

Painted Label Soda Pop Bottle Collectors

PO Box 712, Weston, WV 26452   (304) 842-3773
Dues: Write for details   Contact: Gary Brent Kincade

Paperweight Collectors' Association

20 Old Broadway, Garden City, NY 11040   (516) 741-3090
Founded: 1953   Members: 1200
Dues: $10.00 per year   Contact: Evan Pancake

Collectors of glass paperweights with colorful embedments. Members from 13 states have tried to encourage the production of high-quality paperweights.

Peanut Pals

PO Box 4465, Huntsville, AL 35815   (205) 881-9198
Founded: 1978   Members: 250
Dues: $10.00 per year   Contact: Judith Walthall

Thank goodness, the Planters Peanut Man will live forever! Peanut Pals collect memorabilia and historical information about the Planters Peanut Company and its products.

Pen Fancier's Club

1169 Overcash Dr., Dunedin, FL 33528   (813) 734-4742
Founded: 1977   Members: 1000+
Dues: $25.00 per year   Contact: Cliff Lawrence

Collectors of fancy fountain pens and other antique writing instruments, they publish a monthly magazine but hold no regular meetings.

Pepsi-Cola Collectors Club
PO Box 1275, Covina, CA 91722

Old bottles and advertising paraphernalia.

Pipe Collectors International
Box 22085, 6172 Airways Blvd., Chattanooga, TN 37422   (615) 892-7277
Founded: 1982   Members: 2000
Dues: $15.00 per year   Contact: C. Bruce Spencer

Pipe smokers and collectors, unite! The club runs smoking contests and members receive *Pipe Smoker*.

Plate-o-Holic
478 Ward Street Extension, Wallingford, CT 06492   (203) 265-1722
Founded: 1986   Members: 200
Dues: None   Contact: Adam Selesh

Dealing in limited edition plates and figurine collecting can be profitable. One limited-edition cookie plate sold in Denmark in 1895 for 50¢ now commands $5,000! Plate-O-Holic claims that there are 16.5 million plate lovers around the world.

Police Insignia Collector's Association
15 Pond Place, Cos Cob, CT 06807   (203) 661-3927
Founded: 1973   Members: 700
Dues: $15.00 per year   Contact: James J. Fahy

Most police departments have stopped giving away colorful shoulder badges because of cost, thus their value has skyrocketed for the collector. (The same goes for hats, uniforms and memorabilia.) Most Police Insignia Collectors Association members are law enforcement officers, but the association is open to all. Their newsletter is published bimonthly.

Procurers of Painted-Label Sodas
PO Box 8154, Houston, TX 77004   (713) 523-4346
Founded: 1980   Members: 100
Dues: Write for details   Contact: Victoria Herberta

Painted label bottles have "an enormous impact on life," say these collectors. The Coke or Pepsi bottle with its enameled logo painted onto the glass bottle has changed the way we live. The club publishes the book, *America Goes Pop*.

Rathkamp Matchcover Society

1359 Surrey Road, Vandalia, OH 45377   (513) 890-8684
Founded: 1941   Members: 1800
Dues: $6.00 first year ($5.00/yr. after)   Contact: John C. Williams

Named after Harry Rathkamp who was an early collector of matchbooks, the society has over 30 local groups who swap and sell. A recent issue of the bi-monthly *Voice of the Hobby* reported that the Diamond Match Company, who bought the original patent for the matchbook, is closing its Springfield, Mass. plant! Conventions are held each August.

Reagan Political Items Collectors

Rt. 1, Box 258B, Denison, TX 75020   (214) 465-2514
Founded: 1981   Members: 72
Membership: $10.00 per year   Contact: Rene J. Parenteau

"Dedicated to the collection and preservation of Ronald Reagan memorabilia. In addition, we urge support for President Reagan's programs." Members share and swap campaign buttons and movie posters. Membership entitles you to the quarterly newsletter, *Reagan Review*.

Salt and Pepper Shaker Collectors

RD 2, Watkins Glen, NY 14891
Dues: Write for details   Contact: Marian Boyce

Saltshaker Collectors Club

2832 Rapidan Tr., Maitland. FL, 32751   (305) 629-1168
Founded: 1983   Members: 150
Dues: $10.00 per year   Contact: Dottie and Bill Avery

Society for the Collection of Brand-Name Pencils

603 East 105th Street, Kansas City, MO 64131

Eberhart, Faber Castell, Kentucky Cardinal and others!!!

Society of Inkwell Collectors

5136 Thomas Ave., S, Minneapolis, MN 55410   (612) 922-279[?]
Founded: 1980   Members: 275+
Dues: $22.50 per year   Contact: Vincent D. McGraw

They say there are over 11,000 patents for inkwells....and the Society of Inkwell Collectors should know. Their quarterly newsletter, *The Stained Finger* has the latest on inkwells, from the Statue of Liberty Inkwell to the Great Northern Pacific Railroad Baked Potato Inkwell. These collectors plan their first convention for 1988 (maybe on January 23, National Handwriting Day?)

Society of Political Item Enthusiasts

Box 159, Kennedale, TX 76060   (817) 534-8146
Founded: 1980   Members: 700+
Dues: No membership fee   Contact: Dr. Robert M. Platt

Souvenir Card Collectors Society

PO Box 4155, Tulsa, OK 74159   (918) 747-6724
Founded: 1981   Members: 900
Dues: $15.00 per year   Contact: Dana Marr

Souvenir cards are 8 1/2" x 11" cards that are reproductions of the original steel engraved plates used to make money by the American Bank Note Company and the Bureau of Engravings.

Space Toy Information Center

623 S. Fourth St., Philadelphia, PA 19147   (215) 923-7465
Founded: 1979   Members: 150+

Collectors of "Space Toys" (ray guns, spacemen, and robots), a category of toys that defied definition until a couple of years ago, now have their own information center and trading post. Joel Spicak has over 10,000 of these toys in his private collection, with his favorites being helmets and his 500 ray guns. "Japan is making the most interesting toys," says Spicak. The Japanese are interested in space films that came out of the U.S. in the 1960s and 70s and are creating toys based on them that are not finding their way into this country. (Oh, *please*, Mr. Nakasone, keep the Toyotas, send us the *toys*!)

Spark Plug Collectors of America

PO Box 2229, Ann Arbor, MI 48106   (313) 994-3101
Founded: 1976   Members: 300
Dues: $10.00 per year   Contact: William H. Bond

No joke! These collectors can count over 3000 different brands of spark plugs manufactured since the 1890's. Their semiannual publication *The Ignitor* is filled with electric articles on restoring antique plugs.

Spoon Collecting Club

RR 1, Box 61, Shullsburg, WI 53586
Founded: 1974
Dues: Write for details

Members: 500
Contact: Winifred Rowe

Publishes *the Spooner*.

Stein Collectors International

PO Box 463, Kingston, NJ 08528
Founded: 1965
Dues: $20.00 per year

(201) 329-2567
Members: 1650
Contact: Jack G. Lowenstein

No six-packs here--thanks to a 13th-century potter in Cologne, Germany, there are beer steins in myriad shapes and forms to be collected by these club members. (By the 16th century, wise potters were adding lids to the vessels "to safeguard the contents of the stein from falling leaves, insects, birds...") Jack Lowenstein said with so many steins available, he had to specialize, choosing steins with a picture of the "The Munich Child," the symbol of Munich, Germany. His collection numbers 250 now. SCI publishes a quarterly newsletter, *Prosit*, (formerly *der Gemuetlichkeit*), holds quarterly meetings of the 20 regional chapters and an annual convention in July, and sponsors occasional trips to southern Germany.

Sugar Packet Club

6826 Home City Ave., Cincinnati, OH 45233
Founded: 1976
Dues: $3.50 per year ($4.50 Foreign)

(804) 359-0648
Members: 187
Contact: Paul Aylward

Did you know that...sugar packets from before the 1950s are almost non-existent?...advertising on sugar packets began in the mid-50s?...an average sugar packet collector has about 5,000 packets, cubes and wrappers? ...collectors empty the packets before displaying them? Al Wick does. He founded the first organized sugar-packet-collecting organization in the U.S., in 1965, coining the term, "Sucre Sacologists." Members share and trade information on their passion through *The Sugar Packet*, a warm, chatty quarterly newsletter. Writes a member, new to the U.S.:" I left all my sugar cubes in Paris, secure in metal boxes where they are safe from ants, but not from my mother when she runs out of sugar for her coffee."

Tea Leaf International
PO Box 904, Mt. Prospect, IL 60056
Founded: 1980
Dues: Write for details

Members: 600
Contact: Carolyn Nickerson

Sorry to say, this is not a club of tea leaf readers--they collect tea leaf china.

Teddy Bear Boosters Club
PO Box 520, Stanton, CA 90680

Texas Barbed Wire Collectors Association
1322 Lark, Lewisville, TX 75067
Founded: 1966
Dues: $13.00 per year

(214) 436-6762
Members: 300
Contact: Charlie Dalton

Their big meeting is the first weekend of August (also proclaimed "Barbed Wire Days," by Texas' governor Mark White) Drawings of wires and a price guide for over 1000 wires have been published in *The Barbed Wire Collector* a bi-monthly. One member crafted a barbed wire hat he says is great for an itchy scalp. And the "Barbarian of the Year" Award goes to a deserving barbed wired promoter.

Texas Date Nail Collectors Association
501 West Horton, Brenham, TX 77833
Founded: 1970
Dues: $12.00 per year

(409) 830-1495
Members: 200
Contact: Jerry Waits

At the turn of the century, railroads needed to better manage the replacement of worn railroad ties. Though many methods were tried, the practice of using specially marked and dated nails was started. Each railroad had its own distinctive nails, with round, oval or square heads, raised or lowered lettering, etc. The date-nail practice was abandoned about 20 years ago, but thousands of date nail lie in railroad beds throughout the country. The Texas Date Nail Collectors Association, the only official date-nail club, publishes the bi-monthly *Nailer News* and holds semi-annual meetings.

Thimble Collectors International
PO Box 2311, Des Moines, IA 50310
Founded: 1978
Dues: $15.00 for two years

Members: 800
Contact: Mignon Jeffords

With 25 regional groups such as the "Thimblefools of Northern Illinois" and

"Ohio Thimble Seekers," the organization keeps U.S. and international members up to date with tips on the various aspects of thimble collecting, through its newsletter and biennial thimble convention.

Tin Container Collectors Association

PO Box 440101, Aurora, CO 80014

Founded: 1971 — Members: 1000

Dues: Write for details — Contact: Clark Secrest

Clark Secrest started collecting tin cans after he found a Log Cabin syrup tin from the 1930s at a junk shop. For twenty-five years, food and tobacco manufacturers depended on tin containers as a major form of advertising. While most of the boxes are beautiful with fine lithography, Clark says with a laugh that "some of the rarest ones do happen to be pretty ugly." Members receive *Tin Type* monthly.

Train Collectors Association

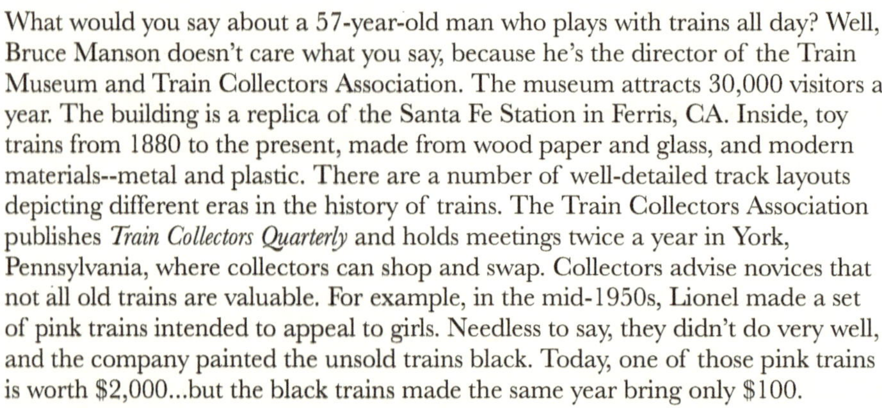

Train Museum, PO Box 248, Strasburg, PA 17579

Founded: 1954 — Members: 600

Dues: Write for details — Contact: Bruce Manson

What would you say about a 57-year-old man who plays with trains all day? Well, Bruce Manson doesn't care what you say, because he's the director of the Train Museum and Train Collectors Association. The museum attracts 30,000 visitors a year. The building is a replica of the Santa Fe Station in Ferris, CA. Inside, toy trains from 1880 to the present, made from wood paper and glass, and modern materials--metal and plastic. There are a number of well-detailed track layouts depicting different eras in the history of trains. The Train Collectors Association publishes *Train Collectors Quarterly* and holds meetings twice a year in York, Pennsylvania, where collectors can shop and swap. Collectors advise novices that not all old trains are valuable. For example, in the mid-1950s, Lionel made a set of pink trains intended to appeal to girls. Needless to say, they didn't do very well, and the company painted the unsold trains black. Today, one of those pink trains is worth $2,000...but the black trains made the same year bring only $100.

T.S.H.I.R.T.S.
The Society Handling the Interchange of Remarkable T-Shirts

2554 Lincoln Blvd. #400, Venice, CA 90291 — (213) 385-5103

Founded: 1976 — Members: 35,000+

Tom Grossa says that the T-Shirt is "one of America's greatest contributions to the world of fashion and popular culture." He should know, with his collection of hundreds of unique T-Shirts. Members not only are collectors, but are designers, manufacturers and dealers.

Universal Autograph Collectors Club

PO Box 467, Rockville Centre, NY 11571 (516) 766-0093
Founded: 1965 Members: 1,000
Dues: $10.00 per year Contact: Herman M. Darvick

Greta Garbo's is worth $675, Christopher Columbus' is worth a million, and Elvis Presley's is worth $75. Not their sunglasses, maps or picks, but...their autographs. Herman M. Darvick, who has the autograph of every US Vice President, says that while autographs can be worth a lot (Caesar's Palace Casino is offering more than $2 million for Julius Caesar's), with a little persistence you can get a famous person's autograph for the price of a stamp, if you send a sincere, handwritten, personal note. The Universal Autograph Collectors Club publishes *The Pen and Quill* bimonthly.

Willow Society

39 Medhurst Road, Toronto, Ontario, Canada M4B 1B2 416-757-0634
Founded: 1978 Members: 550
Dues: $15.00 per year Contact: Conrad Beirnacki

Ever wonder where the expression "blue plate special" came from. Willow Society members know that it was so named originally because it was served on blue willow patterned plates. Members collect willow pattern china, probably the most popular china pattern ever. The pattern, featuring a large willow tree and a bridge, was first created by Josiah Spode about 1810. By 1830, there were over 200 manufacturers using the pattern. The pattern has been copied on draperies, carpets and almost everything else. The society publishes the *Willow Transfer Quarterly* and holds conventions.

World's Fair Collectors Society

PO Box 20806, Sarasota, FL 33583 (813) 923-2590
Founded: 1968 Members: 300
Dues: $10.00 per year Contact: Michael R. Pender

Former Long Island resident and fair lover Michael Pender was director of state exhibitions under Robert Moses at the 1964-65 World's Fair. With an extensive collection of plates, buttons, and giveaways, he and his wife started the World's Fair Collectors Society. Members are interested in preserving the history of fairs, from the Crystal Palace exhibition of 1851 to the World's Fair slated for 1992 in Seville, Spain, marking the quincentennial of Columbus' voyage. Future association projects include a museum and a catalog of historic fair structures that are still standing.

FOR THE SPORT

How's your Barrel-Jumping team doing? Racers, chasers, gamesmen or markswomen, these folks know how to have a good time...in some of the strangest ways you've ever heard of.

All-American Soap Box Derby

PO Box 7233, Akron, OH 44306
Founded: 1933
Dues: Write for details

(216) 733-8723
Members: 100 local clubs
Contact: Wayne L. Alley

For the last 50 years, August in Akron has meant the Soap Box Derby race. Every kid wants to build a soapbox racer at one time during their childhood, but these kids get theirs to work. There are many strict specifications as to how the cars should be built, among them, that parents can't help! The winners have to show the judges that they can take apart and put back together their vehicles without Mom or Dad. Entrants must have won local soap box meets before coming to hilly Akron to compete. Winners receive scholarships ($5000 for first place), and prizes are given for best construction, decoration, and originality in design.

American Alpine Club

113 E. 90th St., New York, NY 10128
Founded: 1902
Dues: Membership by nomination only

(212) 722-1628
Members: 1600
Contact: Frank Delavega

Members have climbed mountains or conducted explorations of Arctic or Antarctic regions.

American Armwrestling Association

PO Box 132, Scranton, PA 18512
Founded: 1971
Dues: Write for details

(717) 342-4982
Members: 500
Contact: Bob O'Leary

Sponsors competitions. Betch a brew.

American Coaster Enthusiasts

PO Box 8226, Chicago, IL 60680
Founded: 1978
Dues: $20.00 per year

(312) 776-8868
Members: 1400+
Contact: Liucija Ambrosiani

You've heard about the best of them: the Texas Cyclone in Houston, The Thunderbolt at Kennywood Park, Mister Twister in Denver, The Cyclone in Coney Island, and The Beast at Kings Island near Cincinnati. American Coaster Enthusiasts know these rollercoasters and others backwards and forwards. They are involved in promoting coasters, developing the art of rollercoaster building and helping to save the old wooden vintage coasters from demolition. They hope to develop a rollercoaster museum with old cars, models and a rehabilitation workshop. Members receive *Roller Coaster!* and *Coaster World*.

American Coon Hunters Association

Box 30, Ingraham, IL 62434   (618) 752-6691
Founded: 1948   Members: 600
Dues: $5.00   Contact: Floyd E. Butler

Git your hound and run a coon up a tree, 'cause hounds are considered "tree'd" (for which they are awarded points) if they repeatedly bark at a raccoon who is sitting, scared to death, in the tree. The association's goals are the conservation of the raccoon and its habitat. Each October, the ACHA holds the World Championship Wild Coon Hunt, bringing coon hunters and their hounds together to a different state each year. Popular hound dog names: Scout, Killer, J.R., Ace, Ranger and the ever-popular Tracker.

American Cryptogram Association

12317 Dalewood Drive, Wheaton, MD 20902
Founded: 1929   Members: 800
Dues: Write for details   Contact: Margaret Blomquist

These puzzle experts were called in to join the war effort, some helping to break enemy codes, and cracking the Japanese code "PURPLE" during WWII. Members collect ciphering devices (hard to come by, because the government supposedly destroys all after use), Publishes the bi-monthly *Cryptogram*. The cover of the journal has an ornamental design, by a member from Holland who goes by the name of HANO---the design is actually a clever and difficult code. The journal also is filled with cryptograms, that about 25% of the membership completes, sending in answers for credit.

American Darts Organization

13841 Eastbrook Avenue, Bellflower, CA 90706   (213) 925-1205
Founded: 1975   Members: 50,000
Dues: $10.00 per year   Contact: Tom Fleetwood

The American Darts Organization is busy setting up darts tournaments with strict code of darts rules, helping members improve their darts game, helping people set up their own darts leagues. The visionary goals of the ADO are to help to get more media coverage for the sport, to try to develop a youth movement in darts, and to arrange low-price hotel and airline rates for traveling darters. Upon request, the ADO will send the official rules for a proper dartboard set-up. Members receive *Double Eagle* newsletter.

American Double Dutch League

PO Box 776, Bronx, NY 10451   (212) 681-2437
Founded: 1973   Members: 40,000
Dues: $10.00 per year   Contact: David A. Walker

Promoting the sport of Double Dutch rope jumping. Members say that the sport requires teamwork, cooperation, creativity and coordination--plus only two ropes!! The Double Dutch Training Film is a must for all serious jumpers. The club was started by a member of the New York City Police Department.

American Kiteflyers Association

3839 Dustin Road, Burtonsville, MD 20866
Founded: 1964   Members: 1550
Dues: $15.00 per year   Contact: Robert Price

Both for builders and flyers. competitions are held, at the annual convention. Members receive discounts at participating kite stores.

American Racing Pigeon Union

13 Glenwood Lane, Grenville, SC 29605   (803) 277-5405
Founded: 1910   Members: 11,000
Dues: $3.50 per year   Contact: Mrs. Edna Scifres

Just imagine if all your friends were taken to the middle of New Jersey and set free to race home to Ohio. Impossible? Not if your buddies are like Mr. Smart, Good Vibrations or The Red Mojo, racing pigeons whose natural urge to fly home is far stronger than Dorothy's in Oz...or even E.T.'s. Pigeon racers take their champion birds 100, 300...even 500 miles away from their homes, set them free and time them, to see who flies home first. Races of 100-600 miles are common for "Old Birds" and 100-300 miles for "Young Birds." A good pigeon will fly 600 miles in one day and one breed, the Racing Homers, can fly 700 miles in a day, over 16 hours at 45 mph. (ground speed)! Pigeons were originally used as messengers and in the World Wars were credited for saving many lives as couriers. The union maintains a large number of highly-bred, virile and tested racing pigeons to be available in times of war. The AU offers free diplomas for race winners, videotapes and films of pigeon races. *Racing Pigeon Bulletin* is America's first and

only racing pigeon weekly, although the sport has over a million "flyers"
internationally and fierce devotees in Belgium, England and Japan.

Balloon Federation of America

PO Box 264, Indianola, IA 50125   (515) 961-8809
Founded: 1961   Members: 3500
Dues: Write for details   Contact: Thomas Sheppard

Members either own their own balloons or belong to a local club with a hot air
balloon. The Federation is involved in ballooning events and competitions around
the country.

Baseball, Football & Sports Hall of Shame

PO Box 6218, West Palm Beach, FL 33405
Founded: 1983   Contact: Bruce Nash

This club is not for your amateur jock. No, you have to be a professional athlete
who has *really* screwed up--committed an embarrassing blooper, boner, blunder or
wacky foul-up of some kind. These infamous stars are inducted into one of the
Halls of Shame. The results of the "induction ceremonies" are printed in books
by the same name, available from Pocket Books.

Bass'n Gal

Box 13925, 3600 West Pioneer Pkwy, Arlington, TX 76013 (817) 265-6214
Founded: 1976   Members: 12,000
Dues: $15.00 per year   Contact: Sugar Ferris

Women fishermen--women fisherwomen?--fishers!

Bicycle Network

PO Box 8194, Philadelphia, PA 19101   (215) 222-1253
Founded: 1976   Members: 100
Dues: Write for details   Contact: John Dowlin

If someone screams "Velorution!," they don't have a weird back ailment, and
they're not trying to overthrow a small country. The Bicycle Network is working
for velorution--the French word for bicycle revolution--on a worldwide basis. The
Bicycle Network advocates bicycles as a healthful, efficient and low-cost form of
transportation. They conduct seminars on how to transport and park bicycles and
promoting cycling for commuters in developing countries. The Network also
offers its quarterly calendar they call *Cycle and Recycle.*

Brown Trout Club

Box 744, Portland, ME 04104   (207) 773-8561
Founded: 1981   Members: 1981
Dues: $14.00 per year   Contact: Hubert J. Hughes

A virtual clearinghouse of information on how and where to catch trout and salmon.

Church of Monday Night Football

PO Box 2127, Santa Barbara, CA 93102   (805) 687-5331
Founded: 1979   Members: 1,000
Dues: $9.00 for each conversion   Contact: Rev. Richard Slade

First there was Moses, then Martin Luther, then Sun Myung Moon and now the Reverend Richard Slade, a marketing man from Santa Barbara, California. With the three wise men spreading the gospel (Frank Gifford, Don Meredith and Howard "The Mouth" Cosell), thousands of converts have found the way home. The Rev says that "every church has a mission, and this is ours. We want a Super Bowl on Monday night." He says, "Monday night football is unique because it is a social event. You generally watch Saturday and Sunday football alone." As the Rev sits behind one, two, even six televisions on Monday, he explains that Sunday is a family day. So, as the church's blessing reads, "Play it on Mondays!"

The Six Commandments of the Church are:
I.   Thou shalt keep Monday Night holy...and tune in early.
II.   Honor thy holy point spread...for it is right on.
III.   Thou shalt not covet thy neighbor's beer.
IV.   Thou shalt not commit adultery during halftime highlights.
V.   Thou shalt stay tuned until the final gun...for the spread may change.
VI.   Forgive those who bet against their home team...for they know not what they do.

The Commandment After...
     Prepare for the day when the Super Bowl is played on Monday Night Football...for on that day there will be heaven on earth.

Those who make the conversion receive the membership card with the sacred schedule of games printed on it, a sacred scroll with the Six Commandments, plus bumper sticker, coaster and full-color divine decal and a subscription to the church's newsletter.

Explorers Club

46 E. 70th St., New York, NY 10021   (212) 628-8383
Founded: 1904   Members: 3200
Dues: Write for details   Contact: Mrs. Eileen Harsch

Professional explorers and scientists.

Fifty-Plus Runners Association

PO Box D, Stanford, CA 94305   (415) 497-6254
Founded: 1980   Members: 1400
Dues: $10.00 per year   Contact: Dr. Peter Wood

This association focuses on the effects of running on health, disability and longevity. While studying the causes of arthritis at the Disease Prevention Center in Stanford, Dr. Wood found that the over-50 runners have an average bone density that is *40% higher* than that of their sedentary counterparts. The *Fifty Plus Bulletin* is filled with inspiring articles, like one on a woman's 100-mile run!

Highamerica Balloon Club

PO Box 99362, Troy, NY 48099   (313) 435-4160
Founded: 1968   Members: 300
Dues: Write for details   Contact: Linden F. Harding

Formerly the Balloon Platoon of America.

Iceberg Athletic Club

3046 West 22nd Street, Brooklyn, NY 11224   (212) 372-8457
Founded: 1918   Members: 25
Dues: Write for details   Contact: Vic Boff

Though he is in his eighties, Vic Boff swims every day, 365 days a year, in the Atlantic Ocean off Coney Island. Vic, the club's third president (the first president was Detective George Lawrence O'Connor of the NYC Missing Persons Bureau) is a health and fitness fanatic. The club's purpose, according to Vic, is to "bring serious winter bathers together. Our philosophy is to live the outdoor life. Most people waste the winter sitting in their homes. We are putting winter back in our lives."

First founded as the Polar Bear Club, in 1901, they reorganized after WWI to become the Iceberg Athletic Club. Other than the Parachute amusement park ride and Nathan's Famous Hot Dogs stand, the Club is Coney Island's oldest landmark or organization still active. Though their passion has been recorded and written about by hundreds of newspapers and reporters, they are adamant about the fact that they don't swim for the publicity (the Icebergs are certainly not the only winter athletic club--winter swimming is practiced around the world in places like Sweden and the Soviet Union.)

Vic, who is also a weightlifter, says that once the body is acclimated, you never catch a cold (he's only had five colds in 25 years.) Some members go as their schedules permit, but others like Vic Boff go every day no matter what. The coldest day in Iceberg history was when the water temperature was 28 degrees. Ice had drifted near the shoreline, and the six brave swimmers had to push the razor-sharp floating pieces away. One member, a postal worker, said, "I don't miss a day, regardless of the weather. You know how the saying goes, 'Through rain and snow and sleet....' We do the same thing with swimming that the post office does with the mail." Vic Boff promises, "It's a tremendous stimulant," but, as the club motto says, "If you turn red, go ahead; if you turn blue, it's not for you."

International Academy of Twirling Teachers

PO Box 266, Janesville, WI, 53547

Dues: $12.00 per year   Members: 9,000

Majorettes everywhere, the demand for good twirling teachers is ever spiraling upwards! Members are sworn "to carry the benefits of baton twirling to the young people of all free countries of the world." Teachers receive *Drum Major*, the original national twirling magazine, with all the news in the wonderful world of twirling.

International Cheerleading Foundation

4425 Indian Creek Pkwy, Overland Park, KS   66207   (913) 649-3666

Founded: 1964   Members: 29,000+

Dues: $5.00 per year   Contact: Randy Neil

Give me a J! Give me an O! Give me an I! Give me an N!
What do you get?!?

2020 Update:
ACTIVE

International Sled Dog Racing Association

PO Box 446, Nordman, ID 83848   (208) 443-3153

Founded: 1966   Members: 1500

Dues: $10.00 per year   Contact: Donna Hawley

Want to be a musher? Sled dogs were originally used by Eskimos and Indians for companionship and transportation and later by white men to transport the mail and news to remote areas. (In 1925, sled dogs saved the stricken village of Nome, Alaska from diphtheria by quickly transporting antitoxin across the interior of Alaska and the Bering Sea icecap.) Today, the sled dog is being replaced by aircraft and snowmobile, but the sport of sled dog racing has been growing steadily. (The longest racecourse is the 1,100 mile Iditarod Trail race from Anchorage to Nome.) The Alaskan husky can pull the wooden sleds up to 25 miles per hour over short distances. Some sled dog events test speed, some endurance and the weight pulling contests (pulling up to 2000 pounds on a sled) test strength.

International Unicycling Federation

16152 Kinloch, Redford, MI 48240

Founded: 1982   Members: 150

Dues: $15.00 per year   Contact: Al Hemminger

"Anyone who can learn to walk can learn to ride a unicycle," said William Jenack, the father of modern unicycling. Backing up that fact was Nini Hall, the youngest unicyclist ever--at 18 months, she made her stage unicycling debut in diapers. John Lizza, the first blind unicyclist on record might also agree. One of the events in the 1987 World Unicycling Convention in Japan was the attempt to break American champ Floyd Beattie's 100-mile unicycling record of 7 hours, 18 minutes and 55 seconds. (Hundred miles seem long? On a homemade five-foot high "giraffe" unicycle, Pietro Biondo of Montreal covered 12,193 miles in 1982. Five feet sound tall? The world's tallest unicycle was 101 feet high, weighing 1400 pounds, built and ridden by Steve McPeak of Nevada.) The IUF is trying to achieve Olympic status for unicycling. Members receive a one-year subscription to *Unicycling* magazine, discounts to many conventions, and a membership card.

Jersey Rag Racers

Medford Lakes, NJ   (609) 654-8672

                                                Members: 30

Dues: Write for details   Contact: Jack McManus

Dedicated to the old English sport of whippet racing. These swift-running dogs look like greyhounds, only a little smaller. One handler holds the dog, the other waves a rag to attract the whippet's attention. The dogs race to the owners, and first one there wins.

National Association of Left-Handed Golfers

10149 Hammerly, No. 714, Houston, TX 77080   (713) 464-8683

Founded: 1936   Members: 1300

Dues: $17.50 per year   Contact: Kenneth R. Ahrens

Other than being a male southpaw wielding a club, this group only requires a member "to be a good guy." You can tell who the group members are on the golf course, says Ken Ahrens, because, "they are the only ones standing on the right side of the ball," even in Tasmania and Taiwan. Left-handed golfers have a distinct advantage, too: "Nobody knows enough about your swing to give you advice." (Ahrens also reported that the club is the same age as Mickey Mouse and Alcoholics Anonymous, although no conclusions should be drawn.) Each year, NALG sponsors the National Amateur Open and Senior Championship. A newsletter of activities is available, and there'll be a club song if the "lefty" running for mayor of Reno has time to complete it.

National Baton Twirling Association International

2020 Update: ACTIVE

Box 266, Janesville, WI 53545   (608) 754-2238
Founded: 1947   Members: 15000
Dues: Free   Contact: Don Sartell

Sponsors the annual twirling championships.

National Contesters Association
3205 Hillsdale Drive, Des Moines, IA 50322
Founded: 1937   Members: 750
Dues: Write for details   Contact: Jewell Wintermeyer

No, it's not a social club for ex-Wheel of Fortune contestants. The NCA sponsors "skill" writing competitions, with prizes for the winners.

National Jousting Association
328 Bush Chapel Rd., Aberdeen, MD 21001   (301) 272-3086
Founded: 1968   Members: 10 local clubs
Dues: Write for details   Contact: Alice M. Blum

Modern jousters don't kill their opponents. In ring tournaments, the mounted jousters spear small rings with their lances.

2020 Update: ACTIVE

National Pigeon Association
Box 3488, Orange, CA 92665   (714) 637-6285
Founded: 1920   Members: 1600
Dues: $10.00 per year   Contact: James R. Larinore

Pigeon raisers and racers.

2020 Update: ACTIVE

National Puzzlers League
325 Middlesex Rd., Buffalo, NY 14216   (716) 876-3227
Founded: 1883   Members: 300
Dues: $8.00 per year ($2.00 initiation fee)   Contact: Marjorie B. Friedman

The meeting grounds for crossword puzzlers and other word puzzle lovers.

National Speleological Society

Cave Avenue, Huntsville, AL 35810
Founded: 1941

Members: 6500

Dues: Write for details

Contact: Paul Stevens

This cave-fanciers' society has its own private cave--the subject of an intense conservation effort because it has a unique collection of specially-adapted small cave animals, including blind salamanders, and blind fish. The most incredible thing about this limestone cave is that it's located smack in the middle of Huntsville, Alabama--right under the First National Bank!!

North American Tiddlywinks Association

10416 Haywood Drive, Silver Spring, MD 20902 (301) 681-9345
Founded: 1967

Members: 125

Dues: Write for details

Contact: Larry Kahn

Imagine a room of perpetual college students sitting around a table at MIT, or Cornell, speaking with a strange vocabulary: "I can't pot my nurdled wink, so I'll piddle you free and you can boondock a red. But if Sunshine gromps the double, I'll lunch a blue next time." The subject is tiddlywinks, a game that was purportedly invented by one Joseph Assheton Fincher of London. Fincher patented the game in 1888 and trademarked the name "Tiddlewinks" a year later. The name supposedly is taken as a derivation from the name of unlicensed pubs in England in the 1830s, called "Kiddlywinks."

The game was very popular in the 1890s, but interest waned until 1958 when Prince Phillip was challenged to a match. Then the tiddlywinks team from Oxford challenged teams from American Ivy League schools...and that's where it stands today, with most American winkers coming from these Northeastern schools. The game differs in many respects from the children's game of tiddlywinks that merely consist of flipping a chip.

Winkers have their own nicknames: Horsemeat, Dragon, Bozo. Some of them, like Sunshine and Ferd, use only their nicknames in everyday life. NATwA sponsors Tiddlywinks tournaments, with the typical winking season consisting of three championships. The association publishes *Newswink* and maintains close ties with the English Tiddlywinks Association.

Over the Hill Gang, International

13791 East Rice Place, Aurora, CO 80015

(303) 699-6404
Founded: 1977

Members: 1400

Dues: $50.00 per year

Contact: William Vandersluis

Three gray-haired Colorado skiing instructors founded this club to combat declining interest in skiing among older people. Today, there are more than a dozen "gangs" around the country, recreational clubs for people over 50 years old. The most popular sport still is skiing, with lift ticket discounts available for members, but members get into bike riding, rafting trips, camping, sailing, tennis and golf...even hot air ballooning. The average age of the members is about 57, with the oldest member being 94 and the most famous member being former President Jerry Ford. Members can join at large or can join an existing gang like "The New Jersey's Gangsters" and "Chicago's Silver Fox Gang." The club's quarterly newsletter is called *The Legend*.

The club motto: "Once you're over the hill, you pick up speed!"

Riders of the Wind, Field Event Players Association

PO Box 43, Wallops Island, VA 23337   (301) 651-DISC
Founded: 1982   Members: 150+
Dues: $7.50 per year   Contact: Michael D. Conger

Throwing a Frisbee® is not just fun and games anymore. Riders of the Wind promote the Frisbee® for sporting and recreational events. The Pegasus Award is given to the best Frisbee player each year.

Scrabble Crossword Game Players

4320 Veterans Memorial Hwy, Holbrook, NY 11741 (516) 588-7781
Founded: 1972   Members: 9000
Dues: $10.00 per year   Contact: James A. Houle

With over 200 local groups around North America, the club sanctions tournaments and supervises the compilation of the Official Scrabble Players Dictionary. Starting a local Scrabble group is serious business, though. Directors of local groups must take a 58-page test and score above 90 percent to qualify for the job. The Games themselves last one hour and turns are held to a strict three-minute limit "If you have to go to the bathroom and it takes longer than three minutes, you lose your turn," said one club director. You even have to fill out special forms in order to challenge a word--the Official Scrabble Player Dictionary decides the answer. The top five players receive cash awards and the winner gets a trip to England to play against the British national Scrabble champion--the tournament is held every two years (next one in 1989.) A newsletter is sent every two months to members.

Seventy Plus Ski Club

104 East Side Dr., Ballston Lake, NY 12019   (518) 399-5458
Founded: 1977   Members: 2,800
Dues: $5.00 lifetime membership   Contact: Lloyd T. Lambert

Lloyd Lambert, a writer and reporter on skiing since 1944, was concerned when some septuagenarians said they couldn't afford to ski because they were on fixed incomes. To that end, Lambert formed the Seventy Plus Ski Club, to offer free or discount skiing to active downhillers over the age of 70. Members now hail from 47 states and a dozen countries overseas. The club runs a ski trip to Europe each winter. Lambert himself has been skiing for *over 70 years...since 1915*! He is an interesting character who has appeared on national television and radio, for not only skiing, but recreational boating as well. He was employed as a sign painter and department store display director, and as a young man went into vaudeville for a year (he was a natural...his father sold Charlie Chaplin his derby hats.)

Skate Sailing Association of America

R.D. 2, Box 429, White House Station, NJ 08889 (201) 534-9287
Founded: 1922   Members: 150
Dues: $3.00 per year   Contact: Ron Palmer

This is the club for the growing winter sport of racing on a sled with a sail on a frozen pond or lake.

Society of Saunterers International

2461 Whitehouse Trail, Gaylord, MI 49735
Founded: 1985   Members: 300
Dues: $15.00 per year   Contact: Anthony Jenckes
Morse

Sauntering may be the exercise of the future. No joke! It doesn't take any special equipment, except the occasional walking stick or umbrella, can be done anywhere without attracting attention and anyone who can walk...can saunter. The first sauntering society was formed by a group of philosophy students who pointed out that in ancient Greece, Aristotle lectured his students during walks to stimulate thought. One enthusiast said that sauntering is the perfect outdoor sport for her because "I've never been in a hurry to get anywhere." What is the difference between ambling, sauntering and just walking? No one is quite sure-- except that sauntering is pointless. Practiced on the decks of passenger liners and city sidewalks after dinner or theater, the more mindless it is, the better. The Society of Saunterers, International proposes that walking "most perfectly serves the person, saves the planet, and vice versa." *The Saunterer* monthly emphasizes the literary and philosophical aspects of the joys of sauntering.

Their motto: "Walk and go, even now, even so."

The Stone Skipping and Gerplunking Club

Unicorn Ltd. Conglomerate, Lake Superior State College
Office of College Relations, Sault Ste. Marie, MI 49783   (906) 635-2315
Founded: 1968   Members: 500
Dues: Write for details   Contact: W. T. Rabe

On the shores of Mackinac Island, MI, with its abundance of flat stones, the Grand Old Man of Stone-Skipping, U.S. Navy Commander E. M. Tellefson, (who started skipping stones in 1932) proclaims "Let he who is without Fisbee cast the first stone." Thus starts the Mackinac Island Open Stone Skipping Tournament each July 4th. Entrants have paid a fifty-cent fee to toss plinks, pittypats, plunkers, agnews and skronkers. (Plinks are clean cut long skips, pittipats are short skips at the end of a run, a plunker is a stone that skinks, an agnew is a stone that lands in the crowd and a skronker is a stone that never hits the water.) They're all looking for that stone which will skip forever and win them the coveted "Little David Trophy," a 75- pound mounted rock *and* 52 pounds (a pound per week) of Ryba's Fudge, a Mackinac Island delicacy. The world record for skipping was 24 skips (in 1975 and 1977.) This is a family sport, with adults having no discernible advantage over children. Technique is fairly important, too. Founder W. T. Rabe says, "it's all in the foot and the arm. Swing from the shoulder, keep the stone low, breathe deeply and let 'er rip." Rabe says the club's motto is "Leave no stone unskipped."

Unicycling Society of America

Box 40534, Redford, MI 48240   (313) 533-4677
Founded: 1973   Members: 500
Dues: $6.00 per year   Contact: Carol Brichford

The USA sponsors local and national unicycling meets. "Contrary to popular belief, just about anyone can learn to ride, including several blind person and people well over 60 years of age." Members receive *On One Wheel Magazine*.

U.S. Amateur Tug of War Association

PO Box 9626, Madison, WI 53715   (608) 845-9312
Founded: 1978   Members: 500+
Dues: $15.00 per year or $100 for life   Contact: Robert Pulfer

When tug-of-war was deleted from the Olympic line-up in 1920, Americans almost forgot about this historic team sport. That was until Robert Pulfer came along and formed the U.S. Amateur Tug of War Association. In 1984, he hosted the World Championship Tug-of-War competition in the spirit of the Olympics, with 16 countries, including India and Israel, pulling together in Oshkosh, Wisconsin. In competition, a team competes against another of equal total weight. (Unfortunately for some of us onlookers, the rules state that each team member must weigh in wearing non-transparent shorts only.)

Tug-of-war has a long history, first as part of ancient rituals in tribes and cultures. In Indonesia and Burma, winning the tug-of-war was taken as an omen of rain. As early as 2500 B.C., tug-of-war became a sport activity, showing up in Egypt, China, and Turkey among other countries.

Pullers can purchase bumper stickers ("Tug on this" or "Pull till you puke!"), caps and necklaces.

U.S. Barrel Jumping Association

16220 Chatham, Detroit, MI 48219   (313) 535-5999
Founded: 1977   Members: 50
Dues: Write for details   Contact: Bennett W. Sipes

This has nothing to do with a drop over Niagara Falls, though if anyone wants to start that kind of barreling club, please tell us. The United States Barrel Jumping Association promotes the sport of jumping over barrels while on ice skates. The barrels are lined up in a straight line and jumpers try to jump over as many as possible without breaking their necks.

U.S. Boomerang Association

Box 182, Delaware, OH 43015   (614) 353-8332
Founded: 1980   Members: 500
Dues: $10.00 per year   Contact: Chet Snouffer

Promoting the sport of boomerang science, the USBA runs competitions and members receive *Many Happy Returns* quarterly.

U.S. Disc Sports

462 Main Street, West Hampton Beach, NY   11978   (516) 634-3040
Founded: 1967   Members: 100 clubs
Dues: $12.00 per year   Contact: Eric Wootten

Formerly the International Frisbee Disc Association. They are now members of the World Flying Disc Federation in Sweden.

U.S. Hang Gliding Association

PO Box 66306, Los Angeles, CA 90066   (213) 390-3065
Founded: 1971   Members: 8000+
Dues: $29.50 per year   Contact: Amy C. Gray

U.S.M.A. (Unofficially, the U.S. Monopoly® Association)
26097 Hendrie, Huntington Woods, MI 48070   (313) 963-3542
Founded: 1963   Members: 1000
Dues: Write for details   Contact: Lee Avery Weisenthal

"Go directly to jail, do not pass go and do not collect $200."

This is a rowdy group of Monopoly® players who compete against each other.
Since Monopoly® is a registered trademark of Parker Brothers, they can't use it in
the club name.

U.S. National Marbles Tournament
City Hall, Cumberland, MD 21502   (301) 722-2000
Founded: 1923   Contact: Eugene Mason
When: A week in the middle of June   Where: Wildwood, New Jersey

The national tournament for kids between 8 and 14 years old, with trophies and a
$500 prize for the champions. These kids play a game known as "Ringer,"
knuckling down on a shooter, putting a backspin on it, and plunking it into the
ring. Girls have had their own championship since 1948.

U.S. Orienteering Federation
PO Box 1039, Ballwin, MO 63011   (314) 394-2869
Founded: 1971   Members: 4000+
Dues: $15-$20.00 per year   Contact: Robert L. DeFer

Orienteering involves going deep into the woods--where most of us would be
hopelessly lost--and finding your way back to civilization with the use of a map
and a compass. Orienteering has become the "natural" sport of the 1980's--a
good alternative to hunting or bulldozing.

U.S. Othello Association
PO Box 342, Falls Church, VA 22046
Dues: $6.00 per year   Contact: John A Storer

Othello is a game of strategy, using black and white chips on a checkerboard. The
association publishes the "world-renowned" *Othello* quarterly, holds Othello
tournaments, maintains player's ratings.

U.S. Parachute Association

1440 Duke Street, Alexandria, VA 22314   (703) 836-3495

Founded: 1957   Members: 16,000

Dues: $29.50 per year ($3.00 1st time fee)   Contact: Bab Eyk

2020 Update: ACTIVE

"The United States Parachuting Association has just one job--to keep you jumping." A division of the National Aeronautic Association, it was founded to promote safety in skydiving. Membership includes public liability/property damage insurance and a 12-month subscription to *Parachutist,* which features regular reports of fatal and non-fatal accidents (falling onto a parked car, jumping into Lake Erie and drowning.) The USPA will help you "Spread Your Wings," selling decals, patches, clothing and updating your skydiving library with books on night jumps, water jumps, first-jump certificates. It will also provide you--at no cost--with your very own fatality report form. You might buy *D.B. Cooper Dead or Alive?* a book about the fate of a legendary skydiver who jumped from a Boeing 727 with $200,000 in his pocket. As their motto reads, "Blue skies and soft landings!"

U.S. Trivia Association

720 Rockhurst, Lincoln, NE 68510   (402) 483-1759

Founded: 1977   Members:

Dues: Write for details   Contact: Ron Hicks

Home of the National Trivia Hall of Fame and library with thousands of books on Trivia. Members receive the monthly *Trivia Unlimited* Magazine

U.S. Twirling Association

PO Box 24488, Seattle, WA 98124   (206) 623-5623

Founded: 1958   Members: 10,000

Dues: $14.00 per year   Contact: Kathy Forsythe

2020 Update: ACTIVE

Competitors, judges and teachers of baton twirling.

World Championship Cutter & Chariot Racing Association

824 Southwood Dr., Murray, UT 84107   (801) 266-3131

Founded: 1964

Dues: Write for details   Contact: K. B. Bud Anderson

2020 Update: ACTIVE

Has Ben Hur been here?

World Footbag Association

1317 Washington Avenue, Golden, CO 80401   (303) 278-9797
Founded: 1983   Members: 2700
Dues: $5.00 per year   Contact: Bruce Guettich

Since 1977, over six million footbags have been sold worldwide. The footbag is made of leather, weighs a little more than an ounce, is about two inches in diameter and is filled with plastic pellets. The basic object in a footbag game is to try and keep the bag off the ground by kicking in with the feet. The world record is now held by Andy Linder from Illinois who kicked his footbag 32,598 times in less than five-and-a-half hours without dropping it once! For those who are wondering, "Hacky-Sack" is the brand name of the original footbag now distributed by Wham-O, Inc. The WFA is dedicated to promoting, educating and stimulating interest in all footbag games and footbags. They provide info of how to kick a footbag, and on care and maintenance of your footbag. WFA co-founder Greg Cortopassi has put together a collection of over 1,400 footbags from the original Hacky Sack® prototype, to footbags covered in exotic materials like snake, mink, weasel and eel. Some of his bags are filled with cherry pits, rubber bands, walnuts, and even human hair. WFA offers a full line of footbag merchandise (T-shirts, videotapes, bumper stickers, and of course, over a dozen brands of footbags.)

World Sauntering Society

Unicorn Ltd. Conglomerate, Lake Superior State College
Office of College Relations, Sault Ste. Marie, MI 49783   (906) 635-2315
                                                 Members: 7,000
Dues: $3.00 per year   Contact: W. T. Rabe

"Start Slowly, Saunter Slowly, Finish Slowly, Live Longer! (Maurice Chevalier)

World Sauntering Society is a scion society of the Unicorn Hunters of Lake Superior State College. The headquarters is on the world's longest front porch (660 feet in length) on The Grand Hotel on Mackinac Island, Michigan. The group sponsors "World Sauntering Day," the fourth Friday of August when 800 to 1000 saunterers on the front porch of the Grand Hotel make sauntering a bit difficult. (See Society of Saunterers International.) Members receive a subscription to *The Woods-Runner*.

THE ARTS ACADEMY

Culture vultures, this is your big moment. Dust off your tuba, don your clogs, and don't let Br'er Fox get you!

Amateur Organist Association International
5101 Park Dael Drive, Minneapolis, MN 55416   (612) 593-0692
Founded: 1972   Members: 13,000
Dues: $18.50 per year   Contact: Ernie Sampson

Organ players, who own home organs. Members receive *Hurdy Gurdy* magazine.

American Accordion Musicological Society
334 S. Broadway, Pitman, NJ 08071   (609) 854-6628
Founded: 1970   Members: 175
Dues: $3.00 per year   Contact: Stanley Darrow

Accordion players and collectors.

American Accordionists Association
580 Kearny Ave., Kearny, NJ 07032   (201) 991-5010
Founded: 1938   Members: 2000
Dues: Write for details   Contact: Maddalena Belfiore

Promoting the accordion.

American Banjo Fraternity
2665 Woodstock Rd., Columbus, OH 43221   (614) 451-3462
Founded: 1948   Members: 300
Dues: $5.00 per year   Contact: William C. Kentner

Collectors and players of the classic five-string banjo.

American Guild of English Handbell Ringers
601 W. Riverside Dr., Dayton, OH 45406   (513) 223-5065
Founded: 1954   Members: 3,200
Dues: $25.00 per year   Contact: Andrew L. Flanagan

Imagine 16 children ringing more than 60 finely-tuned bells in perfect tempo and harmony. Founder Donald Allured says, "A good handbell choir makes the Pittsburgh Steelers look like a kindergarten." He contends that his little bellringers are athletes of sorts, because of the strength it takes to ring a bell perfectly.

American Hobbit Association
PO Box 2546, Northbrook, IL 60065
Founded: 1977 — Members: 200
Dues: Write for details — Contact: Renee Alpen (Arwen)

Honoring J.R.R. Tolkien and his famed trilogy, *The Lord of the Rings*, Renee Alpen started this group with the name "Minas Aearon" (Tolkienese for "Tower by the Sea")--but she quickly changed it when no one could pronounce it. Renee also changed *her* name--to Arwen (a Tolkien character), and that change stuck pretty well. "We have several regularly scheduled costume parties," says Arwen, where members dress up like their favorite Tolkien character. "We play games and we eat like hobbits--hobbits eat a lot--and everybody just sort of pigs out. Every September we have the Hobbit Dinner, as close to September 22nd as we can get, because that's the birthday of Bilbo and Frodo." (Bilbo and Frodo are two of the main hobbits in the stories.) Arwen, who first read the books in elementary school feels that they are literature's "best romantic adventure." Members are sent the bi-monthly *The Rivendell Review*, with all the latest news on the hobbits.

American Old Time Fiddling Association
6141 Morrill Avenue, Lincoln, NE 68507
Dues: Write for details — Contact: Delores De Ryke

They enjoy hearing, collecting and performing historic fiddling tunes.

American Recorder Society
596 Broadway, #902, New York, NY 10012 — (212) 966-1246
Founded: 1939 — Members: 4,000
Dues: $20.00 per year ($15.00 student) — Contact: Waddy Thompson

Many members begin with the recorder, then branch out to study historical flutes, and other early instruments. Workshops, listings of new music, newsletter and quarterly magazine.

American Science Fiction Association
421 East Carson #95, Las Vegas, NV 89101 — (702) 732-9329
Founded: 1954 — Members: 27,000+
Dues: $25.00 per year — Contact: Patricia G. Silvers

Known for its large annual convention, the American Science Fiction Association helps new science fiction writers with monthly workshops and bestows the Android Awards to the best works in science fiction and fantasy.

American Society of Ancient Instruments

1205 Blythe Ave., Drexel Hill, PA 19026   (215) 789-1205
Founded: 1929
Dues: Write for details   Contact: Frederick J. Stad

The oldest organization of its kind in the United States, The American Society of Ancient Instruments is a historical center of Renaissance and Baroque period music and instruments. The yearly festival is performed on authentic 17th and 18th century viols. Guest performers are featured on antique harpsichord, Baroque oboe, violin, flute, piccolo, trumpet, waldhort, lute and recorder. The society maintains a library of 1500 chamber music compositions.

American Tolkien Society

PO Box 373, Highland Park, MI 48031   (313) 887-4703
Founded: 1975   Members: 400
Dues: $5.00 per year   Contact: Philip Helms

Fantasy fiction lovers, who are dedicated to studying the work of J.R.R. Tolkien.

Ayn Rand Institute

13101 Washington Blvd., Los Angeles CA 90066   (213)306-9232
Founded: 1985   Contact: Dr. Michael S. Berliner

The institute is also "The Center for the Advancement of Objectivism," establishing Objectivist clubs in over 60 colleges around the country. Objectivism, a philosophy that Ayn Rand expounded in her books (*The Fountainhead, Atlas Shrugged* and others) says that each individual must live by his own mind and for his own sake, neither sacrificing himself to others nor others to himself. The campus clubs sponsor debates, defending Capitalism against Socialism and explaining why nuclear arms treaties with totalitarian governments are wrong.

Bloomsday Club

Old York Books
122 French St., New Brunswick, NJ 08901   (201) 249-0430
Founded: 1975   Members: 100

Dues: Write for details   Contact: Mrs. E.T. Hopkins

Studying the works of Irish writer James Joyce, Bloomsday members meet on
December 6, the day that Joyce's works were first allowed to be published and
circulated in the United States.

Blues Foundation
W. C. Handy's Home   (901) 527-BLUE
Memphis "Home of the Blues," TN 38103
Founded: 1980
Dues: $15.00 per year   Contact: Joe Savarin

"Dedicated to the Preservation and Perpetuation of America's Original
Indigenous Musical Art Form...the Blues," this non-profit group includes B.B.
King on its Board of Directors (and awards a "Lucille" award to promising young
amateurs.) Each year on W. C. Handy's birthday, at the National Blues Music
Awards Show, the Foundation hands out the "Handys," named in honor of the
father of the blues. And if your children start talking about "Blues in the
Schools," they're not unhappy at all--they're learning the history and structure of
this all-American art form in an innovative program for fifth- and sixth-graders in
the Memphis area.

Burlesque Historical Society
c/o Exotic World
29053 Wild Road, Helendale, CA 92342   (619) 243-5261
Founded: 1963   Members: 500
Dues: Write for details   Contact: Jennie Lee

Affiliated with the Exotic Dancers League of North America, located at the same
address.

Catgut Acoustical Society
112 Essex Ave., Montclair, NJ 07042
Founded: 1963   Members: 800
Dues: $25.00 per year   Contact: Dr. Carleen Maley
Hutchins

Musical instrument makers as well as musicians, physicists and engineers, these
folks are interested in making better violins with better acoustics. (Authors note:
They probably don't socialize a lot with the previous group.)

Dickens Society

c/o Dept. of English
University of Massachusetts, Boston, MA 02125 (617) 237-2330
Founded: 1970 Members: 800
Dues: $15.00 per year ($400 lifetime) Contact: Susan R. Horton

Lovers of the work of Charles Dickens. Members receive *Dickens Quarterly.*

2020 Update:
ACTIVE

Duke Ellington Society

Box 31, Church St. Sta., NY 10008 (201) 461-0267
Founded: 1959 Members: 300
Dues: $15.00 per year

Lovers of the Duke's jazz. Chapters in Chicago, Washington and Toronto.

Guild of Carillonneurs in North America

3718 Seattle Rd., Cincinnati, OH 45227 (513) 271-8519
Founded: 1936 Members: 500
Dues: Write for details Contact: Richard D. Gegner

People who are interested in bells and chimes as musical instruments.

Happy Hours Brotherhood

87 School St., Fall River, MA 02720 (617) 672-2082
Founded: 1925 Members: 400
Dues: $10.00 per year Contact: Edward T. LeBlanc

These collectors of 19th Century popular literature include dime-store novels, and story papers. "A lot of people think a dime novel is a cheap novel selling for a dime, but that's it exactly," says club president Edward LeBlanc. "There was a snobbish attitude by some university libraries, and there's still some lingering of it. But Harvard and Yale have dime-novel collections, except that Yale doesn't like to advertise it too much, I think."

2020 Update:
ACTIVE

Horatio Alger Society

4907 Allison Drive, Lansing, MI 48910
Founded: 1961 Members: 235
Dues: Write for details Contact: Jack Bales

Alger was the most popular author in America from 1870 to 1900, with his moral tales of poor boys pulling themselves up by the bootstraps. But not everyone loved Horatio Alger. *Library Journal,* in 1879, attacked his work as sensational, unrealistic and painting a picture of America that was not feasible. In 1907, the library in Worchester, Mass., near his home, banned his books. The Horatio Alger Society was formed so that "Alger's ideals should not die," as collector Jack Bales says. Bales has all 120 of Horatio Alger books, including some translated into other languages. Bales and other book collectors meet at a yearly convention and stay in touch throughout the year through the *Newsboy*.

International Chain Saw Wood Sculptors Association

14041 Carmody Drive, Minneapolis, MN 55344
Founded: 1985   Members: 50

Wielding a chain-saw can be fun say these sculptors. They encourage the turning of tree stumps into works of art (too bad the American pioneers didn't know about this group.) Their next big project is a chain saw sculpting television commercial.

International Churchill Society

PO Box 385, Contoocook, NH 03229   (603) 746-5606
Founded: 1968   Members: 1000
Dues: $15.00 per year   Contact: Richard M.
Langworth

Orator, statesman, military strategist, painter, journalist and author, Winston wrote more than 1,000 articles and 37 books in his lifetime, winning him the Nobel Prize for Literature. With offices in the U.S., Canada, Great Britain, Australia, and New Zealand, the International Churchill Society keeps the memory and the legacy of William Churchill alive. Members collect books, stamps, coins and other objects memorializing the man, and the society hosts the Churchill tours of England.

Kafka Society of America

German Department
Temple University, Philadelphia, PA 19122   (215) 787-8270
Founded: 1975   Members: 350
Dues: $15.00 per year   Contact: Maria Luise-Caputo-
Mayr

Those interested in the work of writer Franz Kafka.

Legacy

2149 Dahil Circle, Verona, WI 53593   (608) 845-6622
Founded: 1973   Members: 300+

Dues: $15.00 per year   Contact: Vera Chestnut

Leaders in the square dancing field, promote the 3 "C's"--coordination, cooperation and continuity. Legacy is taken from LEaders GAthered for Commitment and Yak.

Lewis Carroll Society of North America
617 Rockford Road, Silver Springs, MD 20902
Founded: 1974   Members: 375
Dues: $20.00 per year   Contact: Sandor Burstein

A first edition of "Alice in Wonderland" goes for $200,000 (only 19 exist.) But Charles L. Dodgson, (a.k.a. Lewis Carroll) wrote 180 books during his life, on everything from philosophy to mathematics and logic (his books on symbolic logic have been influential in the field.) LCSNA members not only collect books, but Carroll ephemera, too. A newsletter is published.

Lute Society of America
Box 1328, Lexington, VA 24450   (703) 463-5812
Founded: 1966   Members: 650
Dues: $26.00 per year   Contact: Mary Hinely

Lutists worldwide, including some in the Far East and some behind the Iron Curtain. A newsletter, journal and seminars are available.

Mark Twain Association
245 West 25th St., New York, NY 10001   (212) 255-9640
Founded: 1926
Dues: $15.00 per year   Contact: Alice Dauer

Humorist, satirist, and one of the most prominent figures of nineteenth-century America, the cultured Mr. Clemens was also a pianist who loved to perform chamber music. The association holds a Sunday meeting and "tea," with a speaker on Twain, plus guest musicians or actors. The group also leads Twain walking tours around New York City.

Musical Box Society, International
Box 205, Route 3, Morgantown, IN 46160   (812) 988-7545
Founded: 1949   Members: 2800
Dues: $20.00 per year ($5 initiation fee)   Contact: Clarence W. Fabel

Collectors of antique musical boxes, player pianos, barrel and paper roll organs.

National Association for the Preservation & Perpetuation of Storytelling

PO Box 309, Jonesborough, TN 37659   (615) 753-2171
Founded: 1975
Dues: $25.00 per year   Contact: Jimmy Neil Smith

Sponsoring the first festival devoted entirely to the oral tradition, NAPPS brings together storytellers from different backgrounds, even different cultures. With the Great Smokey Mountains as their backdrop, spinners of yarns, weavers of tall tales, or the more formal folklorists and oral historians take their place at the swapping ground each October. (Maybe Jackie Torrance will tell of the Bell Witch, or 6' 7" Ray Hicks will talk of finding his wife via a fortune-teller's coffee grounds...or children'll learn to play the "Old Bloody Bones" game.) The organization is responsible for the rebirth of storytelling, with approximately 200-300 people now making all or part of their living from the art in the U.S. Founder Jimmy Neil Smith said, "The South has produced as many storytellers as any region...It's not Grimm's Fairy Tales that keep us sitting around the table. It's the stories of our family." Besides hosting festivals, NAPPS publishes a quarterly magazine, a newsletter and a storyteller's directory.

National Clogging and Hoedown Council

PO Box 1214, Cary, NC 27511   (919) 467-6861
Founded: 1970   Members: 850+
Dues: $16.00 per year   Contact: Ruth Landis

Promoting "mountain dancing." The National Clogging and Hoedown Council sponsors festivals and contests, plus they are compiling a history of the various styles of the dances. Members receive *Toe Tappin' Talk* twice a year.

National Flute Association

805 Laguna, Denton, TX 76201   (817) 387-9472
Founded: 1973   Members: 4,500
Dues: $20.00 per year ($12.50, students)   Contact: Myrna Brown

Flutists of all levels convene each year for four days, attending discussions on the flute, hearing performances by leading artists and attending masterclasses by renowned teachers. Maintains world's most extensive collection of flute music and publishes *The Flutist Quarterly*.

Nockian Society

30 South Broadway, Irvington, NY 10533   (914) 591-7230
Founded: 1963   Members: 800
Dues: Write for details   Contact: Edmund A. Opitz

Founded to honor the ideas of American writer-philosopher Albert Jay Nock
(1883-1945.)

North American Guild of Change Ringers

#405-1172 Yates St., Victoria, BC, Canada V8V 3M8   (604) 386-3990
Founded: 1972   Members: 300+
Dues: $12.00 per year   Contact: Michael H. J. Batten

This club has nothing to do with walking down the hall loaded down with nickels
and dimes. Change ringing is the art of ringing a set of tuned bells--like English
handbells or in a church tower.

Poe Foundation

1914-16 Main St., Richmond, VA 23223   (814) 648-5523
Founded: 1921
Dues: $10.00 per year   Contact: Dr. Bruce V. English

Dead mysteriously at the age of 40, Poe was already a famous man. The Poe
Foundation and its Poe Museum have a full collection of Poe's works and work to
set the record straight about his life. Members receive the annual literary
magazine, *The Poe Messenger*.

Sweet Adelines

PO Box 470168, Tulsa OK 74147   (918) 622-1444
Founded: 1947   Members: 33,000
Dues: $50.00 per year   Contact: Peggy Chambers

The Adelines are women interested in singing in barbershop quartets and in four-
part harmony. Regional clubs around the country meet at the annual convention
and a newsletter is available.

Tolkien Fellowships

329 N. Avenue 66, Los Angeles, CA 90042
Founded: 1977   Members: 300
Dues: Write for details   Contact: Bill Spicer

Lovers of J.R.R. Tolkien's works, unite! Local meetings and events include the
Crowning of King Elessar in April, the Bilbo and Frodo Birthday Picnic in
September and the Tokienmoot and Yulemoot, both larger conventions.
Costumes are encouraged at the meetings.

Tubists Universal Brotherhood Association (T.U.B.A.)
School of Music,
University of Kentucky, Lexington, KY 40506   (606) 257-8189
Founded: 1973
Dues: $25.00 per year   Contact: Skip Gray

Hundreds of tubas meet at the regional, national and international conferences.
All members receive the *T.U.B.A. Journal* quarterly and all members have access to
the tuba resource library and unpublished manuscripts library with its tuba music
collections.

Uncle Remus Museum
PO Box 184, Eatonton, GA 31024   (404) 485-6856
Dues: Write for details   Contact: Madeleine Gooch

The ten-foot high rabbit stands in the middle of Eatonton, Georgia as a
monument to the town's most famous citizen, Joel Chandler Harris. Chandler was
the storyteller who gave life to Uncle Remus, Br'er Rabbit, Br'er Fox and "all de
critters." Friends of the museum can visit an old slave log cabin, just like the one
Uncle Remus would have lived in!

United Serpents
PO Box 8915, Columbia, SC 29202   (803) 254-2708
Founded: 1983   Members: 140
Dues: $5.00 per year   Contact: Craig Kridel

These people have nothing to do with handling snakes...no, the serpent was an
end-blown wind instrument of the 17th to 19th centuries, that looks much like a
serpent, with many twists and turns. The United Serpents are trying to generate
interest in the instrument, staging concerts and helping people to study the
serpent.

Visual Lunacy Society
PO Box 308, Great Falls, VA 22066   (703) 860-8235
Founded: 1980   Members: 1000
Dues: $12.00 (includes 3 stamps)   Contact: Carl T. Herman

You receive a letter in the mail stamped with these words "DESTROY BEFORE
OPENING"--you open the letter carefully, pulling out a sheet of paper stamped
with a goofy-looking face and the words "APPROVED--IMPERIAL YOYO."
Welcome to the Visual Lunacy Society. These are the rubber stamp people--an
organization dedicated to "stamping out boring mail." Located in Washington,
the stamping grounds of hundreds of wild bureaucratic-rubber-stampers--the

Visual Lunacy Society was formed to spoof bureaucracy. Some of the best stamps from a recent newsletter/catalogue: a picture of a knight on horseback with the words "GOVERNMENT OF ITALY•EXPRESSO MAIL"; "HOME FOR THE BEWILDERED"; a picture of a fish with the words "KANSAS SCHOOL OF OCEANOGRAPHY--LOCATED MIDWAY BETWEEN THE ATLANTIC AND PACIFIC OCEANS"; "REJECTED• GOVERNMENT OF SRI LANKA--TRY IT AGAIN"; "WINNEBAGOS OVER WICHITA"; and "RESUBMIT IN ARABIC."

Founder Carl Herman says the power of the rubber stamp is amazing. One member sent a letter to a Swedish woman stamped with an official-looking notification reading, "MAIL DELAYED DUE TO WAR IN AFGHANISTAN." Well, the Swede hadn't heard from her American friend for a while, and she became so concerned that she persuaded the Swedish Consulate to make a call to the U.S. State Department and ask why it was that the Russians were causing U.S.-Sweden mail delays. The Washington Post was brought in to help, and they traced the stamped message back to the American friend and his VLS stamp pad.

Correspondence art and rubber stamp art is very popular in Europe and has been displayed in museums since the late 1800s. Membership entitles you to pick three rubber stamps, and receive a membership card, plus the catalog/newsletter and all future ones. Each catalog has a theme--the first one celebrated Micronesia, the second one, an equally remote area...Kansas, and the third one announces the Visual Lunacy Society's pulling out of South Africa. Orders over $100 are rewarded with a free veal cutlet. (If you qualify, let us know if it's breaded.)

HELPING HAND

Caring for others takes some wonderfully creative forms. Take these *good works* for example...

A Child's Wish Come True
PO Box 1067, Webster, MA 01570   (617) 797-4141
Founded: 1983   Members: 141
Tax deductible gifts accepted   Contact: Mary Girardin

Over 1000 wishes have been granted to terminally ill children since the group's beginning, including a visit with President Reagan, a visit to the Washington zoo to see the pandas, and a teenager's wish for a horse of her own. One child wanted to catch "the largest fish in the world." After some creative imagining, the answer was clear, and the youngster was off to Universal Studios and a chance to meet the famous "Jaws!" A Child's Wish Come True also works to reunite and reunite emotionally-drained families by throwing Christmas and birthday parties.

A Wish With Wings
PO Box 110418, Arlington, TX 76007   (817) 261-8752
Founded: 1982   Contact: Pat Skaggs
Tax deductible gifts accepted

Much the same as A Child's Wish Come True, and others.

American Blind Bowling Association
3500 Terry Drive, Norfolk, VA 23518   (804) 857-7267
Founded: 1951   Members: 3000
Dues: Write for details   Contact: Gilbert A. Baqui

American Blind Skiing Foundation
610 S. William St., Mt. Prospect, IL 60056   (312) 253-4292
Founded: 1972   Members: 200
Tax deductible gifts accepted   Contact: Sam Skobel

To imagine a blind person cross-country skiing is easy, but the ABSF also encourages downhill skiing!! Blind and visually handicapped skiers are taken to ski areas around the country and special races around the world. Truly amazing.

Brass Ring Society

5155 East 51st St. #112, Tulsa, OK 74135   (918) 496-2838
Founded: 1983   Members: 300
Tax deductible gifts accepted   Contact: Ray Esposito

What joy in helping terminally ill children in the United States and Canada to grab the "brass ring" of life and make their dreams come true.

Buxom Belles, International

27856 Palomino Dr., Warren, MI 48093   (313) 754-5731
Founded: 1956   Members: 1700
Dues: Write for details   Contact: Joan Klauka

A weight loss and therapy group.

Christic Institute

1324 N. Capitol, Washington, DC 20002   (202) 797-8106
Founded: 1978   Members: 20,000
Dues: Write for details   Contact: Sara M. Nelson

Christic is a public law firm and information center. Though not connected with any religious group, Christic "connects religious principles to public policy." Christic started the Karen Silkwood case after she mysteriously died while exposing the unsafe conditions at the Kerr McGee nuclear processing plant in Oklahoma. Christic also initiated legal action after four anti-Klan protesters in Greensboro, NC were killed in an attack that had been allegedly aided by police. Christic is working on protecting citizens from exposure in the Three Mile Island reactor cleanup. The Institute researches theological underpinnings of public policy concerning nuclear weapons and energy.

Claustrophobia: Life Extension

5047 Southwest 26th Drive, Portland, OR 97201

Help for those who have been cooped-up too long with their life-threatening disease.

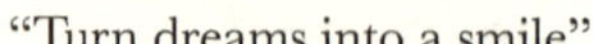

The Dream Factory

PO Box 188, Hopkinsville, KY 42240   (502) 443-2143
Founded: 1980   Members: 82,000
Tax deductible gifts accepted   Contact: Charles G. Henault

"Turn dreams into a smile"

Started by Charlie Henault and some fellow South Central Bell employees, the Dream Factory has granted the wishes of over 1,100 terminally ill children between the ages of 3 and 13 years old. There are 21 chapters in eight states, no paid salaries and 90% of the money raised goes to pay for dreams. With children, dreams are simple and quite easy to fulfill: a pet, a bicycle, a trip to Disneyworld or a visit from a favorite television star. Often, the dream brings smiles and sometimes miraculously (contrary to what the medical community says), a brief improvement in the child's health. One child got a visit from Superman, another took a trip to Memphis to see Elvis' home, and another was visited by actress Jill Whelan of "The Love Boat." The newest project is Camp Rainbow, a free one-week summer camp for these special children.

Earthwatch

Box 127, Belmont, MA 02178 617) 489-3030
Founded: 1971 Members: 26,000+
Dues: $25 per year Contact: Brian Rosborough

Each year, nearly 3000 Earthwatch volunteers participate in adventures from living with orangutans to climbing into a volcano for study to uncovering a Viking Burial to mapping shipwrecks off Majorca. Earthwatch is made up of civilians, unskilled in fieldstudy, working with research scholars and scientists on a diverse range of projects. "Earthwatch supports the efforts of scholars to preserve the world's endangered habitats and species, to explore the vast heritage of its peoples, and to promote world health and international cooperation."

Volunteers, who range in age from 16 to 85, help defray the cost of the expedition, thus providing a bright light in a dark time for funding. Saving the leatherback turtle from the threat of extinction has been one of the most popular programs. In the Virgin Islands, leather-backs who weigh up to 1,300 pounds are killed for their oil and their eggs, which are a claimed to be an aphrodisiac. Volunteers follow the turtles as they lay their eggs on the beach and save them from the predators. "One of the big problems I see today is the helplessness people feel about the way the world is going, says Linda Dyar, psychotherapist and a turtle project volunteer. "The best thing about Earthwatch is that it lets us feel we can make a difference."

Members receive four newsletters and four magazines per year, plus are eligible to participate in an expedition of their choice.

Elderhostel, Inc.

80 Boylston St., Boston, MA 02116 (617) 426-7788
Founded: 1974 Contact: William D. Berkeley

Based on the belief that retirement does not mean withdrawal, Elderhostel has given over a quarter of million older Americans a taste of the college life in over 850 colleges and universities around the world. Inspired by the youth hostel and folk schools of Europe, Elderhostel gives folks over 60 a chance to live in the dormitories, take specially-designed courses, eat in the cafeteria and reach out for new experiences. Most programs are one to three weeks long, in schools from the New Hampshire to the Northwest Territories of Canada, from Ireland to Israel. The cost of the programs is low, and the hefty catalogs are sent free of charge.

ELF--Elf Lore Family

PO Box 1082, Bloomington, IN 47402
Dues: Write for more information

E.L.F., or the Elf Lore Family is a group that is working toward the protection of nature. The elves have get-togethers through the year on the holidays and solstices, equinoxes etc. The ELFs "believe in Ecology, Multidimensional consciousness and common sense." They have just established LOTHLORIEN, a "green haven for elfinfolk" It consists of a nature sanctuary, survival education center, and woodland meeting grounds located near the Hoosier National Forest of Southern Indiana.

Experiment in International Living

Brattleboro, VT 05301   (802) 257-7751
Founded: 1932   Dues: $40.00 registration fee

Spend one week to ten months in another family's home in England, Korea or 40 other countries and learn the customs and languages of others. American families do reciprocate.

Floating Hospital

275 Madison Ave., New York, NY 10016   (212) 685-0193
Founded: 1866   Members: 35
Tax deductible gifts accepted   Contact: Elayne Weinbaum

One of New York City's more innovative ideas, the Floating Hospital is a medical and dental clinic at sea. Children, adults and senior citizens board the Floating Hospital in the morning, and while they are provided with testing services and health education, the hospital is cruising them around New York Harbor. Each year the clinic serves more than 75,000 people,

Friend Finders International

314 Lloyd Bldg., Seattle WA 98101   (206) 697-1401

Founded: 1984
Dues: $20.00 registration fee,
  $30.00 90 day search   Contact: Janice Wisbey

Herbert V. Farmer the group's founder, was a prisoner in Stalag 17, a German prisoner-of-war camp during WWII. After the war, he tried to find the friends he was imprisoned with and realized there was no organization devoted to pairing lost buddies, so began Friend Finders International. The brains of Friend Finders is a computer name bank that cross-checks all names that sound alike. FFI also has a tracking division that conducts investigations. Friend Finders brought together a family that had not been together in 23 years. They helped a 70-year-old woman from Brooklyn find a friend that she had lost track of ten years before. Three sisters were reunited who hadn't seen each other since 1945. In some cases, people just lose track of each other, in some cases, the courts have assigned new names and identities to family members. Other times, wars or catastrophic events will have been the breaking point. And sometimes the reason for someone's disappearance remains a mystery...even after the person is found.

Good Bears of the World

Box 8236, Honolulu, HI 96815   (808) 946-2844
Founded: 1969   Members: 10,000
Dues: $8.00 per year or $100 for life   Contact: Jim Ownby

Teddy Bear lovers of the world, this club is yours. Bearo's (as members are called) donate Teddy Bears to children in hospitals and institutions, and to other worthy recipients. This includes the elderly in nursing homes, the crew of the USS Theodore Roosevelt and the Toledo Police Department which received 80 bears to be given to abused children. Good Bears either operate at large, giving bears as the spirit moves them, or they form into dens (there are dens in 23 states.) These dens raise money collectively to buy bears (GBW has its own official bear, made exclusively by R. Dakin and Company) The quarterly magazine is called "Bear Tracks," and the monthly newsletter called *The Good Bearer* is filled with events around the country (bear days at the zoo, bear conventions) and news from the local "dens." October 27th, Teddy Roosevelt's birthday was selected as "Good Bears of the World" Day.
Club motto: Have you offered a good bear hug today?

Good Fellows

384 Penobscot Bldg., Detroit, MI 48226
Founded: 1914

Former newspaper boys get together once a year and hawk papers, raising money to create "A Christmas for Every Needy Child." Other groups just like this exist in other cities.

Ground Zero Pairing Project

PO Box 19049, Portland, OR 97219   (503) 245-3403
Founded: 1982   Members: 1500 local groups
Tax deductible gifts accepted   Contact: Earl A. Molander

Providing community-to-community links between the Soviet Union and the United States, paired communities send each other "community portraits" as a way of learning about the similarities between people and lives here and in the USSR. Group visits between linked communities are also planned.

Handicapped Scuba Association

1104 El Prado, San Clemente, CA 92672   (714) 498-6128
Founded: 1975
Dues: $20.00 per year   Contact: Jim Gartacre

With the motto, "Accept the Challenge," the handicapped move out of their wheelchairs into a world of gravity-free, 3-dimensional movement. "There aren't any observers in the Handicapped Scuba Association," as handicapped and able-bodied are taught together, mastering skills together. *Freedom in Depth* is a video that will "make you re-assess what you presumed were the limitations of physical capability." Their quarterly publication, *Squid*.

Holiday Project

765 California St., San Francisco, CA 94108   (415) 391-9911
Founded: 1976   Contact: Rita Saenz

Members visit and bring gifts to nursing homes, orphanages, mental hospitals, juvenile detention homes and prisons, on Christmas, Chanukah, Easter and other holidays. Their motto: "Be the Gift."

Hospital Audiences, Inc.

220 W. 42nd St., New York, NY 10036   (212) 575-7676
Founded: 1969   Contact: Michael Jon Spencer
Tax deductible gifts accepted

Music, theater and dance are brought to people in prisons, hospitals, nursing homes, and mental health institutions. Also, loans artworks and brings art classes into the facilities.

Hug-A-Tree and Survive

6465 Lance Way, San Diego, CA 92120   (619) 286-7536
Founded: 1981   Contact: Jacquie Beveridge

Jimmy Beverage, a nine-year-old boy, died after being lost in the mountains near San Diego. That prompted the development of Hug-a-tree and Survive. "Hugging a tree and even talking to it calms the child and prevents panic." The program teaches children how to stay in one place, keep warm and dry and make it easier to be spotted by searchers. The program is now conducted in 26 states.

The Hug Club

PO Box 453, Laguna Beach, CA 92652   (714) 494-3971
Founded: 1980   Members: 7000
Dues: Write for details   Contact: John Thrash

The Hug Club says a hug a day keeps the doctor away. The proven therapeutic benefits of hugging are stress reduction, diminished anger, and a strengthening of relationships. Lots of Hug Club mugs, bumper stickers and t-shirts are available.

International Fire Buff Associates

7509 Chesapeake Ave., Baltimore, MD 21219   (301) 477-1544
Founded: 1953   Members: 6000
Dues: Write for Details   Contact: Roman A. Kaminski

with over 80 local clubs around the country, the Fire Buffs are interested in fires and the welfare of firefighters. They act as a sort of public relations arm for firefighting companies. They can be found on the scene serving coffee and food, or operating ambulances. Each year they present the "Fireman of the Year Award" as well as the "Fire Buff of the Year Award."

International Hug Center

115 Glenfield Drive, Pittsburgh, PA 15235   (412) 795-0147
Founded: 1982   Members: 1000
Dues: Write for details   Contact: John McKenzie

June 15th is "Hug Day"--a day when everyone should hug ten people, emphasizing the "interdependence of the human race" through the embrace. On Hug Day, the club announces their pick for the "ten most huggable people in the world."

International Wheelchair Road Racers Club

165-78th Avenue, NE, St. Petersburg, FL 33702   (813) 521-3420
Founded: 1981   Members: 300
Dues: $5.00 per year   Contact: Jeanette K. Parke

Promoters of the sport of wheelchair racing.

L.A.D.I.E.S. (Life After Divorce is Eventually Sane)

PO Box 2974, Beverley Hills, CA 90213
Founded: 1983   Members: 20

A society to help women in Beverly Hills who have been divorced from the rich and famous.

2020 Update:
ACTIVE

Make-A-Wish Foundation of America

4601 N. 16th St., Suite 205, Phoenix, AZ 85016   (602) 234-0960
Founded: 1980
Tax deductible gifts accepted   Contact: Linda Dozeretz

"From the time we're small, we wish upon stars and pennies in fountains. Fulfilling dreams in part of the joy of life." Make-A-Wish Foundation was started when seven-year-old Chris Greicius had a dream of being a policeman. The Arizona Department of Public Safety helped make the dream come true. Chris spent a day at the headquarters, was given a specially-made uniform with a helmet, badge and toy gun. He rode in a patrol car, flew in the helicopter and became the state's first "honorary patrolman." A few days later Chris died of leukemia.

National Deaf Bowling Association

9244 East Mansfield Ave., Denver, CO 80237   (303) 320-1700
Founded: 1964   Members: 300
Dues: $6.00 per year   Contact: Don Gene Warnick

For individuals and groups, they sponsor the World's Deaf Bowling Championship.

National Foundation for Happy Horsemanship for the Handicapped

Box 462, Malvern, PA 19355   (215) 644-7414
Founded: 1967
Contact: Maudie Hunter-Warfel

Membership by invitation only.

National Foundation of Wheelchair Tennis

15441 Red Hill Ave., Suite A, Tustin, CA 92680   (714) 259-1531
Founded: 1980   Members: 700
Dues: $12.00 per year   Contact: Bradley A. Parks

Promoting wheelchair tennis.

National Odd Shoe Exchange

Rural Route 4, Indianola, IA 50125

Founded: 1943

Dues: $7.50 per year ($15.00 initial fee)

(515) 285-1832

Members: 15,000

Contact: Jeanne Sallman

Founded by a woman who wore 6B on the left and 4B on the right, The National Odd Shoe Exchange helps the extra shoes of owners of mismatched feet not go to waste. For example: if an amputee who wears 9C on the left joins, NOSE will match him with another amputee who wears 9C on the right! The same procedure applies for those with two mismatched feet. (The problem with mismatched feet can be troublesome and expensive...you need to buy two pairs of shoes to fit one pair of feet.) The club tries to find mates of the same age group and tastes in shoe styles. The club motto:

"When Odd Shoes Are Left...to Trade Them is Right"

2020 Update: ACTIVE

Operation Identity

13101 Blackstone Rd., NE, Albuquerque, NM

Founded: 1979

(505) 293-3144

Members: 150

Contact: Sally File

Reunites parents and children who've been separated by adoption or divorce.

2020 Update: ACTIVE

Operation Liftoff

1171 Kings Ave., Ben Salem, PA 19020

Founded: 1978

Tax deductible gifts accepted

(215) 639-1586

Contact: Ernest Bischoff

Sends hundreds of terminally ill children to Disneyworld.

Operation Suburbia

PO Box 1625, Hartford, CT 06101

Contact: Edward T. Coll

(203) 249-7523

Sends "slum youths" to the suburbs for two-week vacations in an effort to "educate suburban families and to break down the walls of racial polarization on a grass roots level."

Orphan Voyage

2141 Road 2300, Cedaredge, CO 81413

Founded: 1953

Tax deductible gifts accepted

(303) 856-3937

Members: 500

Contact: Jean M. Paton

Helps orphans and adults who were adopted children find their roots.
Jean Paton, an adoptee herself, has spent the better part of her life helping others
find lost relatives without salary or monetary compensation.

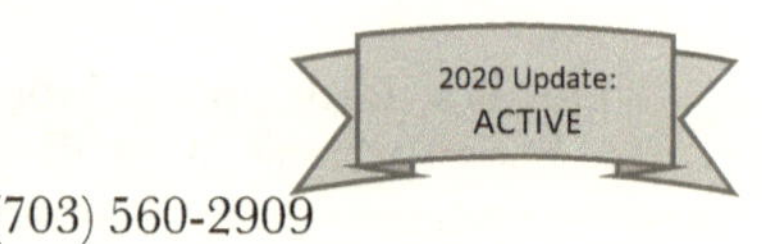

People-Animals-Love
4835 MacArthur Blvd., Washington, DC 20007   (703) 560-2909
Founded: 1981   Contact: Earl Strimple
Tax deductible gifts accepted

PAL provides the elderly and institutionalized with pets, with love. PAL sends
these trained dogs and cats with a volunteer who monitors the pet's health plus,
PAL provides food and care for the pets. PAL has shown that pets may positively
affect a person's blood pressure and general well-being. Prisoners with pets often
require less disciplinary action and medical attention, and in nursing homes,
hospices and mental institutions pets serve to lessen loneliness, hopelessness and
boredom.

People-to-People International
501 East Armour Blvd., Kansas City, MO 64109
Founded: 1956
Dues: $15.00 per year   Contact: Julian Niemczyk

Founded by President Dwight D. Eisenhower as a response to the Cold War,
People-to-People promotes international understanding and friendship by direct
people-to-people contacts, without governmental intervention. The programs
consist of visiting people in other countries, homestays by foreigners visiting the
U.S., pen pals, and youth exchanges. People-to-People has chapters in 33
countries.

Performing Arts for the Handicapped (PATH)
PO Box 3106, Carlsbad, CA 92008   (619) 438-3498
Founded: 1980   Contact: Bob Cole

PATH runs workshops to assist talented and motivated disabled actors in getting
work in theatre, TV, films, etc. "We don't sell handicaps, we sell talent," says Cole,
who is the father of two deaf children. Board members include Tom Bosley, Ron
Howard, Burt Reynolds and Henry Winkler.

Poetry Therapy Institute
PO Box 70244, Los Angeles, CA 90070   (213) 963-4992
Founded: 1973   Contact: Anne Ross Silver

Psychologists, psychiatrists, and educators exploring the use of poetry as a
therapeutic tool.

Project Orbis

330 West 42nd Street, New York, NY 10036 (212) 244-2525
Founded: 1982 Donations accepted

Project Orbis is the world's only flying eye hospital. Twenty million dollar's worth
of ultra-sophisticated medical equipment is housed in a white passenger jet that
zig-zags around the world, making stops in Latin America, Africa, Europe, China
and the Middle East. Unpaid volunteers, mostly American ophthalmologists and
other doctors, have treated 2,000 patients and more importantly, trained 1,500
local ophthalmologists in surgical techniques not previously known in the
developing world. Project Orbis, (Orbis is the Latin word for eye), costs four
million dollars per year. It is funded by the USAID, and private and corporate
donations. Hotels provide the Orbis staff with free or discounted rooms,
governments contribute medical supplies, and local airlines give free tickets to
doctors and staff who are returning to the US. The 25 year old DC-8 was
donated by United Airlines. With over 42 million blind persons in the world,
Project Orbis provides badly needed service.

React International

3653 Woodhead Dr., Northbrook, IL 60062 (312) 291-0922
Founded: 1962 Members: 20,000
Dues: Write for Details Contact: Gerald H. Reese

Monitoring citizen band radio stations for local emergency response. REACT
stands for Radio Emergency Associated Citizens Teams. These CBers work with
local authorities in getting help for car accidents and the like.

Reunite, Inc.

PO Box 694, Reynoldsburg, OH 43068 (614) 861-2584
Founded: 1980 Members: 300
Dues: Write for Details Contact: Paula M. Burdette
Members are adoptees, birthparents, foster children and judges working towards
adoption reform. They also help with birthparent searches when adopted children
turn of legal age.

Share Your Birthday Foundation

National Press Bldg., Washington, DC 20045 (202) 393-0300
Founded: 1954 Contact: Elizabeth Heller

American elementary school children send birthday presents to other school-age children in foreign countries. The exchange is mutual, with the foreign children sending a birthday gift back to their American friends. The only stipulation is that the gifts not be guns or war toys. The hope of the program is that "today's children may tomorrow exchange gifts, not bullets and bombs."

Sister Cities International

2020 Update: ACTIVE

Town Affiliation Association of the US, Inc.
1625 Eye Street, Washington, DC 20006 (202) 293-5504
Founded: 1967 Members: 740 cities
Dues: Write for Details Contact: Thomas W. Gittins

More than 700 American cities are linked with 1200 foreign cities in 85 nations. The hope is that the city-to-city contact will foster better international understanding in education, economic and social relationships.

2020 Update: ACTIVE

Ski for Light

1455 W. Lake St., Minneapolis, MN 55408 (612) 827-3232
Founded: 1975 Contact: Dr. Raymond Keith

Sighted instructors take up to 250 blind people at a time on cross-country trails. "Ski for Light is not just a learn-to-ski experience. It is a program that allows individuals to overcome insecurities regarding blindness and a time when sighted people shed misconceptions they hold about blind people."

Spendermenders International

PO Box 15000-156, San Francisco, CA 94115 (415) 775-9754
Contact: Sandi Gostin

A self-help group for people who can't stand to let a sale pass them by without emptying their wallets.

Stepfamily Association of America

602 East Joppa Road, Baltimore, MD 21204 (301) 823-7570
Founded: 1977
Dues: $45.00 per year Contact: Roger B. Burt

This association aids in the working through and sharing of the problems (and pleasures) of being a stepparent. Books and educational materials on step-parenting are also available. With chapters in 21 states, they also meet for an annual conference. Having established the first Sunday in October as Stepparent's

Day in California, they are now working toward establishing a National Stepparents Day.

Terrap Network for Agoraphobics
1010 Doyle St., Menlo Park, CA 94025   (415) 329-1233

Treatment for people who are deathly afraid of open-spaces.

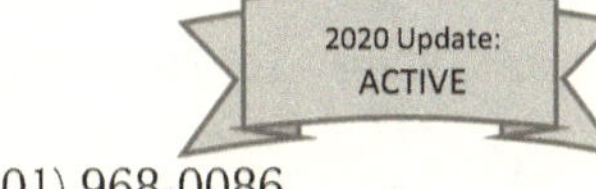

Therapy Dogs International
1536 Morris Pl., Hillside, NJ 07205   (201) 968-0086
Founded: 1980   Members: 1,000 trained dogs
Dues: $10.00 per dog ($2.00 each add. dog)   Contact: Milt Winn

Phila, a German Shepherd was the first certified therapy dog. When Elaine Smith, a registered nurse, saw how her dog Phila changed the attitudes of patients in the Hillside, NJ area, she started Therapy Dogs International to bring together and recognize other "dogs of service." Therapy dogs visit the sick and frail in hospitals and nursing homes, children without families, the mentally retarded -- all people who suffer from isolation. "People who have shown no interest for living will suddenly, without provocation, reach out for the friendly paw of man's best friend." In some states, Therapy Dogs now have the same privileges as seeing-eye dogs on public transportation and in stores. Dogs of all breeds can be used as therapy dogs. Human members receive an identification card and a big yellow tag stating "I am a Therapy Dog" for four-footed members.

Their motto: "Paws Awhile for Love"

TOPS Club
4575 S. Fifth St., Milwaukee, WI 53207   (414) 482-4620
Founded: 1948   Members: 320,000
Dues: $12.00 per year   Contact: Gail Schemberger

"Take Off Pounds Sensibly" was founded by former pie-cooking champion Esther S. Manz when she weighed in at 208 lbs. In 1985, TOPS members lost 885 tons (that's 1,769,105.89 lbs.) Weight loss competitions are held and achievers are crowned as king or queen, but more important is the support members give one another. TOPS run retreats to get away from it all and help members follow a strict diet. The club also helps members *keep* off pounds sensibly (KOPS) and sponsors KOPS charm, beauty and greatest achievement awards. At the TOPS International convention each year, an International King and International Queen are picked, some of them having lost over 150lbs! In the words of their song (to the tune of "Ach Du Lieber Augustine"):
    The more we get together, together, together

The more we get together, the slimmer we'll be
For your loss is my loss
And your loss is my loss
The more we get together, the slimmer we'll be.

Travel and Fly Without Fear

310 Madison Ave., New York, NY 10017   (212) 697-7666
Founded: 1969   Members: 50+
Fees: $5.00 membership & $15.00 per session   Contact: Carol Cott Gross

Nate Cott was Plane Scared. He couldn't get off the ground without white
knuckles. After a lot of goading, he placed a small ad in the New York Times
looking for others with his phobia and found out that he wasn't alone. With the
help of psychotherapists, he founded Fly without Fear. Members meet at La
Guardia or J.F.K. Airport once a week. They speak with flight attendants and
pilots, they sit in the aircraft. Later, they taxi down the runway and graduate with
a short conditioning flight. There are said to be 25 million aviaphobiacs in the
U.S., many of whom are not only afraid to fly but to travel in any non-controllable
situation (tunnels, elevators, trains.) Travel and Fly without Fear members learn to
desensitize and demystify their fears.

Trees for Tomorrow

PO Box 609, Eagle River, WI 54521   (715) 479-6456
Founded: 1944   Contact: Henry H. Haskell

"We have not inherited the earth from our fathers, we are borrowing it from our
children" sums up the philosophy of Trees for Tomorrow. Trees for Tomorrow is
an ecological education center started by nine Wisconsin paper-mill owners. Its
purposes are to educate the public on the environment and encourage private
reforestation. The Center runs programs such as ski-touring, winter ecology, fish
and wildlife study, and photography sessions. The state of Wisconsin which *had*
been known for the finest white and red pines in the nation, was an ecological
disaster when Trees for Tomorrow was started. The region had literally been
deforested--cut to its stumps. When the stumps were cleared for farming, the soil
couldn't support crops. Then fires swept the barren land and the humus was
burned, making reforestation difficult. The paper mill owners during World War
II were concerned that they had to haul wood from Canada and the Northwest to
keep their mills going. They started with a public relations drive to encourage
reforestation, but it was clear that what was really needed was an education center.
Trees for Tomorrow has achieved the planting of an incredible 25 million pine
trees since its establishment. A quarter of a million people have taken part in
Trees workshops since it opened (about 5,000 went in 1986) two-thirds of them
students and teachers. Trees is funded by private industry, by civic groups, and by
individual Tree members.

USA Toy Library Association

104 Wilmot Road, Suite 201, Deerfield, IL 60015 (312) 940-8800
Founded: 1984   Members: 300
Dues: $35.00 per year   Contact: Sylvia Lurie

How many parents buy a new toy for a child and within hours, maybe minutes, that expensive piece of plastic is ignored for something else? At toy libraries, toys are loaned just like books are loaned from the library. Toy libraries have a number of advantages: They carry a large selection of toys, loaned free or for a nominal fee, the "toy librarians" are trained in child development and the role of "playtime," they can provide specially adapted toys for children with special needs (there are over 100 toy libraries in the US that cater to disabled children.) The USA Toy Library Association brings together toy librarians, teachers, therapists, toymakers, toy sellers and parents. Members receive the quarterly *Child's Play* newsletter, a free copy of *Guide to Good Toys*, and a directory of all the toy libraries in the United States.

World Gratitude Day Foundation

132 West 31st Street, New York, NY 10001
Contact: Edna Fuerth Lemle

The World Gratitude Day Foundation promotes gratitude gatherings around the country and around the world, "To unite all people in a positive emotion."

FAN CLUBS

Who said Americans have no heroes? Whether it's James Bond...Mae West...Mr. Ed...or Captain Kirk, these loyal fans love their idols deeply. (Even Millard Fillmore? You bet!)

Abbott and Costello Fan Club
PO Box 262, Carteret, NJ 07008
Founded: 1968

Members: 2800
Contact: Billy Wolfe

Who's on First? newsletter and hall of fame for these stars of stage, screen and radio.

The Andy Griffith Show Appreciation Society
PO Box 330, Clemmons, NC 27012

Dues: $5.00 per year

(919) 998-2860
Members: 2,000
Contact: John Meroney

This noble band is urging local TV stations to bring the 249 episodes (49 of them in color) to every TV set in America (with less commercial interruption.) Members' mailboxes are filled quarterly with *The Mayberry Gazette*, plus sweatshirts, buttons, and videotapes available from Weaver's Department Store with "The Best Selection in Mayberry."

The Andy Griffith Show Rerun Watchers Club
1313 21st. Ave., S. Suite 107-146, Nashville, TN 37212
Founded: 1979
Dues: $3.00 (voluntary) per year

Members: 12,000
Contact: James H. Clark

"Shazam!" and "Floyd's Barbershop" are just two of the many chapters of the Andy Griffith Show Rerun Watchers Club. Founded at James Clark's fraternity in college, where having only *one* television meant a daily stake out against the M*A*S*H watchers (which was on at the same time as Andy), the AGSRWC today has over 300 organized chapters in all 50 states and 8 foreign countries. The purpose: to watch the show...and keep it on the air. (The show, which originally ran from 1960 to 1968, is in reruns in most of the major markets around the country.)

James Clark says he's seen each episode at least 10 times yet watches still the show every day. "It's amazing that a show with no sex or violence is still a success today in reruns." The club rules its membership like Andy ruled Mayberry; membership dues are voluntary, there are no club rules and a newsletter called *The Bullet* that comes out once in a while (usually about two or three times a year.) *The Bullet* was named for the solitary bullet that Andy kept in his pocket. Members can get T-Shirts made the Aunt Bee way, bumper stickers that say "Pipe Down, Otis" or "Nip It in the Bud!," or "Goober Says Hey!." Clark wrote a book on the show that points out a bunch of minor inconsistencies--Andy's address was 14 Maple in one episode, 322 in another *and* Floyd the barber was Floyd Colby in the beginning and Floyd Lawson later on.

Annette Funicello Fan Club
10075 Dedham Drive, Indianapolis, IN 46229   (317) 633-9269
Founded: 1961   Members: 290
Dues: Write for details   Contact: Rita Rose

Why? Because we like you!

Annie People
Box 431, Cedar Knolls NJ 07927
Founded: 1983   Members: 250
Dues: Free   Contact: Jon Merrill

It was the 2,377th and final showing of the Broadway show of *Annie,* on a cold Sunday in January 1983. Fans were standing outside the stage door waiting to greet the stars. Two fans, Jon Merrill and Tricia Trozzi, both from New Jersey, started comparing notes about Annie. When they realized there was no fan club for Annie, they said simultaneously, "Why don't *we* start one?" Leapin' lizards, each has now seen both the show and the movie over 50 times, and each has hundreds of Annie dolls, cut-outs and memorabilia filling their homes! Even former cast members keep in touch with them, receive the free bi-monthly newsletter and come over to visit the virtual Annie museum they've created.

As the World Turns Fan Club
212 Oriole Drive, Montgomery, NY 12549
Dues: Write for details   Contact: Deanne P. Turco

A-Team Fan Club
PO Box 3900, Hollywood, CA 90078

Mr. T says *you* gotta join this club!!

Badfinger Fan Club

5126 Creekbend Circle, Cleveland, TN 37311
Founded: 1984
Dues: $7.50 per year   Contact: Steve Donahue

Providing the only "authorized" newsletter, *Badfinger Connection*, about the rock group.

Baker Street Irregulars

34 Pierson Avenue, Norwood, NJ 07648
Founded: 1934   Members: 2000
Dues: $12.50 per year   Contact: Thomas L. Stik, Jr.

Arthur Conan Doyle's character has been immortalized in the movies and on stage and has been given new life by modern mystery writers, creating new Holmes stories all the time, in the style of Conan Doyle. But Conan Doyle never liked the character Sherlock Holmes, feeling that the stories were trivial and that his real works were being neglected (he had written a number of historical novels and books on spiritualism.) In 1894, he tried to kill the detective off in a story called "The Final Problem." Fans were so outraged that he was forced to resurrect Holmes. The Baker Street Irregulars are devoted to the "legend that Sherlock Holmes is not a legend."

The Baker Street Irregulars is one of the most enduring fan clubs. It was started by Christopher Morley and Edgar Smith as a literary society for studying Holmes' stories, and publishing the *Baker Street Journal* (still printed and sent to members of local chapters.) The main events of the club are the annual "stag" dinner on January 6 (chosen by Morley to be Holmes' birthday) and the sponsoring of a horserace at Aqueduct Racetrack during the summer. Local "scions" meet regularly to read and discuss the infallible man with a nose for clues.

Benedict Arnold Fan Club

2117 West Field, Scotch Plains, NJ 07076   (201) 889-5037
Dues: Write for details   Contact: Kenneth Roberts

Benedict Arnold got a raw deal, these people say. Some members are descendants of the so-called traitor, and others are historians who say that Benny was just looking out for his own best interests.

Big Man's Fan Club

Box 482, Benton, KY 42025   (502) 527-9361
Founded: 1981   Members: 300
Dues: Write for details   Contact: Endice Court

Now the Big Man, saxophone player Clarence Clemons doesn't have to borrow any fan mail from his "Boss" (a certain Mr. Springsteen.)

Boxcar Willie Fan Club
Trainman Productions
Rt. 3, Box 95, Canton, TX 75103
Write for details.

Bram Stoker Memorial Society
Penthouse North, 29 Washington Square W., New York, NY 10011
Dues: $10.00 lifetime membership   Contact: Benjamin Pierce

Hail to Count Dracula's creator! Members receive a membership certificate, a paperback copy of *The Count Dracula Book of Classic Vampire Tales,* copy of *The Count Dracula Fan Club Book of Vampire Stories*, and a wallet-sized photo of Bram Stoker.

Burt Reynolds Fan Club
80 Broadmeadow Blvd., Townhouse #5450, Columbus OH 43214
Contact: Harriette Mullins

Cartoon/Fantasy Organization
401 S. LaBrea Ave., Inglewood, CA 90301   (213) 412-2638
Founded: 1977   Members: 350
Dues: $12.50 per year   Contact: Ann Nichols

Japanese animation lovers, unite! Fans of Gatchaman and the Dirty Pair, konnichi wa! Each of the more than thirty chapters nationwide screen dramatic, science fiction and fantasy animated adventures from Japan. Members say that *these* science-fiction cartoons are more exciting than their American counterparts yet are easy to follow without knowing Japanese.

Circus Fans Association of America
PO Box 69, Camp Hill, PA 17011   (717) 761-4819
Founded: 1926   Members: 2500
Dues: $16.00 per year   Contact: J. Allen Duffield

"We fight anything that fights the circus," said one member. It is the "banding together of youngsters who carried water for the elephants or followed the red wagons down the winding road or over the distant hills to far cities." Today those children have grown up willing to do anything to make it easier for the circus to come to town--every year, in every community--including fighting legislation that raises licensing fees, etc. The state organizations are known as Tents, and the local organizations are called Tops. These dedicated fans expect no reward for their work, no free tickets, thus their motto, "We Pay As We Go!."

Companions of Dr. Who Fan Club

PO Box 56764, New Orleans, LA 70156   (504) 393-0939
Members: 200   Contact: Charles L. Duval

"He's the intergalactic do-gooder," wearing a long scarf and frock coat, accompanied by his robot dog named K-9. Who? Yes, it's Dr. Who, the hero of a 20-year-old British television show with 98 million viewers in 38 countries. Dr. Who club members wear multicolored scarves, fedoras, frock coats too, as well as buttons saying:

    "Brighten the Universe--Kiss a Time Lord"
    "Have TARDIS, will travel"

(TARDIS, for the uninitiated, stands for Time and Relative Dimensions in Space.) The British equivalent of Star Trek, the show is low in budget but high in cult appeal, though Dr. Who fans take their show a little less seriously than Trekkies do theirs.

Count Dracula Fan Club

29 Washington Sq. W., Penthouse N., New York, NY 10011 (212) 533-5018
Founded: 1965   Members: 4000
Dues: $40.00   Contact: Carole Anne Lombardo

Keeps members up-to-date on such news items as the passing of Elsa Lanchester (the lovely "Bride of Frankenstein"), where to purchase "Kiss me I'm a vampire" pins and vampire coloring books. Special divisions include The Moldavian Marketplace, which contains items of unusual interest such as Dracula stationary, pins, and mobiles, The Research Library, The Bram Stoker (Count Dracula's author) Memorial Collection of Rare Books, The Unicorn Unit and others. Count Dracula Fan Club Pen Pal Network is available, too, by writing to:

    Miss Debra Gail Hatfield
    6000 Eurper Lane
    Fort Smith, Arkansas 72903

The group sponsors movie screenings and trips. They also publish new vampire stories--"Dracula Made Easy," "Further Perils of Dracula," "Count Dracula and the Unicorn" and "The Count Dracula Cookbook" are just some of them.

Count Dracula Society

334 West 54th St., Los Angeles, CA 90037   (213) 752-5811
Founded: 1962   Members: 500
Dues: $20.00 per year   Contact: Donald A. Reed

Known as the count of darkness or the bloodsucking wolf--Drac is based on a real character in Rumanian history--Bram Stoker's 1899 novel has been immortalized. Law librarian Donald Reed is Dracula's biggest fan. He started the Count Dracula Society because he felt Dracula deserved recognition and, well, nobody else was doing it. Notable members include Christopher Lee and George Hamilton (remember "Love at First Bite"? The Society gives the Count Dracula award, one each year to a Dracula deservant. The one-foot-high porcelain statue of Dracula has been given to George Hamilton, Bela Lugosi, Christopher Lee, Darren McGavin, to name a few.

Danny Vann Fan Club

PO Box 87222, Canton, MI 48187   (313) 397-1388
Founded: 1979   Members: 80
Dues: Write for details   Contact: Dawne Van Pelt

Vann is named for his impersonations of Elvis Presley.

Dark Shadows Clubs/ Dark Shadows Festivals

6500 Yucca Street, #248, Hollywood, CA 90028
Founded: 1982   Contact: Joseph Collins

"General Hospital" couldn't hold a candle for creepiness next to this chilling daily series. Remembered beyond the grave, its fans hold two or three conventions each year, featuring Dark Shadows cast members. Hard-core fans will jump at the chance to purchase "Original Music from Dark Shadows (Volume 2)" featuring such hits as "Widow's Hill" and "Collins' Mausoleum," plus articles and books on the show. articles and books.

David Letterman Fan Club

2120 NE 204th St., Miami, FL 33179
Dues: $6.00

Elvis Presley Burning Love Fan Club

1904 Williamsburg Drive, Streamwood, IL 60107 (312) 82-1061
Founded: 1983   Members: 325
Dues: $12.00 per year   Contact: Bill DeNight

When the King had a hit with "Teddy Bear," back in 1957, fans began sent him
thousands of teddy bears. Up to his guitar in bears, Elvis rented trucks to take the
furry friends to hospitals and orphanages in the Memphis area. The bears
continued to arrive, and Elvis continued to give them out for the rest of his life.
One of 400 local Elvis groups nationwide, the Burning Love Fan Club raises
money for various charities and distributes teddy bears to hospitalized children on
Christmas, all in fond memory of Elvis.

Enge's Entourage

945 Ward Drive, Santa Barbara, CA 93111   (805) 967-1456
Founded: 1974   Members: 41
Dues: Write for details   Contact: Marge Colvin

Yes, it's hard to believe...but here's another Engelbert fan club....he has 150 of
them worldwide (we won't list all of them.).. but even harder to believe is that he
attends *all* the club parties. Enge's Entourage, with its *large* membership, can count
on the star's presence at the parties they throw three times a year. Now let's
see...three parties, times 150 clubs...that's a lot of parties, Engelbert. (It's a tough
life, but somebody's...)

Enge's Flaming Hearts

1312 Avenue N, Brooklyn, NY 11230   (718) 645-1391
Founded: 1976   Members: 85
Dues: Write for details   Contact: Regina Joseph

Engel's Angels in Humperdinck Heaven Fan Club

3024 Fourth Ave., Carney, Baltimore, MD 21234 (301) 665-0744
Founded: 1971   Members: 82
Dues: $9.00 per year   Contact: Jean Marshalek

The *Guardian Engel* newsletter is published monthly.

Engelbert's Aquarians

1400 S. Douglass Rd. Space 220, Anaheim CA 92806   (714) 634-4939
Founded: 1970   Members: 84
Dues: Write for details   Contact: Mary Jane Lamb

Yet another fan club for the Englishman who started life with the name "Arnold
Dorsey."

Ernest Fan Club

PO Box 23325, Nashville, TN 37202   Members: 1700
Dues: $5.00   Contact: John Cherry

It's the Ernest P. Worrell International Fan Club! Who's Ernest P. Worrell?? Why
he's the guy on all the TV commercials, with the strange face and cap who says
"Hey, Vern! KnoWhutImean?" As far as we can tell, that's all he says...but we
hear that there are many who would like to be members of his fan
club...KnoWhutImean? Members receive a membership card *and* a signed black-
and-white picture of Ernest *and* the authorized Ernest bumper sticker *and* the
KnoWhutImean News. We know there must be some real hardcore Ernest fans out
there who are going to delight in the selection of Ernest posters, greeting cards,
mugs and the videocassette with the best of Ernest 'n' Vern's TV commercials...
KnowWhutWeMean?

First Fandom

2209 South Webster Street, Kokomo, IN 46901   (317) 455-1958
Founded: 1958   Members: 300
Dues: $5.00 per year   Contact: Ray Beam

Collectors of science fiction and fantasy magazines.

Friends of Dark Shadows

PO Box 213, Metairie, LA 70004
Founded: 1973
Dues: $15.00 per year   Contact: Sharida Rizutto

Members receive *The Collinwood Journal* and *The Collinwood Report*.

Friends of General Hospital

42 Joy Street, Norwood, MA 02062
Founded: 1986   Members: 430
Dues: $10.00 per year   Contact: Joanne Wroe

Joanne Wroe says, "Fan mail is crucial! Imagine these changes over the years:
      • Luke would have been killed off during his 1st year
      • Joe Kelly would have been on GH a few short months.
      • Holly would have gone back to Luke when he returned from the
"dead"
      • Duke would have been sent to prison, never to be seen again.

But letters changed the course of those storylines. The present project is keeping

Jack Wagner on the show. I'd hate to see what would happen without him!!"
"The General Store" offers video tape rentals of "the best show on television,"
black & white photos taken right from the screen, bumper stickers, and ballpoint
pens, all with the Friends of General Hospital logo. The newsletter is published 6
times a year.

Friends of Veteran Soap Actors
PO Box 6039, Bluefield, WV 24701
Dues: Write for details   Contact: Denise Clifton

Friends of Weird Al Yankovic
8033 Sunset Blvd., Los Angeles, CA 90046

Galactic Hitchhiker's Guild
PO Box 4229, Bremerton, WA 98312-0229
Founded: 1982   Members: 70
Dues: $10.00 per year   Contact: Brian McNett

"I just can't keep quiet when standing in line. In an all-too-frequent moment of
utter boredom, I began reciting lines from this bizarre radio show I'd been
listening to," said Brian McNett, one of the three club founders, describing his
zeal for *The Hitchhiker's Guide to the Galaxy*. Writer Douglas Adams' story has been
adapted into a radio show, book, T.V. series, and computer games. Open to all
sentient life-forms, the club currently holds a semi-annual meeting and publishes a
quarterly newsletter (when they get around to it.)

Galaxy Patrol
22 Colton Street, Worcester, MA 01610
Contact: Dale L. Ames

Grab your space helmet and ray-gun, the Galaxy Patrol is coming. With its *Space-
O-Gram*, the club specializes in all the news of science-fiction films and stories of
the pre-high-tech genre. Everything from Flash Gordon to Lost in Space is
included...anyone flying through space in a tin can and crash landing on Mars
counts.

General Hospital Association
7890 Blairwood Circle S., Lake Worth, FL 33467
Dues: Write for details   Contact: Barbara Williams

Gone with the Wind Society
364 North May Avenue, Monrovia, CA 91016
Founded: 1981   Members: 1000+
Dues: $25.00 per year   Contact: Cynthia Molt

What would you say about someone who has seen "Gone With the Wind" over
500 times and owns the world's second largest collection of Gone With the Wind
memorabilia with over 2000 pieces? (Some might say she has Scarlett fever.)
Cynthia Molt is a "Gone with the Wind" expert, who started the Society and
plans to start a Gone With the Wind Museum to be located somewhere in
California. *Wind Magazine* is published bi-monthly. And, fans of Miss O., Rhett,
and Ashley, don't miss the get-together in Atlanta in 1989 for the fiftieth
anniversary of the film.

Good Day Sunshine
Liverpool Productions
397 Edgewood Avenue, New Haven CT 06511   (203) 865-8131
Founded: 1978   Members: 3000
Dues: $8.50 per year   Contact: Charles F. Rosenay

GDS hosts two major Beatles conventions per year, complete with sound and look
alike bands, Beatles collectible, games and contests. Publishes a bi-monthly
magazine and runs the yearly "Good Day Sunshine Magical Mystery Tour to the
Beatles Land" for fans who want to see where it all started for the Fab-4.

Guiding Light Fan Club
2855 Stevens St., Oceanside, NY 11572
Founded: 1981   Members: 850
Dues: $12.00 per year   Contact: Chris Mullen

It all started in January of 1937, more than 50 years ago, when Irna Phillips
originated a 15-minute radio drama, "The Guiding Light." Procter and Gamble
and other soap manufacturers were the original sponsors, thus coining the name
"soap opera." The show was dropped briefly in 1941, but fans demanded it back.
It moved to the CBS network in 1952 (though it continued on radio until 1956)
and now it's the longest-running drama in broadcast history. The fan club
publishes a regular newsletter and holds an annual luncheon with lots of Guiding
Light stars.

Hermania
641 Denning Place, Charlotte, NC 2821
Dues: Write for details   Contact: Tom Calhoun

The one and only Herman's Hermits fan club!!

The Higher We Fly John Denver Fan Club

7304 16th Avenue, Kenosha, WI 53140   (414) 658-4977
Founded: 1984   Members: 350
Dues: Write for details   Contact: Cindy Marx

Fans meet at the biennial "Denver Day" celebration. Newsletter available.

Humper Dears

1939 S. Roanoke Ave., Springfield, MO 65807   (417) 881-5444
Founded: 1971   Members: 100
Dues: Write for details   Contact: Velma Miles

The most memorable moment of Velma Miles' life was the 20 minutes that she and the Hump spent holding hands on a piano bench in Chicago. Velma, who has attended over 100 of Englebert's concerts, saves money to finance her concert trips by sewing her own clothes. Velma's husband doesn't mind having competition from the English singer...it gives him more time to go fishing. Velma says that before Enge came into her life, she was sick and depressed. Humper Dear is one of Engelbert's *131* fan clubs (!), many of whom raise money for charities. Publishes *The Humper Dear Happening* newsletter monthly.

International Federation of Elvis Presley Fan Clubs

PO Box 16948, Memphis, TN 38116   (901) 345-1425
Dues: Write for details   Contact: Norine Mitchell

Want to know if there is a Elvis club in your very own home town? Well, there probably is, but you'll have to ask the International Federation of Elvis Presley Fan Clubs to find out.

International Frankenstein Society

Penthouse North, 29 Washington Square W., New York, NY 10011
Dues: $10.00 lifetime membership   Contact: Robert G. Lane

Members receive an official membership card, club button, synopsis of the original *Frankenstein* by Mary Shelley, color wallet photo of Christopher Lee as the Monster, a color postcard of Mary Shelley and other goodies.

International Irwin Allen Fan Club

2111 E. 65th St., Brooklyn, NY 11234

Dues: Write for details   Contact: Joel Eisner

Writer, producer and director Irwin Allen is best known for his television series of
the 1960s, "Land of the Giants," "Lost in Space" (our all-time fave), "The Time
Tunnel" and "Voyage to the Bottom of the Sea."

International Mae West Society

PO Box 2623, Beverly Hills, CA 90213
Founded: 1981
Dues: $12.00 per year   Contact: Robert De Nend

"Too much of a good thing can be *wonderful*, " said Mae West, and her apartment
in Hollywood reflected that philosophy. The furniture was elegantly designed to
conform to the shape of Miss West's figure. At this apartment, hundreds of
famous show-biz people responded to the famous invitation, "Why don't you
come up and see me sometime?" The Mae West Society was founded a year after
the sex goddess' death, to create a museum dedicated to preserving the memory
of Miss West, taking much of its collection from the spacious apartment that she
left behind.

International Order of the Sons of the Desert

5151 White Oak Avenue, Encino, CA 91316   (818) 894-7718
Founded: 1964   Members: 3000+
Dues: $6.00 per year   Contact: Rick Greene

"Stan Laurel gave us our constitution just before he died...there is a provision for
cocktails in every bylaw," says Bob Satterfield, grand sheik of the Los Angeles
tent. Insisting they are not a fan club, they are a group of buffs, with more than 75
local groups called "Tents," each named after one of the Laurel and Hardy films
(including The Way Out West Tent of Los Angeles, The Saps at Sea Tent of San
Diego, The Bacon Grabbers of Chicago and the Two Tara Tent of Philadelphia.)
Each Tent is lead by a Grand Sheik. Laurel dictated that "everyone has a hell of a
lot of fun" with an ambiance of "half-assed dignity" being maintained. Sons of
the Desert (which gets its name from a 1933 feature...many say it was the duo's
best) members sing the club theme song, not once but twice at each tent meeting.

> *We are Sons of the Desert/Having the time of our lives/*
> *Marching along, two thousand strong/*
> *Far from our sweethearts and wives/*
> *God bless them/Tramp, tramp, tramp, the boys are marching,*
> *and dancing to this melody/*
> *Sons of the Desert are we!*

Members from around the world keep in touch through the quarterly *Intra-Tent*

Journal. At the yearly convention members and Grand Sheiks bring their own red fezzes to what turns out to be a Laurel and Hardy film festival party, screening some of the 105 films they made together during their career.

International Space: 1999 Alliance
810 Garrard St., Covington, KY 41014

(606) 261-1181

Founded: 1977

Members: 250+

Dues: Write for details

Contact: Rose Marie Badgett

Lovers of the television show *Space: 1999*.

International Wizard of Oz Club Inc.

220 N. 11 Street, Escanaba, MI 49829

Founded: 1957

Members: 2,000

Dues: $10.00 per year

Contact: Fred M. Meyer

Celebrating Frank Baum's Oz books and the popular film, IWOOC holds three sprightly-named times a year: the Ozmopolitan in Zion, IL, the Winkie in Asilomar, CA and the Munchkin in Wilmington, DE. The *Baum Bugle* is issued three times a year, the *Baum Trading Post* provides collectors with trading opportunities, and *Oziana* magazine includes original writing.

James Bond 007 Fan Club

PO Box 414, Bronxville, NY 10708

Founded: 1972

Members: 2200

Dues: $13.00 per year

Contact: Richard Schenkman

Founded by Richard Schenkman and friend at the young age of 13, the James Bond 007 Fan Club still exists with its predominantly male membership. Interviews with producer Alfred R. Broccoli, producer Kevin McClory and actor George Lazenby have appeared in the club newsletter *Bondage* (published about twice per year.) The club plans a convention. One club member from New Orleans throws a birthday party for Bond in November. Fans can correspond with each other.

Trivia Question: Who was the first person to play James Bond? The answer: actor Barry Nelson in the 1954 television version of "Casino Royale" on CBS.

Jim's Neighbors
4201 Wichita Avenue, Cleveland, OH 44109

Dues: $10.00 first year ($5.00 after)

Contact: Cheryl Yurcak

"Gaw-lly!," Gomer Pyle was actually discovered by Andy Griffith at a nightclub in Santa Monica in 1962. Andy saw Jim Nabors and asked him to try out for a part on his new T.V. show. The club keeps members up-to-date on Jim's recording and performing career through *Nabor's News*.

King of our Hearts Elvis Presley Fan Club

6117 Silberman, San Jose, CA 95120   (408) 268-4754
Founded: 1968   Members: 500+
Dues: Write for details   Contact: Rosemary Luci

Leave it to Beaver Society

9346 East 29th Street, Tucson, AZ 85701
Dues: Write for details   Contact: Teri Edwards

Leonard Nimoy Fan Club

17 Gateway Drive, Batavia, NY 14020
Founded: 1982   Members: 460
Dues: $12.00 per year   Contact: Barbara Walker

Leonard gave the club his authorization to be his *official* fan club. Members get *Quest II* bi-monthly.

Little Rascals Society

Box 262, Carteret, NJ 07008
Dues: Write for details   Contact: Russell Crocl

The Lunarians--The New York Science Fiction Society

1171 East 8th Street, Brooklyn, NY 11230   (212) 252-9759
Founded: 1956   Members: 50
Dues: Write for details   Contact: Walter R. Cole

Science fiction lovers meet at the annual Lunacon (in March or April.)

Maltese Falcon Society

PO Box 22544, San Francisco, CA 94122   (415) 665-7644
Founded: 1981   Members: 150+
Dues: Write for details   Contact: Jayson Wechter

Members say that the "Tough, slick and cynical" detective who is "principled in the face of a callous corrupt world" is a distinctly American invention that premiered in *Black Mask Magazine* in the 1920s and 1930s. Members are fans of the works of detective writers such as Raymond Chandler and Dashiell Hammett (*The Maltese Falcon* was written by Hammett.) The group holds a convention and publishes a quarterly magazine called *Hard Boiled*, after the characters it reveres.

Marx Brothers Study Unit

Darien 28, New Hope, PA 18938

(215) 862-9734

Founded: 1978

Members: 400+

Dues: $7.00 per year

Contact: Paul G. Wesolowski

Groucho Marx said that he wouldn't join any club that would have him as a member, but the Marx Brothers Study Unit might have been the exception. Founder Paul Wesolowski had never seen a Marx Brothers film before 1974, but after the first one, he was hooked. He started to amass what--according to his business card--is, "The Most Complete Marx Brothers Research Facility on This Planet," today containing over 3,000 photos, 28,000 magazine and newspaper articles and posters filling every inch of wall space in his museum/home. *The Freedonia Gazette*, published twice a year since 1978, is so named after the name of the fictional country Groucho ruled in the movie "Duck Soup." Currently, the club is working towards the issuance of a Marx Brothers postage stamp celebrating the centennial of Chico's birth (Chico was the oldest brother.) Those who join MBSU will receive the Fredonia Gazette and are invited to the yearly open house at the museum.

Mister Ed Fan Club

PO Box 1009, Cedar Hill, TX 75104

Founded: 1974

Members: 1000+

Dues: $10.00 per year

Contact: James Burnett

Though Mr. Ed died in 1979 at the age of 33, his fans have not forgotten him. The cover of his fan magazine, *The Horse's Mouth* reads, "He's Hot, He's Sexy, and He's Ed." The first and original Edhead, James "Big Bucks" Burnett had never seen one of the 143 Mr. Ed episodes until October 9, 1983. When he was 15, he made up the club name to serve as a false return address...but to his astonishment, Edheads all over wanted to join. The first members were the Monty Python Troup, and then rock star Iggy Pop. Even the series' human co-star, Alan Young, who played Wilbur Post has become an official Edhead.

In 1984, Burnett held Edstock, the world's first-ever Mr. Ed music festival, held in Dallas at Bronco Bowl, a horseshoe-shaped arena. Edstock was a bit of disappointment, (because of low attendance, Big-Bucks lost $20,000 on the Festival.) But progress marches on. Today, the club lives with its three-pronged goals of Joyism Forever, Getting out of Debt, and Better TV. Presently, the club is undertaking "Project Edstar": to have Ed's own star embedded on the sidewalk of Hollywood Blvd. Other projects include the creation of the Mr. Ed museum in the Dallas area, and a possible special one hour return of Mr. Ed drama show called "Barnasty."

The club sells lots of merchandise, including "Live Ed" posters, stereo LP's of Tiny Tim and The Gloomchasers singing a very special version of the infamous Mr. Ed. theme song ("A horse is a horse, of course, of course"), available on the Broken Records label. The ultimate goal of all this merchandising is the construction of a city named for the talking horse, "Edtopia," the world's ultimate trailer park. With bold goals like these, the club motto, "One Club, One Horse, One World," is fitting.

Monkees Buttonmania Club
Liverpool Productions
397 Edgewood Avenue, New Haven, CT 06511   (203) 865-8131
Dues: Write for details   Contact: Charles F. Rosenay

The Mouse Club
2056 Cirone Way, San Jose, CA 95124   (408) 377-2590
Founded: 1979   Members: 500+
Dues: $17.50 per year   Contact: Tim & Julie McEuen

Collectors of Goofy, Pluto, Minnie and of course, Mickey Mouserobilia. Disney toys books and games are traded among members. Conventions are...but of course...held in Disneyland and Disneyworld.

National Fantasy Fan Federation

PO Box 713, Webster City, IA 50595
Founded: 1941   Members: 300
Dues: Write for details   Contact: Lola Andrew

Readers and writers of fantasy-oriented books and magazines.

North American Dr. Who Appreciation Society
6642 Andalsol Ave., Van Nuys, CA 91406   (818) 344-2088
Founded: 1979   Members: 6000
Dues: Write for details   Contact: Michael Shubin

Though the television program Dr. Who has been running since 1963 in England, members of this Society were only able to get it on the air in the United States a couple of years ago.

Old Soldiers of Baker Street of Two Saults

Unicorn Ltd. Conglomerate, Lake Superior State College
Office of College Relations, Sault Ste. Marie, MI 49783   (906) 635-2315
Dues: Write for details   Contact: W. T. Rabe

An outgrowth of the Baker Street Irregulars, these Old Saults sponsor a breakfast
on Sherlock Holmes' birthday (the first Friday in January.)

Old Time Western Film Club

PO Box 142, Siler City, NC 27344
Founded: 1970   Members: 500
Dues: No membership fee   Contact: Milo Holt

Promoting old-time westerns, and related memorabilia (1903-1955.) The club
hosts a three-day Western film festival each July in Charlotte, NC.

Pee-Wee Herman Fan Club

Box 48423, 7610 Beverly Blvd., Los Angeles, CA 90048
Dues: $5.00 per year

This is a really cool club! Members receive an autographed photo of the Pee-Wee
man himself plus a one year's subscription to the newsletter. For $10.00 members
can get a pair of giant (size 60) souvenir underpants. That's right, it's those undies
you've been hearing about--classic white color, durable, 100% cotton, Hanes
silkscreened with a picture of Pee-Wee in blue and red. Life isn't worth *living*
without these!

Praed Street Irregulars

17 Mt. Lassen Dr., San Rafael, CA 94903   (415) 479-6554
Founded: 1966   Members: 3600
Dues: No membership fee   Contact: Ted G. Schulz, Lord
                                                 Warden of the Pristine

Marshes

Mr. Solar Pons of 7B Praed Street, London, W., a "clever consulting" detective
created by Wisconsin writer August Derleth, has loyal fans in these "Solarians," as
they call themselves. Admirers of Sherlock Holmes as well, the group is loosely
associated with the Baker Street Irregulars and the August Derleth Society.

R.A.L.P.H. (Royal Assoc. for the Longevity & Preservation of the Honeymooners)

LIU/CW Post College, Greenvale, NY 11548   (516) 299-2622
Founded: 1982   Members: 12,000+
Dues: $7.00 per year   Contact: Peter Crescenti

One of the first projects was a fundraising drive to buy a precious artifact at auction: Ralph Kramden's size 51 Gotham Bus Company uniform for $650.00. Today Honeymoonies hail from 49 states and nine countries around the world. The 1987 annual convention highlights include a photo opportunity with the *actual Kramden kitchen* (another prize that RALPH bought), a chance to stand near the Kramden uniform, a vote for the best of the lost episodes, the famous "Honeymooners costume contest," and the always popular "Bang-Zoom" lessons...do it right or don't do it at all. RALPH offers a wide range of merchandise to its members--from the "The Honeymooners Game," T-Shirts, videotapes of the lost episodes, to Ralph and Norton dolls. New members receive an official RALPH button, newsletter, and trivia quiz:

> Q: Ralph Kramden drives a bus for the Gotham Bus Company. What is his usual route?
> A: The Madison Avenue Bus.
> Q: What is Ralph Kramden's salary?
> A: $62.00 per week.
> Q: "Trixie" is only a nickname. What is Norton's wife's real name?
> A: Thelma.

RALPH has succeeded in returning "The Honeymooners" to the sets of millions in many US markets, making it more popular today than ever. Founder Cresenti believes that the show could be very popular in Japan or England, where they love American culture.

Rocky Horror Picture Show Fan Club

204 W. 20th Street, New York, NY 10011
Dues: Write for information.

The one and only! Members devote their lives to living out the script from the "Rocky Horror Picture Show" movie. Recently, in Chicago, two devotees of the club were married after their 100th time acting out the script in costume. (Was it Franky and Brad???)

Sgt. Pepper's Lonely Hearts Club

Two Birch Hill Ave, Wakefield, MA 01880

Founded: 1976

(617) 944-3998

Members: 4500

Contact: Tom McDonald

This is truly a lonely-hearts club for Beatlemaniacs who want to correspond as pen pals with each other.

Shoes Fan Club

PO Box 404, Zion, IL 60099

Founded: 1978

(312) 746-2947

Members: 500

Contact: Chuck Fieldman

Keeping fans informed about their favorite rock group "The Shoes," offering unreleased live Shoes cassette recordings, Shoes memorabilia and the quarterly "Shoes News."

Six of One Club; The Prisoner Appreciation Society

PO Box 172, Hatfield, PA 19440

(215) 822-6286

Founded: 1977

Dues: $30.00 per year

Members: 1500

Contact: Bruce A. Clark

"The Prisoner" is considered by the Boston Globe to be number 3 on its list of the most popular "cult TV" shows of all time...and the only one on the list not made in America. It was created by and starred Patrick McGoohan, who played Number 6, a rebel in a Orwellian society. Only 17 one-hour episodes of "The Prisoner" were created. A convention is held each year in Portmeirion, Wales, the village where the series was filmed. This is an international organization, that accepts membership through the U.K. headquarters (PO Box 66, Ipswich IP2 9TZ England.)

Slim Whitman Appreciation Society of the US

1002 W. Thurber, Tucson, AZ 85705

Founded: 1970

Dues: $8.00 per year

(602) 887-8384

Contact: Loren R. Knapp

Bumper stickers, T-shirts, lapel pins, posters, rare LP's and a newsletter are available.

Starfleet

PO Box 843, Newton, IA 50208-0843
Founded: 1972
Dues: $8.00 per year

Members: 2100
Contact: Steven L. Smith

"United in appreciation of Star Trek - the greatest human adventure" . Members hold a fictional rank and position, attend the Starfleet Academy and Starfleet conventions and receive the newsletter, *Communique*.

Star Trek Welcommittee

481 Main St., Hatfield, MA 01038
Founded: 1972
Contact: Shirley S. Maiewski

(413) 247-5339
Volunteer Workers: 100

The Welcommittee is not really a club, but a non-profit, volunteer information service answering questions about the 300 clubs, 400 fan magazines, plus the books, conventions and sale items relating to Star Trek.

Straight-Arrow Fan Club

301 East Buena Vista Avenue, North Aurora, SC 29841
Founded: 1986
Contact: Joe Harper

Straight-Arrow was a radio series from 1948-1951, sponsored by Nabisco, and then a syndicated comic strip. This is Straight-Arrow's first fan club. *Pow-wow*, the club's newsletter has included a feature on how to build a tee-pee.

Tara Collectors Club

PO Box 1200, Jonesboro, GA, 30236

Terry and the Pirates/John Cipollina Fan Club

PO Box 4355, Arlington, VA 22204
Founded: 1980
Dues: Write for details

(703) 920-6577
Members: 600
Contact: Mike Somavilla

The official fan headquarters for other rock-n-roll bands, too, like the Dinosaurs, Zero and Thunder and Lightning. *Silverado News* is the newsletter.

Three Stooges Fan Club

710 Collins Ave., Lansdale, PA 19446
Founded: 1974
Dues: $6.00 per year

Members: 2000+
Contact: Gary Lassin

With most members voting for Curley as their favorite Stooge, the club
perpetuates Stooges trivia. "This Date in Stooge History," is a regular feature in
the quarterly *3 Stooges Journal*. (i.e., "*A Pain in the Pullman* released, June 27, 1936.")
The journal reviews books, provides updates to collectors and includes lots of
lively comments from members. Yearly convention, T-shirts, books, tapes and
memorabilia available. (More fun than a poke in the eye....)

U.N.C.L.E. HQ
2710 Rohlwing Rd., Rolling Meadows, IL 60008 (312) 392-4869
Founded: 1976   Members: 500
Dues: $7.00 per year   Contact: Susan Cole

Fans of the television show, "The Man From U.N.C.L.E." and the short-lived
spin-off "The Girl from U.N.C.L.E." (U.N.C.L.E. stands for United Network
Comman for Law and Enforcement.) Members receive the newsletter, and each
year meet at the Spycon Convention (with fans from other undercover police
television series--"The Avengers," "Rat Patrol," "The Professional," etc.)

We Love Lucy...or...
The International Lucille Ball Fan Club

PO Box 480216, Los Angeles, CA 90048   (213) 475-0137
Founded: 1977   Members: 1000
Dues: $10.00 per year   Contact: Thomas J. Watson

The official fan club for the world's funniest, most lovable redhead publishes *The
Lucy* newsletter, chock full of photos, about four times per year.

The Wool Hat Society
20 Spruce Street, New Rochelle, NY 10805
Dues: Write for details   Contact: Donna Ferrara

One of the many fan clubs revering The Monkees.

Working Class Hero
3311 Niagara Street., Pittsburgh, PA 15213
Founded: 1970   Members: 500+
Dues: $6.50 per year   Contact: Barb Whatmough

Originally called "The Beatle Peace Followers," then called "The Beatles Live
Peace in Pepperland," "Working Class Hero" (taken from the title of a John
Lennon song) publishes a quarterly newsletter.

World of Dark Shadows

PO Box 2262, Mission Station, Santa Clara, CA 95055   (408) 984-2817
Founded: 1975   Members: 500+
Dues: Write for details   Contact: Kathleen Resch

Fans of the television show Dark Shadows (1966-1971.) Members have been writing the National Academy of Television Arts and Sciences in hopes of presenting the show with a special Emmy Award.

World Science Fiction Society

c/o Southern Cal. Institute for Fan Interests
PO Box 8442, Van Nuys, CA 91409   (213) 559-1622
Founded: 1939   Members: 12,000+
Dues: Write for details   Contact: Craig Miller

Held on Labor Day weekend, the World Science Fiction Convention is the largest science fiction convention of its kind. There, the Hugos are awarded to different categories of science fiction expertise, including books, radio, movies, television, and magazines.

ZOSO

1390 Market St., Suite 2115, San Francisco, CA 94102
Dues: $2.00

WHEELS, WINGS AND WATER

Gyrocopters...Checker cabs...houseboats...getting there with this crowd is more than half the fun.

Airport and Aircraft Enthusiasts Club
18 Lambert Ave., Lynn, MA 01902   (617) 592-3390
Founded: 1986   Members: 878
Dues: $23.00 per year   Contact: Robert B. Redden

Publishes The Aircraft and Eye, journals, and newsletters, and holds annual conventions.

All-American Indian Motorcycle Club
25801 Clark Rd., Wellington, OH 44090
Founded: 1971   Members: 225
Dues: Write for details   Contact: Ernest Hartman, Jr.

Owners of the American-built Indian motorcycles, manufactured until 1953.

American Association of Private Railroad Car Owners
969 Santa Ysable Ave., Baywood Park, CA, 93402 (805) 528-7533
Founded: 1977   Members: 400
Dues: $250.00 per year   Contact: Gordon L. Crosthwait

Members own their own railroad cars.

American British Cab Society
4470 Cerritos Ave., Long Beach, CA 90807   (213) 424-4302
Founded: 1972   Members: 250
Dues: $5.00 per year   Contact: Dr. D. Cameron
Paschall

Dennis Leslie is a railroad buff who has driven streetcars, double-decker buses, movie-lot stagecoaches and once helped build a bulletproof, watertight Pullman car for F.D.R. But more than any of the preceding vehicles, Leslie loved his Austin taxicab, which Dr. Paschall helped him buy for $100. It had 700,000 miles on it, had been driven around the streets of London for ten years, and had been sitting in a field with weeds growing out of it. Yet with the oil and battery changed and the tires pumped up, the old 1957 Austin diesel started right up.

In love with their stalwart steeds, the two men set out to find other American owners and fans of British cabs. Though there are about 12,000 cabs operating on the streets of London, only right-hand-steering cars built before 1968 may be imported, by U.S. Federal Law.

The design of the British cabs is specified by Scotland Yard, which rules that it must be high enough so that a man doesn't have to take off his top hat to ride in comfort, that it's strong enough to withstand a severe collision and that it won't tip over, no matter how you spin it around. The London taxi drivers are no less prepared--they are all full-time cabbies and some are second-generation drivers. Drivers must spend 18 months walking, biking or moped-ing around London to acquire "The Knowledge," studying literally every alleyway in preparation for a rigorous exam. The cabbies are then re-inspected regularly by Scotland Yard. (This may sound merely sensible to a non-New Yorker...but the very thought brings tears of envy to a Manhattanite's eyes.) British cabs are hard to come by in the US but Lewis reports that a man in Northern California who owns 19 of them has changed the fare meters from pounds to dollars and operates them as a business.

Club members receive a membership card, window emblem, newsletter and sheets of reproductions of interior signs and Metropolitan London police license plates. They also "keep tabs on the cabs" by asking members for snapshots of their treasured autos.

American Bugatti Club

2366 Huntington Dr., San Marino, CA 91108-2675   (818) 286-5377
Founded: 1960   Members: 214
Dues: $40.00 per year   Contact: Thomas Perkins

These owners and ex-owners of Bugatti cars, manufactured from 1909 to 1956, dedicated to preserving the art and legend of Ettore Bugatti. Annual meetings, and occasional sponsorship of an international road rally.

American Truck Historical Society

PO Box 59200, Birmingham, AL 35259   (205) 879-2131
Founded: 1971   Members: 6500
Dues: Write for details   Contact: Ms. Zoe S. James

American Truck Racing

500 Northridge Rd. #300, Atlanta, GA 30332
Founded: 1980   Contact: N. Linn Hendershot

Bobtail and pick-up truck racing.

Amphibious Auto Club of America

3281 Elk Ct., Yorktown Heights, NY 10598   (914) 245-7541
Founded: 1974   Members: 100
Dues: No membership fee   Contact: Fred Marsh

Members exchange views in the *Waterlogged News* and meet each year at the annual auto-swim-meet.

Amphicar Owners Club

382 Vassar Rd., Poughkeepsie, NY 12603
Founded: 1976   Members: 200
Dues: $10.00 per year   Contact: Jim Nichols, Jr.

Borgward Owners' Club

77 New Hampshire, Bay Shore, NY 11706   (516) 273-0458
Founded: 1974   Members: 100
Dues: $15.00 per year   Contact: Dyck Livant

Owners of the German-built Borgward cars from the 1950s.

Bricklin International

119 Old Sherman Hill Road, Woodbury, CT 06798
Founded: 1976   Members: 700
Dues: Write for details   Contact: E. V. Clisby

Owners of Bricklin automobiles.

Bus History Association

965 McEwan, Windsor, Ont. N9B 2G1
Founded: 1963   Members: 300
Dues: $20.00 per year   Contact: Bernard Drouillard

The association publishes of *Bus Industry Magazine*, each issue with a "Transit Profile" detailing routes and schedules in a selected city, plus a color postcard of a bus or coach. For a behind-the-scenes look at local bus operations, the annual convention in a different city each year gives members a chance to exchange bus memorabilia. Club members also enjoy visits to bus manufacturing plants, and in-depth talks with bus drivers and industry leaders.

Cadillac Convertible Owners of America

Box 269, Ossining, NY 10562
Founded: 1977
Dues: $35.00 per year

Members: 300
Contact: Roberta Lynne

Caddy convertible owners.

Cartercar

10208 Aviary Dr., San Diego, CA 92131
Founded: 1975
Dues: Write for details

(619) 578-4526
Members: 24
Contact: Jack Bryant

There are only 25 Cartercars in existence today out of the hundreds that were produced from 1904 to 1914. Byron Carter assembled the first one at the Michigan State Prison, where he was superintendent. After that, the president of General Motors secured the rights to produce them.

Checker Club

469 Tremaine Avenue, Kenmore, NY 14217
Founded: 1983
Dues: $5.00 per year

Contact: Don McHenry

Practically synonymous with taxicab, Checker Cabs were those big, boxy cars that could fit six of your friends or you and your cello in the back seat. Each Checker was road-tested before being sold as a taxicab, airport limousine, etc. In 60 years of production (until 1982), there were only 7 body styles. (King Hussain still uses a 1963 model.) It wasn't until 1962 that Checker started a push to sell the auto to the general public, initially offering it in 96 colors! Club members complain that when they drive their prized car, they are constantly being hailed. Despite the final closing of the Checker plant, a club newsletter is published three times a year.

Circumnavigators Club

24 E. 39th St., New York, NY 10016
Founded: 1902
Dues: Write for details

(212) 724-4448

Contact: Helen Jost

Founded by two Americans who were sailing across the Indian Ocean at the turn of the century, the Circumnavigators Club brings together those who can prove that they have completely circled the globe, crossing all meridians in one direction. Past members have included Robert Peary, John Philip Sousa, Generals Douglas MacArthur and John Pershing, and President William Howard Taft. Most members today are business and professional people, belonging to chapters in a number of states and in several nations of the world. (If you have four globetrotting buddies, you may be able to start a group in your area.) Members receive the bimonthly newsletter and, from time to time, the club sponsors group trips. Their traditional farewell, "Luck to you!"

Club Elite of North America

6238 Ralston Ave., Richmond, CA 94805   (415) 465-4040
Founded: 1970   Members: 250
Dues: $20.00 per year   Contact: Michael Ostrov

Owners of the beautiful Lotus Elite automobile handmade from 1959 to 1963.

Curved Dash Olds Owners Club

Seven Kiltie Drive, New Hope, PA 18938   (215) 862-2353
Founded: 1956   Members: 40
Dues: Write for details   Contact: James Staats

These people won't part with their Curved Dash Oldsmobiles!

Davis 3-Wheel Club of America

3033 Crestline Rd., Bakersfield, CA 93306   (805) 871-2548
Founded: 1978   Members: 25
Dues: $10.00 per year   Contact: Richard Kelley

Members have tracked down 15 of the 17 three-wheeled cars built by the Davis Car Company in the late 1940s in California. The founding member, Tom Wilson, found *his* Three-Wheeler sitting abandoned in a vacant lot.

DeLorean Club International

PO Box 23040, Seattle, WA 98102   (206) 324-6569
Founded: 1980   Members: 1000
Dues: $25.00 per year   Contact: Tom Wilson

DeLorean Motor Club of America

18552 Metzler Lane Ste. A, Huntington Beach, CA 92647   (714) 847-9940
Founded: 1982   Members: 3200
Dues: $50.00 initial ($35.00 yearly after)   Contact: Patti Nolan

Two members' vanity license plates read "NO COKE" and "2-HOT."

Accessories for the auto and books on John Z. DeLorean are available, plus the monthly newsletter, *De Gull Wing*.

DeLorean Owners Association

10568 Ashton Ave., Los Angeles, CA 90024   (213) 474-8194
Dues: $39.00 per year   Contact: Dick Shipman

Technical assistance, parts, information and *DeLorean World* magazine.

Edsel Owner's Club

R#1, West Liberty, IL 62475   (618) 754-3516
Founded: 1968   Members: 1438
Dues: $15.00 per year   Contact: Perry E. Piper

Perry Piper owns 23 Edsels. He bought his first one in 1958. "It was unbelievable how people hid them in their garages or behind their farms. They didn't want their neighbors to know they'd been suckered in." The entire car seemed too long--poorly-proportioned. The famous grill was likened to a horse harness, a toilet seat or the mug of a person sucking a lemon. The upholstery on the inside looked like it belonged on the headboard at the local cheap motel. But Perry loved his Edsel and the way it handled and when he gave it up, he realized he had lost a good thing. Ever in search of the big E, Piper not only regained his dream car, but was contacted by Edsel Henry Ford of California--supposedly no relation to the carmaker, whose affiliation with the club helped turn the 5-member Edsel Car Club of Liberty, Illinois into a thriving organization. Today there are about 12 active chapters all around the country **and** an Edsel in mint condition now brings top dollar. The next convention in Indiana in 1988. Says Piper: Happy Edseling!

Escapees

Rt.#5, Box 310, Livingston, TX 77351   (409) 563-4974
Founded: 1978   Members: 7600 families
Dues: $40.00 per year ($45.00 joining fee)   Contact: Cathy Sipult

Home is Where You Park It reads the title of a club publication, dedicated to the "Special Kind of People Who Share the RV Way of Life." Devotees of RVs (recreational vehicles) are rewarded with free parking at special retreats and RV rallies held around the country. Escapees helps RVers who are retired or on a budget, providing advice on RVing in Europe and other destinations. Other services include mail forwarding, and publications like *Survival of the Snowbird*.

Experimental Aircraft Association

Wittman Airfield, Oshkosh, WI 54903   (414) 426-4800
Founded: 1953   Members: 280,000
Dues: $30.00 per year   Contact: John C. Burton

With 700 chapters throughout the world, EAA caters to sport aviation hobbyists, including pilots, aircraft designers and all others interested in aviation. There are three special interest divisions: The Antique/Classic division for planes built before 1955, the Warbirds of America, for those interested in vintage WWII aircraft and the International Aerobatic Club for those interested in competitive aerobatics. All EAA members receive *Sport Aviation Magazine* and there are frequent "fly-in" meetings among members.

Facel Vega Owners Club

1311 San Pablo Avenue, Redlands, CA 92373   (714) 792-8326
Founded: 1980   Members: 200
Dues: $35.00 per year   Contact: Bert J. Davidson, MD

The first stainless steel sports car ever made was not the DeLorean--it was the Facel Vega, produced in France from 1954 to 1964 in limited numbers.

Graham Brothers Truck & Bus Club

9894 Fairtree Drive, Strongsville, OH 44136   (216) 238-4956
Founded: 1967   Members: 80
Dues: Write for details   Contact: Edwin L. Brinkman

A club for collectors of **school buses**! Graham Brothers also made trucks (from 1923-1929.)

High Speed Rail Association

1625 Eye Street, NW Suite 1015, Washington, DC 20006   (202) 296-8001
Founded: 1983   Members: 165
Dues: $150.00 per year   Contact: Donald M. Deer

With one goal and one goal only: to promote high-speed train construction in the United States. Members, who hail from a number of related industries, are certain that trains traveling 150, 180 even over 200 miles per hour are on their way--it's just a matter of time. Planning is underway for the corridors between major metropolitan areas, with trains modeled after ones now used in Europe and Japan. *Speedlines* is the bi-monthly newsletter.

Helicopter Club of America
1400 Eye St., NW, Suite 550, Washington, DC 20005 (202) 898-1313
Founded: 1970   Members: 140
Dues: $27.50 per year   Contact: Col. A. J. Rankin

Sponsors helicopter events to enthusiasts who fly the whirly-birds for sport.

International Bus Collectors Club
18 Lambert Ave., Lynn, MA 01902   (617) 592-3390
Founded: 1979   Members: 1275
Dues: $23.00 per year   Contact: Robert B. Redden

A club for collectors of buses and models of buses. *The Red Ghost* is the club's own
bus, equipped with video lounge and bar, that takes members on trips. The "Bus
Bash" is held twice a year, a gathering of famous and antique coaches.
Membership includes a quarterly journal. Founder Robert Redden is a master
photographer of both buses and planes, with 150 magazine covers to his credit.

International Edsel Club
PO Box 86, Polo, IL 61064   (815) 946-3036
Founded: 1969   Members: 990
Dues: $8.00 per year   Contact: Paul and Ethel Yount

"Edsel was a car years ahead of its time," joke club members who own the
infamous auto or have a strong interest in it. Say the Younts, "Ford dropped $350
million in the Edsel fiasco, but the Edselers are a proud clan and inclined to think
it all worthwhile." The club has a monthly *Edseletter* and annual meetings.

International Hot Rod Association
PO Box 3029, Bristol, TN 37620   (615) 764-1164
Founded: 1970   Members: 20,000+
Dues: $20.00 per year   Contact: Larry Carrier

Sanctions over a dozen drag races around the U.S. each year.

International Human Powered Vehicle Association

PO Box 51255, Indianapolis, IN 46251-0255
Founded: 1975   Members: 1500
Dues: $15.00 per year   Contact: Marti Daily

If you're planning on pedaling to Peoria, the IHPVA keeps track of advancements
in human powered vehicle design. On land, a human-powered tandem tricycle

has gone 63 miles per hour, and at sea, in 1979, the "Gossamer Albatross" was pedaled across the English Channel in three hours. IHPVA members are kept up-to-date through the publications *HPV News* and *the Human Power*.

International Popular Rotorcraft Association

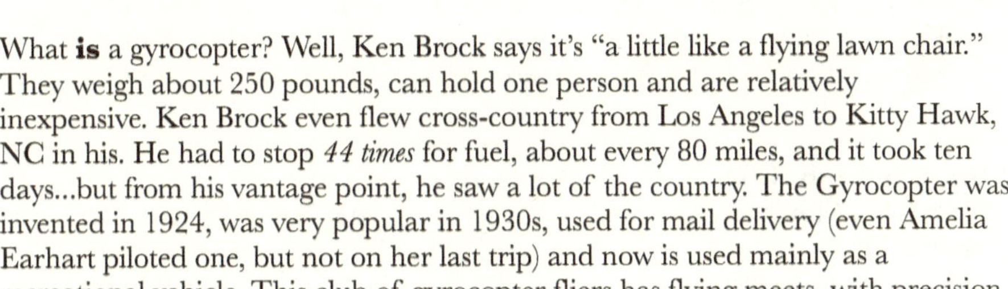

11852 Western Avenue, Stanton, CA 90680
Founded: 1962
Dues: $18.00 per year

Members: 1,800
Contact: Ken Brock

What **is** a gyrocopter? Well, Ken Brock says it's "a little like a flying lawn chair." They weigh about 250 pounds, can hold one person and are relatively inexpensive. Ken Brock even flew cross-country from Los Angeles to Kitty Hawk, NC in his. He had to stop *44 times* for fuel, about every 80 miles, and it took ten days...but from his vantage point, he saw a lot of the country. The Gyrocopter was invented in 1924, was very popular in 1930s, used for mail delivery (even Amelia Earhart piloted one, but not on her last trip) and now is used mainly as a recreational vehicle. This club of gyrocopter fliers has flying meets, with precision take-off and landing contests. The "bomb drop," where you throw objects out of the plane and try to hit a target on the ground, is a popular event.

Lighter-Than-Air Society

1800 Triplett Blvd., Akron, OH 44306
Founded: 1952
Dues: $10.00 per year

(216) 884-9926
Members: 1300
Contact: David L. Hill

Members are interested in the history of balloons and other forms of lighter-than-air transportation. At the yearly summer picnic, members bring models of balloons and prizes and trophies are awarded to the best inventive new designs and advances in hot-air-ballooning.

Loners on Wheels

808 Lester Street, Poplar Bluff, MO 63901
Founded: 1970
Dues: Write for details

(314) 785-2420
Members: 3500
Contact: Dick March

Single RV, motorhome and camper owners meet at rallies and campouts--if they get married, they become ex-LOWS.

Milestone Car Society

PO Box 50850, Indianapolis, IN 46250
Founded: 1971

Dues: $20.00 per year

Who could forget those "great postwar cars" from 1945 to 1970?

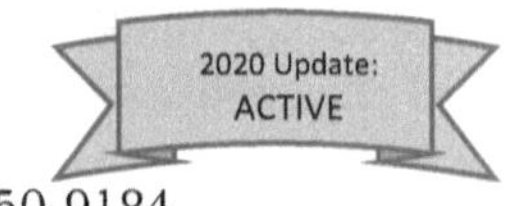

Military Vehicle Collectors Club

Box 33697, Thornton, CO 80233

Founded: 1976

Dues: $25.00 per year

(303) 450-9184

Members: 5000+

Contact: James E. Herrick

Are you interested in restoring a World War II jeep? Are you content to spend a whole day in a surplus store? Members collect and restore all types of military vehicles---know anyone with a tank in their backyard? They hold a yearly convention, and publish *Supply Line* newsletter and *Army Motors* magazine.

Mini Car Club, USA

172 Park St., Montclair, NJ 07042

Founded: 1966

Dues: Write for details

(201) 746-0015

Members: 100

Contact: Boris Kwaloff

The Morris 850, Morris Cooper, B.M.C. Mini and Austin 850--they're definitely not cars for professional wrestlers or basketball players, but club members do enjoy them.

Morgan Three-Wheeler Club

PO Box 99, Old York Rd & Larison Ln., Ringoes, NJ 08551   (201) 782-7053

Founded: 1948

Dues: Write for details

Members: 700

Contact: Alec Knight

One of the only three-wheeled cars ever made in the United States.

Morris Minor Registry

PO Box 6484, Stanford, CA 94305

Founded: 1977

Dues: $10.00

Members: 800

Contact: John Voelcker

"It's a small British auto that looks rather like a pregnant VW Beetle," says founder John Voelcker. The rage in Britain from 1948 to 1971, they are a little hard to find today, although more Morrises survive on the less-humid West Coast (*Morris Minor News* is published monthly.)

Motor Bus Society

Box 7058, West Trenton, NJ 08628

Founded: 1948

Members: 1200

Dues: $25.00 per year   Contact: John P. Hoschek

Some members collect real buses, some collect timetables, transfers, maps, signs or other things. Some are just interested in buses. Library of well over 100,000 photos of buses, terminals, depot signs, and drivers caps. Two meetings are held per year and a monthly magazine, *Motor Coach Age*, is published.

National Corvette Restorers Society
6291 Day Road, Cincinnati, OH 45247   (513) 385-8526
Founded: 1974   Members: 6,900
Dues: $21.00 per year   Contact: Gary Mortimer

The most sought after "'Vette" is the 1953 model--the first one made--with only 200 of the original 300 surviving. These cars go for more than $50,000. The NCRS helps enthusiasts restore Corvettes to their original condition, using original parts when available and reproductions of parts otherwise.

National Hot Rod Association
PO Box 150, North Hollywood, CA 91603   (213) 985-6472
Founded: 1951   Members: 54,000
Dues: $34.00 per year   Contact: Dallas J. Gardner

Wheels start burning rubber, the squeal of other cars is deafening and as you sprint down the track the speedometer climbs to 230 miles per hour! Then, as quickly as it began, it is over. The rowdy crowd yells, popping another brew out of the cooler: this is the world of Drag Racing. Professionals like "Big Daddy" and "The Snake" race Cameros, Chargers, alcohol-burning dragsters and funny cars, with cars being pitted against other cars based on horsepower and weight. The National Hot Rod Association promotes drag racing, with 14 major races around the country each year, publishing the weekly *National Dragster* with the latest from this fast world.

National Tractor Pullers Association
Worthington, OH 43085   (614) 436-1761
Founded: 1969   Members: 2000
Dues: $25.00 (for NTPA Fan Club)   Contact: Mike Allen

Tractor pulling has its roots in horse pulls, the once-popular agricultural contests that tested the strength of the animal. Today, tractor pulling has many variations, though it's basically a simple contest, where tractors try pulling a load of rocks on a steel pan a certain distance before the weight overcomes the power of the tractor. Tractors that fail to pull the dead weight are disqualified. More and more weight is added, until one tractor is left as the winner. Once simple machines, today's tractors are high-performance with some pullers putting 6 or more engines in their machines, some putting out in excess of 6000 horsepower and some installing jet engines for more power (you can't do *that* with a horse.) The NTPA sanctions pulling events, publishes *The Puller, Tire Tracks* and *Pull!* Differently-priced memberships are available for spectators, crew members and competitors.

National Woodie Club

5522 W. 140th St., Hawthorne, CA 90250
Founded: 1974
Dues: $45.00 for three years

(213) 644-9262
Members: 1200
Contact: Will O'Neil

Owners and restorers of wood-bodied cars.

The Ninety-Nines

Will Rogers World Airport
PO Box 59964, Oklahoma City, OK 73159
Founded: 1929
Dues: Write for details

(405) 685-7969
Members: 6,000
Contact: Loretta Jean Gragg

On July 2, 1987, the fiftieth anniversary of Amelia Earhart's disappearance, the Ninety-Nines held the symbolic "Search for Amelia Earhart." Thousands of women pilots around the world in the air at the same time transmitted the message "Let there be peace on earth." The club of international women pilots possessing active licenses, takes its name from the number of original charter members. Those members elected Amelia Earhart as the first President. Today members fly from 33 countries. Virtually all women of achievement in aviation have been members of The Ninety Nines including astronaut Sally Ride and Jeana Yeager (co-pilot of the historic Voyager flight.) The Ninety-Nines sponsor the "Powder-Puff Derby," a cross-country racing event. They award the Amelia Earhart scholarship plus grants, educational programs and hold "fear of flying" clinics. The club sponsors *75 percent* of all the FAA pilot safety programs in the US. *Ninety-Nine News* is published--with nine issues per year, of course.

NSU-USA

20477 Nolina Court, Johnstown, CO 80534
Founded: 1971
Dues: Write for details

Members: 125
Contact: Charles Marsh

The NSU is an obscure German car sold from 1956 to 1972. It is very innovative, having an air-cooled Wankel (rotary) rear engine, front wheel drive, and a low coefficient of drag, but it was marketed poorly and only 3,500 found their way here. Members of NSU-USA swap hard-to-find parts.

Peerless Motor Car Club

1749 Baldwin Dr., Millersville, MD 21108   (301) 923-2606
Founded: 1975   Members: 250
Dues: Write for details   Contact: Bob Giles

The three P's of luxury from 1907 to 1920 were Pierce Arrow, Packard, and the Peerless. The Peerless Motor Car Company in Cleveland produced these high quality cars for thirty years before closing its doors in 1932. Members are owners and restorers.

Police Car Collectors Association

PO Box 112256, Tacoma, WA 98411   (206) 457-7354
Founded: 1984   Members: 200
Dues: $15.00 per year   Contact: Ken B. Richmond

Ownership of a police car is **not** required. And you'll receive the bimonthly newsletter, *Dispatch*.

The Professional Car Society

PO Box 09636, Columbus, OH 43209
Dues: Write for details   Contact: Ed Skrocki

Members worldwide collect *hearses*! Ed Skrocki has three hearses and he collects Flower Cars, too (they're also used in funerals.)

Seven Seas Cruising Association

Box 38, Placida, FL 33946   (813) 475-7280
Founded: 1952
Dues: $18.00 per year   Contact: Ginny-Lea Osterholt

Though now open to associate members with an interest in cruising, originally the club was only open to "Commodores"--members whose sailboats are their home. Many Commodores have lived aboard their cruising sailboats for more than ten years and some over *45 years*. Over 200 members have circled the earth in their home. The *Commodores Bulletin* is published monthly.

Slocum Society

PO Box 76, Port Townsend, WA 98386
Founded: 1955   Members: 1500
Dues: $36.00   Contact: Don Holm,
Commodore

The society is named for Joshua Slocum, an out-of-work captain, who rebuilt "a derelict oyster smack given to him as a joke," and left at the age of 51 to sail around the world from 1895-1898--the story of his journey became a bestseller and is still in print. Founder Richard McCloskey has spent his life documenting over 125 important continent-to-continent solo voyages, between 1857 and 1957. In the 1880s, it was the fad for British fisherman to try and *row* across the ocean to America--some of them actually made it!! Since the 1960s, the number of people making solo voyages has quadrupled, making the adventure far too commonplace for study (but still no easy feat.)

Members of the Slocum Society are either historians studying one- or two-man voyages across the ocean or prospective adventurers who can find out what route to take, how much food to bring, etc. The Slocum Society Sailing Club is open to all boat owners. In 1955, McCloskey started the first single-handed transatlantic race. It still goes on today, though he is no longer connected with it. Their journal, *The Spray*, is named for Slocum's boat, and includes logs of members' journeys. (Slocum himself left for South America in 1909 in 'The Spray', and was never heard from again.)

Soaring Society of America

Box 66071, Los Angeles, CA 90066   (213) 390-4447
Founded: 1932   Members: 17,000
Dues: $35.00 per year   Contact: John P. Dezzutti

For lovers and builders of gliders and sailplanes.

Steamship Historical Society of America

414 Pelton Avenue, Staten Island, NY 10310
Founded: 1935   Members: 3500
Dues: Write for details   Contact: Alice S. Wilson

Publishes *Steamship Bill* quarterly.

Traditional Wooden Boat Society

1101 Wing Point Way, Bainbridge Is., WA 98110   (206) 842-5802
Founded: 1975   Members: 300
Dues: Write for details   Contact: Robert B. Chapel

Helps amateur and professional boatbuilders build the traditional skills needed to construct wooden boats.

Tucker Automobile Club of America

982 Doerner Rd, Roseburg, OR 97470
Founded: 1972
Dues: $15.00 per year

(503) 673-0765
Members: 152
Contact: Jane A. Lemmo

Only 52 Tuckers were ever built in 1948 by Preston Tucker. The club has located all but one! An annual convention is held, and a newsletter is published monthly.

United Sidecar Association

PO Box 8119, Van Nuys, CA 91409
Founded: 1976
Dues: $20.00 per year

(818) 780-5542
Members: 3500
Contact: Doug Bingham

The sidecar was invented in 1903, based on a whimsical cartoon suggesting that women would be happiest riding in a buggy attached to the side of a motorcycle. The association holds many meets and publishes *The Sidecarist* monthly.

Vintage Volkswagen Club of America

818 Main Street, Portage, PA 15946
Founded: 1976
Dues: $15.00 per year

(814) 736-4343
Members: 900
Contact: Terry Shuler

Owners of Vintage Volkswagens (25 years old or more) or anyone who wants to know more about the revolutionary "Bug" is invited to join. The club holds regular meets and publishes a monthly newsletter, with information on where to find original parts.

Whirly-Girls

1725 DeSales St., NW, Washington, DC 20036
Founded: 1955

(202) 429-4648
Members: 500
Contact: Jean Ross Howard

Women rotorcraft or helicopter pilots.

Wills Sainte Claire Owners Club

721 Jenkinson, Port Huron, MI 48060
Founded: 1959
Dues: $15.00 per year

(313) 987-2425
Members: 125
Contact: William L. McKeand

Chief engineer to Henry Ford, C. Harold Wills manufactured his own automobile on the banks of the St. Clair river from 1921-1927. Of the 14,000 cars produced, only 80 survive. The car was the first to incorporate back-up lights and was remembered for its Flying Gray Goose radiator emblem. Bill McKeand, who owns three Wills Sainte Claires, publishes *The Gray Goose* newsletter and is planning a reenactment of the 1926 coast-to-coast non-stop transcontinental record of 83 hours and 12 minutes!

Women on Wheels

PO Box 14187, Phoenix, AZ 85017   (602) 269-1403
Founded: 1982   Members: 2500
Dues: $15.00 per year   Contact: Kathleen Burden

No rude comments now...this is an association for women motorcycle enthusiasts. Members receive the monthly *Wheeler*.

World Airlines Hobby Club

3381 Apple Tree Ln., Erlanger, KY 41018
Founded: 1975   Members: 1200
Dues: Write for details   Contact: Paul F. Collins

Commercial airline memorabilia...airline schedules, plastic models of planes, postcards---these people trade them all.

A BLAST FROM THE PAST

There's more to history than just the escapades of Benedict Arnold and Lizzie Borden (that cutup!) Family-tree-climbing(you *could* be a Royal Bastard), antique collecting and other non-trivial historic pursuits follow.

THE ANTIQUE SHOP

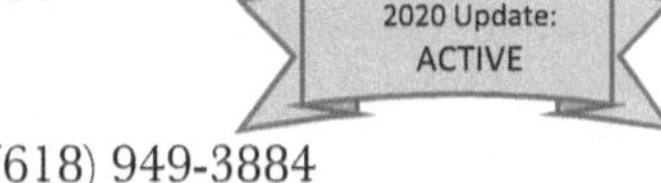

Aladdin Knights of the Mystic Light
R-1, Box 125, Simpson, IL 62985　　　　(618) 949-3884
Founded: 1973　　　　　　　　　　　　Members: 900
Dues: $15.00 per year　　　　　　　　Contact: Dr. J.W. (Bill) Courter

These Knights collect kerosene lamps made by the Aladdin Company of Kansas City, as well as by other companies. These lamps were revolutionary in the "bright white" light they gave, and even in the advanced designs of their later electric models. Writes one member, "Aladdin removed the stopper from the "Genie" vessel and I found a new world inside. Collecting has given me many hours of enjoyment, new friends, and has taken over a disproportionate amount of space in our home." The bi-monthly newsletter is *The Mystic Light of the Aladdin Knights* and a convention called the "Gathering" occurs each summer. The Bright Knight, founder Bill Courter is also a collector of outhouses and a specialist in small fruits and vegetables.

Antique Phonograph Collectors Club
502 E. 17th St., Brooklyn, NY 11226　　(718) 941-6835
Founded: 1973　　　　　　　　　　　　Members: 1800
Dues: $13.00 per year　　　　　　　　Contact: Allen Koenigsberg

Bring back the age of Edison's wax cylinder recordings, wind-up gramophones and "his master's voice" on the label! The monthly newsletter has recordings, catalogues and posters for sale.

Antique Telephone Collectors Association
Box 94, Abilene, KS 67410　　　　　　(913) 263-1757
Founded: 1971　　　　　　　　　　　　Members: 700
Dues: $25.00 per year　　　　　　　　Contact: Caren Lowery

Antique Toy Collectors of America

Carter, Ledyard and Milburn,
2 Wall St., Suite 15, New York, NY 10005 (212) 732-3200
Founded: 1965 Members: 200+
Dues: Write for details Contact: J. W. Cantey Johnson

Publishes *Toy Chest* quarterly, and holds semi-annual meetings to which everybody totes their antique toys and games.

Association of American Military Uniform Collectors

446 Berkshire Rd., Elyria, OH 44035 (216) 365-5321
Founded: 1977 Members:
Dues: $12.50 per year Contact: Gilbert Sanow, II

The AAMUC or "amuck" is dedicated to the collection and study of American military uniforms. *Footlocker* is their quarterly newsletter.

California Early Day Gas Engine and Tractor Association

c/o Antique Gas and Steam Engine Museum
2040 N. Santa Fe Ave., Vista, CA 92083 (619) 941-1791
Founded: 1969 Members: 1000
Dues: $12.00 per year Contact: Heather Johnson

With an interest in restoration of steam and gas engines used in farming, the Association .started a 40-acre museum. Preserving old equipment, they operate a blacksmith shop, and a farmhouse with a kitchen and parlor--showing 20,000 visitors a year farming life of 50 to 100 years ago. Annual events include the Threshing Bee and Antique Engines shows.

Carriage Association of America

RD #1, Box 115, Salem, NJ 08079
Founded: 1960 Members: 3,000
Dues: $30.00 per year Contact: Jill Ryder

Here's a group of "buggy nuts" who collect, restore and drive horse-drawn vehicles. One of the founding members, Horace Sowles, has a collection of 400 or so carriages. "I have all kinds of two-and four-wheeled and sleigh vehicles," he says. Two of the most interesting pieces in the collection are a sleigh originally belonging to John Quincy Adams (the country's sixth president) and a 12-passenger stagecoach from about 1850. CAA has a yearly convention, newsletter and quarterly journal with its swap and sell section called "The Carriage Trade."

Cast Iron Seat Collectors Association

RR #2, Box 229, Le Center, MN 56057   (612) 357-4815
Founded: 1973   Members: 685
Dues: $5.00 per year   Contact: Wilmar H. Tiede

Do you have the most beautiful painted seat? Members of the Cast Iron Seat Collectors Assoc. clean, paint and judge these agricultural artifacts. Factories that stopped casting cannons after the Civil War started making cast iron seats. No longer did farmers need to walk behind their horses and hoes; they now could ride in comfort. More than 1600 different varieties were created between 1865 and 1900, when manufacturing switched to stamped metal. "Some had round holes, some had frills, curves and some with lace effects," describes the membership brochure, "it is a form of Agrarian Art to us." The seats were made rare due to scrap metal drives of WWI and WWII, thus a prime specimen can be worth over $1,000 today. The association newsletter is quarterly, and there's an annual meeting the third weekend of July, in conjunction with the Central Hawkeye Threshing Show, Waukee, Iowa.

Club of the Friends of Ancient Smoothing Irons

PO Box 215, Carlsbad, CA 92008   (619) 729-1740
Founded: 1972   Members: 100+
Dues: Write for details   Contact: Edna M. Glissman

An international group of smoothing iron (also known as "sad irons") collectors.

Early Typewriter Collectors

3615 Watseka Avenue #101, Los Angeles, CA 90034 (213) 559-2368
Founded: 1987   Members: 200
Dues: $15.00 per year   Contact: Darryl C. Rehr

A new organization, they're devoted to the collection of pre-electronic typewriters. The first typewriter was produced by the Remington gunmakers in 1873, and by the time Underwood standardized it with four rows of keys in 1895, there were over a hundred models on the market "many of them looking as weird as the Lunar Landing Module." For the most part, it is these pre-Underwood models that are the real collectibles. The first machines were a commercial flop, partly because they weren't *needed* yet, and partly because they were so poorly designed that the typist had to pick up the machine and look *underneath* it to see what was typed! Many of these strange machines can be bought cheaply, though a few rare ones have price tags over $1000.

Fan Association of North America

505 Peachtree Road, Orlando, FL 32804
Founded: 1982
Dues: $20.00 per year

Members: 200
Contact: Mrs. Colin Johnson

Ivory, mother-of-pearl, silk, feather or lacquered wood fans from the 18th century until about 1920 are prized collectibles. The association publishes a quarterly journal and holds yearly meetings.

Fire Marks Circle of the Americas

1708 Highland Drive, Silver Spring, MD 20910
Founded: 1972
Dues: Write for details

Members: 300
Contact: Henry Kroll

Fire marks were the trademark of insurance companies in the 1700s and 1800s. Metal tags were attached to a building to prove that it was insured against fire. When the volunteer fire department put a fire out, the marks would still be there and the firemen would know which insurance company would pay the reward for the job. About the time of the Civil War, for-pay fire companies came into existence, and fire marks became collectors' items. Today, they can go for thousands of dollars--even reproductions are valuable.

Historical Construction Equipment Association

485 S. Hillside Drive, Canfield, OH 44406   (216) 533-4018
Founded: 1986
Dues: $10.00 per year

Members: 300
Contact: Harry E. Young

Collectors of old steam shovels, dredging equipment, bulldozers, cranes and dump trucks (these people obviously don't live in the middle of New York City; imagine waking up to repark your favorite bulldozer because of alternate side-of-the-street parking regulations!) The first meeting in Peoria, "the earthmoving capital of the world," included a trip to the local Caterpillar manufacturing facility and a tour of a local strip mine!! Newsletter for members.

International Club for Collectors of Hatpins and Hatpin Holders

15237 Chanera Ave., Gardena, CA 90249   (213) 329-2619
Founded: 1977
Dues: $24.00 per year

Members: 150+
Contact: Lillian Baker

In 1908, American suffragettes took the hatpin as a symbol of emancipation; that was after a group of suffragettes in the British courtroom were ordered to remove their pins to avoid their possible use as a weapon. The order, causing these women to expose their heads, was a great embarrassment, thus, the outrage. The invention of the pin machine and the manufacture of hatpins had freed women from the binds of bonnets tied under the chin. The new hats were more like men's and symbolized equality.

Collectible hatpins made from 1850 to 1925 were made longer and longer (up to about 14" in length.) Fearing accidental stabbings, many cities ensued laws against wearing them in public. Hatpins and accompanying holders were very ornate, with figures of animals or brooches at the end of the wire. The club, founded by historian Lillian Baker, publishes the *Points* newsletter.

International Society of Antique Scale Collectors
111 North Canal Street, Chicago, IL 60606   (312) 372-7020
Founded: 1976   Members: 300
Dues: Write for details   Contact: Bob Stein

Special scales have been designed for everything from weighing home-made bread to an opium scale to an egg scale, to a hand-crafted tobacco scale.
Some members are scholars or authors on metrology, the science of measurement. Their annual convention features the unusual "scale talk" and a scale auction. Quarterly publication called *Equilibrium*.

Lock Museum of America
130 Main St., Terryville, CT 06786   (203) 589-6359
Founded: 1971   Members: 1200
Dues: Write for Details   Contact: Regina D. Klimas

Lock collectors, locksmiths and lock and key manufacturers interested in building an exhibit of early American security devices.

Magic Lantern Society of the US and Canada
96 Charles River Rd., Watertown, MA 02172   (617) 926-9741
Founded: 1978   Members: 100+
Dues: $15.00 per year   Contact: Richard Balzer

Magic lanterns were the first "movie cameras." Lantern slide projectors were once used by teachers and lecturers to project glass-plate photographic transparencies. Slide types include glass, wood bound and hand-painted. Some are more than 500 years old, dating back to the Middle Ages.

Midwest Sad Iron Collectors Club
500 Adventureland Drive, Altoona, IA 50009
Dues: Write for details   Contact: Don Davis

National Antique Safe Association

PO Box 110099, Aurora, CO 80011   (303) 340-1524
Founded: 1986   Members: 1,000
Dues: $18.00 per year   Contact: Robert Taylor

The date, about the turn of the century. "It is now possible to construct an absolutely Burglar-Proof safe," read the headlines. Many safe companies, as the P.R. event of the day, would perform public tests of strength, where sticks of dynamite were detonated around the safe to try and crack it or open it. The best of these antique safes were cast in a single piece, out of manganese steel which had to be imported from England. Many small banks that used these safes would build the vault space around them, so once a safe was inside the vault, it was larger than the vault door and couldn't be moved out. Today these one-piece antique safes are worth between $500 and $20,000.

The National Antique Safe Association was started by Robert Taylor, a safe technician, who's been restoring antique safes for 25 years. Half of the association's members are safe technicians and half are safe collectors. Membership to the N.A.S.A. includes the identification and evaluation of one antique safe.

National Depression Glass Foundation

PO Box 11123, Springfield, MO 65808   (414) 632-7915
Founded: 1974   Members: 531
Dues: $10.00 per year (single)   Contact: JoAnn Schliesmann

Pretty in pink, red, yellow, green, or deep hues of cobalt, colored glassware were mass-produced from the late 1920s through the 1940s. Much of it was given away by merchants: punch bowl sets were given away with an oil change, cake plates with the purchase of flour, bowls and dishes with the purchase of tea or oatmeal. "Dish Night" at the movies was popular, too.

National Privy Diggers Association

3532 Copley Rd., Akron, OH 44321   (216) 666-8170
Founded: 1983   Members: 53
Dues: $10.00   Contact: Don Dzuro

Sounds strange? Well, these folks don't have outdoor plumbing, no, they locate and excavate hidden holes from one or two centuries back. What's the point of looking for the filled-in privies of the past and digging them out? Well to Don Dzuro, these now filled-in privies not only were covered by the outhouse, but some were used as the local dumps. The privies of yesteryear are the treasure troves of today, serving up bottles, housewares, and other artifacts. Before the days of common trash pick-up and city dumps, people would toss their garbage out the window--filling any hole in the earth they could find. Dzuro has found lots of bottles (he's an avid bottle collector), a pair of dismembered doll legs, and a World War I German helmet.

Don't get the idea that these guys don't have fun. There are much easier ways of finding things, but privy digging is...exciting. And when members are ready to toss in the shovel for a while, they get together for the Medina, Ohio Summer Fair's Outhouse Race. Teams race around a course pulling an outhouse on wheels (occupied?) Contestants name their outhouses--there's "Loose Goose," "Pooh Pushers"(with a picture of Winnie on the front), "Penski Poopers Outhouse Race Team" and one with a steeple on top - "The Chatham Community Churches."

Their present project is a book on the essential whos, whats, and wheres in privy digging. Membership requirements? None at all, but to receive a Ph.D. (Privy Hole Digger), you must send a picture of yourself digging a privy. Membership entitles you to a membership card, digging release form, and monthly newsletter. The club symbol: the outhouse. The Club motto: "See you down in the hole!"

National Stereographic Association
PO Box 14801, Columbus, OH 43214   (614) 895-1774
Founded: 1973   Members: 1,900
Dues: $20.00 per year   Contact: John Waldsmith

From 1850 to 1930, stereographs were common as in American homes as the television is today. Stereographs were double-image photographs mounted on a card that when viewed through a stereographic viewer, looked like a 3-D picture. Thousands of stereographs were produced on every conceivable subject, and they serve as an important historical record of the times. Stereographs can be had for next to nothing, and found at flea markets or tag sales. Members of NSA are stereograph collectors and photographers. *Stereo World Magazine* reports on new 3-D technology as well as research on historic stereographs. A recent edition had an article called "Stereotombs," on stereo pictures of tombs and graveyards, and an article called "Beached Whales Then & Now," stereo pictures of whales that had strayed ashore on Cape Cod. Annual convention in August.

Occupied Japan Collectors Club
3325 Breckinridge Lane #3, Louisville, KY 40220(502) 267-7427
Founded: 1979   Members: 150
Dues: $10.00 per year   Contact: Sissie Jackson

They collect anything marked with the words, "Made in Occupied Japan," manufactured during the years of US occupation (1945-1952.) The monthly newsletter is called *The Upside Down World of an OJ Collector.*

Old Mine Lamp Collectors Society of America

4537 Quitman St., Denver, CO 80212
Dues: No membership fee

Members: 350
Contact: Henry Pohs

Partisan Prohibition Historical Society

PO Box 2635, Denver, CO 80201
Founded: 1963
Dues: Write for details

(303) 572-0646
Members: 800
Contact: Earl F. Dodge

The Prohibition movement had its roots in the Prohibition Party founded in 1869.
As they gained steam towards the ratification of the 18th Amendment in 1919,
the group produced plenty of campaign buttons, books, pictures and the like.
Members collects these items, plus keep the memory of the Prohibition Party alive
(with alcohol-free temperance parties maybe?)

Self Winding Clock Association

PO Box 7704
3736 Atlantic Ave, Long Beach, CA 90807
Founded: 1980
Due: $20.00 per year

(213) 427-8001
Members: 200
Contact: Bengt E. Honning

Collectors of clock information, particularly on the Self Winding Clock Company
of New York City (1886 to 1972.)

Society for the Preservation & Appreciation of Antique Motorized Fire Apparatus

749 E. South St., Jackson, MI 49203
Founded: 1958
Dues: Write for details

Members: 2000
Contact: Kenneth Soderbeck

Started by a volunteer fireman, the society publishes *Engine Engine* quarterly.

Still Bank Collectors Club of America

401 East 84th Street, Apt. 5-A, New York, NY 10028
Founded: 1966
Dues: $25.00 per year

Members: 350+
Contact: Carl White

Before the age of mechanical banks, still banks were the rage. Collectors have still
banks that date back to pre-Christianity--some are worth thousands of dollars.
These are more than just your usual plain piggy...still banks have been sculpted to
look like bibles, churches, imps, even Charles de Gaulle and Winston Churchill.
Members receive the *Penny Bank Post*

Stretch Glass Society

4426 Point Comfort Dr., Akron, OH 44319   (216) 644-2597
Founded: 1974   Members: 100+
Dues: $6.00 per year   Contact: Alma Magenau

Manufactured in the 1920s, stretch glass has a glow to it that looks like it was stretched. Some say the glass looks like iridescent onion skin. One company has started to produce it again, but the original is still coveted.

Telephone Artifacts Association...or...The Telephone Museum

Bell Building, Two E. First St., Monroe, MI 48161   (313) 243-6227
Founded: 1974   Members: 80+
Dues: $20.00 per year   Contact: Robert K. Lusch

Members are interested in the history of the telephone.

Thermometer Collectors Club of America

6130 Rampart Dr., Carmichael, CA 95608   (916) 966-3490
Founded: 1980   Members: 150
Dues: $5.00 one time membership   Contact: Warren Harris

"I never know what the temperature is," says Warren Harris. That's because none of his 500 thermometers are in sync with each other. The collection dates from around 1820 to about 1940, with wares from six countries. Harris eschews thermometers used as advertising because after 1940, thermometers "were mass-produced, usually plastic and ugly." Though there are 150 club members, Harris says that only a few dozen are real "thermometarians." "Our group is often contacted by research analysts who need to find the correct answer to a thermometer question they plan to ask a contestant on a TV game show." In October 1989, the group plans to have its first national convention, in Sacramento, California.

HISTORICAL GROUPS

Aaron Burr Association

RD #1, Route 33, Hightstown- Freehold Rd., Hightstown, NJ 08520
Founded: 1946   Members: 1,000
Dues: $10.00 per year   Contact: Samuel Burr

Wasn't he a womanizer, a rogue, a traitor...that guy who killed Alexander
Hamilton in a duel? "Wait! Stop!" says his descendant Samuel Burr, "Aaron has
been misunderstood and misrepresented."

Ever since grade school, when Samuel's teacher went into a tirade about Aaron
Burr trying to cheat Jefferson out of the presidency and being a no-good atheist,
the modern-day Mr. Burr has tried to defend his ancestor's honor. (Burr knows
Aaron was a relative, although he can't quite trace the lineage.) He sends the
Chronicle of the Aaron Burr Association to association members who have supported
his cause. (Burr's received only two nasty letters in all the years of his work--one
from a man who challenged him to a duel.)

Abraham Lincoln Association

Old State Capitol, Springfield, IL 62701   (217) 782-4836
Founded: 1908   Members: 360
Dues: $15.00 per year   Contact: Harlington Wood, Jr.

Holds an annual symposium on Abe's birthday, February 12th.

American Canal Society

117 Main Street, Freemansburg, PA 18017
Founded: 1972   Members: 819
Dues: $12.00 per year   Contact: Charles Derr

The area adjacent to the Chesapeake and Ohio canal would have been a
superhighway today, if not for the intervention of Charles Derr and The
American Canal Society. Today, the towpath of the canal, where mule teams once
silently pulled boats up the canal is a very popular National Park, used for jogging
and hiking. The Canal Society is interested in the preservation of canals around
the country for their historical significance, although many are in a serious state of
disrepair. Charles Derr also suggests joining the Pennsylvania Canal Society
(1,356 miles of canal were dug there, more than any other state.)

American Spelean Historical Association

711 E. Atlantic Ave., Altoona, PA 16602   (814) 946-3155
Founded: 1968   Members: 125
Dues: $5.00   Contact: Jack H. Speece

"Caves have served as shelters for not only the Indians but also the early colonists and pioneers," so spelean (cave) historians are recording folktales, facts, and legends of the voids beneath the ground and relating it to the development of this country. Researchers speak with people living near caves, because "those who have the stories to tell will not wait much longer." About one-third of the membership is specifically interested in Kentucky's Mammoth Cave. At 212 miles long, it's the longest cave in the world. Mammoth has been the source of hundreds of tales and legends. Dozens of mummified Indians dating back to 100 A.D. have been found in the cave. In 1842, because of the cave's constant temperature, it served as the country's first hospital for tuberculosis patients. Club members receive the quarterly "Journal of Spelean History." Their annual meeting is held in conjunction with the National Speleological Society.

Association for Gravestone Studies

46 Plymouth Road, Needham, MA 02192
Founded: 1977   Members: 700
Dues: $15.00 per year   Contact: Rosalee F. Oaklee

Gravestones are in danger! Vandalism, the elements, theft and neglect are quickly ruining these markers of the past. The Association for Gravestone Studies is encouraging members to "adopt a graveyard" and make it their own, recording the headstones and preserving the information in the ASG archives. Accomplished members can tell, even from a moving car, in which century a gravestone was carved by the shape of the stones. (Members' moving cars might even sport an association bumper sticker reading, "I Brake for Old Graveyards.")

Daniel Farber, the current president, has photographed over 10,000 gravestones. He's also notated the data on the stones, computerized them by location, subject, carver, and name of the deceased. The logo of the association is taken from an actual gravestone found in Williamstown, Mass, carved in 1771. Each year, an award is given to someone who has made a significant contribution to the world of gravestone studies. Other benefits of membership include yearly conventions, with tours of graveyards, seminars on interpreting gravestone data, and "how to rub a gravestone safely," a quarterly newsletter and a yearly magazine, *Markers*.

Circus Historical Society

800 Richey Rd., Zanesville, OH 43701   Members: 1,400
Dues: Write for details   Contact: Fred Pfening

The first United States circus was Rickett's in 1800, with horseback acts and acrobats. Of course, P.T. Barnum made the circus what it was, starting in the 1870s. During the heyday of the circus, 1890 to 1910, there were 25 shows that traveled by train and another 50 that traveled overland. The Circus Historical Society is a group of collectors and historians who publish *Bandwagon* quarterly.

Civil War Press Corps.

PO Box 856, Colonial Heights, VA 23834
Founded: 1958   Members: 500
Dues: Write for details   Contact: Lt. Col. Joseph
Malcolm

These writers, journalists and other media professionals are interested in ensuring that the Civil War gets "fair treatment" by the news. Staff members take military titles.

Fire Bell Club of America

150 E. 23rd St., New York, NY 10010   (212) 505-2681
Founded: 1939   Members: 130
Dues: Write for Details   Contact: Frank Donnelly

They're called fire buffs, sparks or fire fans--they are people with a common interest in firefighting, fire equipment and fires.

First Flight Society

Box 1903, Kitty Hawk, NC 27949   (919) 441-3761
Founded: 1927   Members: 500
Dues: $20.00 per year   Contact: Gene E. O'Bleness

Each December 17th, members gather at the Wright Brothers National Memorial located in the town of Kill Devil Hills, on the outer banks of North Carolina just south of Kitty Hawk, and walk the 120-foot-length of the Wright Brothers' first flight. They also honor those who have made outstanding "firsts" in aviation by naming them to the "First Flight Shrine." Members receive *Flyer* newsletter quarterly.

Frederick A. Cook Society

c/o Sullivan County Historical Museum
PO Box 247, Hurleyville, NY 14747   (914) 434-8044
Founded: 1977   Members: 90
Dues: $10.00 per year   Contact: Warren B. Cook, Sr.

Contrary to popular belief, Frederick A. Cook was the discoverer of the North Pole in 1908, the first to climb Alaska's Mount McKinley in 1906 and the first American to explore both Polar Regions. The millionaire Admiral Perry, who society members say probably never actually achieved the Pole, waged a campaign to discredit Cook and put his achievement in doubt until his death. The story of how Cook survived the brutal winter of North Pole trip-- trapped in the Arctic, living in an ice cave with his Eskimo friends and with only a moss wick lamp to heat and light the cave is fascinating. The Cook Society and Museum near his birthplace publishes an occasional newsletter and holds an annual convention.

Friends of Cast Iron Architecture

235 East 87th Street, New York, NY 10128   (212) 369-6004
Dues: Write for details   Contact: Margot Gayle

Architectural historians and architectural tour guides get together every so often to speak of how cast-iron has changed their lives--(not to mention the buildings of historical districts like New York City's Soho.)

Friends of Lizzie Borden

Unicorn Ltd. Conglomerate, Lake Superior State College
Office of College Relations, Sault Ste. Marie, MI 49783   (906) 635-2315
Dues: Write for details   Contact: W. T. Rabe

They promote *Lizzie Borden Liberation Day*, each August 4th, the day of the Borden murders, "to underscore that, in spite of a popular misimpression, a jury of her peers indeed found Miss Borden NOT guilty of patricide and matricide."

International Arthurian Society-N.A. Branch

Department of French
Dalhousie University, Halifax, Nova Scotia B3H 3J5   (902) 424-2430
Founded: 1948   Members: 300
Dues: $15.00 per year   Contact: Hans Runte

Studying the folk tales, history and literature of King Arthur.

Leif Ericson Society International

11 South Olive St., Media, PA 19063   (215) 565-3165
Founded: 1926   Members: 999
Dues: $5.00 annual ($2.00 for clerics)   Contact: Ivar Christensen

Membership is limited to 999, allegedly because Norwegians can't pronounce "th." "Honoring America's First Hero," the Society has been planning the

Millennium celebration of Leif Ericson's discovery of America, to be held on October 9 (Leif's birthday) in the year 2003 (tickets are $18.95 now and $95.00 at the door in 2003.) Each year the group announces "The Viking of the Year" award.

Museum of Modern Mythology
275 Capp Street, San Francisco, CA 94110
Write for more information

The final resting home of Speedy Alka-Seltzer, Redi Kilowatt, Mr. Peanut, Tony the Tiger, The Tidy Bowl Man and many, many other 20th Century advertising characters.

National Association of American Observation Balloon Corps Veterans
634 Wagner Rd., Lafayette Hill, PA 19444
Founded: 1932   Members: less and less
Dues: Write for details   Contact: Craig Herbert

During World War I, hydrogen-filled balloons were used for observation purposes by the Americans and British, keeping a tab on German troop movements. These balloons, 92' long and 32' in diameter, held one or two men who wore parachutes in case they were shot down. The balloons were tethered to the ground by a 3/4 mile long cable. The balloons were located with the artillery and used also to regulate artillery fire as well as spot enemy planes. The balloonists first got together in 1931, and in 1932 they formed the NAAOBCV. They publish a magazine called *Haul Down and Ease Off*, referring to the commands that were used in controlling the balloons. Founder Craig Herbert recalls that the job was far from glamorous. They spent 251 days on the front without relief!! (That's the longest of any WWI company.) They never got to shower--never could take their uniforms off, and had to sleep in the mud for five months, getting "gassed" quite often and being stricken by dysentery. The average age of the surviving members is 93. Herbert was instrumental in acquiring a replica of a WWI balloon for display at the U.S. Air Force Museum...regrettably, all the original balloons were destroyed after the war.

National Association of Outlaw and Lawmen History
PO Box 1701, Hamilton, MT 59840   (406) 961-4247
Founded: 1973   Members:
Dues: $20.00 per year   Contact: John Stewart

The Wild Wild West and all the infamous characters that it produced are the subjects of this historic organization.

National Society for the Preservation of Covered Bridges

175 East Main Street, Norton, MA 02766   (617) 756-4516
Founded: 1950
Dues: $9.50 per year   Contact: M. Marion Meyer

During the heyday of the Covered Bridge, the state of Pennsylvania had a couple of thousand authentic wooden bridges. Today there are less than 1,000 left in the whole United States! The Society conducts covered bridge safaris and publishes the *Covered Bridge Topics* newsletter.

Railroad Station Historical Society

430 Ivy Ave., Crete, NE 68333   (402) 826-3356
Founded: 1968   Members: 375
Dues: $7.00 per year   Contact: Janet L. C. Rapp

The 1920s, the age of the railroad, Union Station in St. Louis moved about 269 trains per day! Those days have long past and the Railroad Station Historical Society tries to establish the historical significance of the quickly disappearing railroad station throughout America. Members help designate structures for placement on the National Register of Historic Places, collect and study drawings, plans, and photographs on station histories. "The Bulletin" is published six times a year and "Monograph" once a year. Annual meeting where members look at each other's pictures.

Richard III Society

PO Box 217, Sea Cliff, NY 11579   (516) 676-2374
Founded: 1924   Members: 5000
Dues: $20.00 per year   Contact: William Hograth

Shakespeare described him as "that abortive rooting hog...that poisonous hunchbacked toad...that bottled spider." Credited with murdering his two nephews, the little princes who were heirs to the throne of England, Richard gained all this bad press in his brief two-year reign. Not so, claim members of the Richard III Society who claim his reputation is ill-deserved. They've spent years documenting that he wasn't as brutal or mean as history has portrayed him. Richard was *really* the victim of vicious smears on his character by his Tudor enemies. William Hograth and others, who are judges, lawyers, educators, actors and professionals in the field of criminal justice, say that, "if he had lived, Richard would have been a brilliant king." They see the story of King Richard as one of the first and most brutal political lies of all time. The Richard III Society is an offshoot of the Fellowship of the White Boar in England, which has also dedicated itself to the "restoration of Richard's memory as an intelligent, progressive, and noble king and to erasing his bad reputation." As to the mystery of the murder of his nephews, supporters suggest that they may have been murdered by Richard's enemies in an effort to discredit him. To date, nobody has found any documentation of the maligned king's supposed physical deformity, either. So there, Willie S.

Society for Creative Anachronism

PO Box 360743, Milpitas, CA 95035
Founded: 1965   Members: 11,000+
Dues: $6.00 per year (without newsletters)   Contact: H. Powers

Would you have guessed from the name that this group reenacts the better parts of the Middle Ages, from 650 A.D. to 1650 A.D.? Sword fighting is an important part of the SCA. Members, both men and women, need to be 18-years-old to sword fight--equipment weighs between 60 and 150 lbs. Most of the fighting is hand-to-hand combat, scored by safety marshals. Because of the armor, serious injuries are rare. Members claim it's safer than football and a lot more fun (though wearing a suit of armor in the middle of the summer can be stifling.)

An SCA party features "mock entrails" (nuts and fruits sewn together and baked), eating a 40-course meal out of wooden plates and pewter beakers (things like forks were unknown in the middle ages), and playing dungeons and dragons. Exact authenticity is not required, but members are encouraged to come to SCA meetings in period costume, everything from simple tunics to elaborate court dress. At the sword-fighting tournaments, those who demonstrate great skill in combat may be dubbed Knights by the King. The Tournaments also offer competitions in dance, music, field cookery and arts and crafts.

To the SCA, every person, place and thing in the known World has a new name: Kansas City is the "Barony of the Forgotten Sea" and Missouri is the "The Shire of the Standing Stones." The regions of the United States have been renamed for SCA. "The Known World" is divided into Kingdoms and Kingdoms into Principalities: "The Kingdom of the Middle" (Midwest), "The Kingdom of Caid" (Southern California), "The Barony of the Western Seas" (Hawaii.) SCA sells everything from "Medieval and Renaissance Eyeglasses" to a book called *Saints of the Middle Ages*. The SCA magazine, called *Tournaments Illuminated*, is filled with word games.

Society of the Preservation of Old Mills

1531 Folkstone Ct., Mishawaker, IN 46544   (210) 259-4483
Founded: 1972   Members: 1,600
Dues: $8.00 per year   Contact: Fred Beals

Especially interested in the preservation of grist mills, this society publishes *Old Mill News* quarterly.

Sod House Society

Holdrege, NE 68949
Founded: 1956
Dues: $2.00 per year ($15 for life)

(308) 995-8072
Members: 350
Contact: Mrs. Hal Stevens

Keeping the spirit and history of the Pioneers of early America alive.

Surratt Society

Box 427, 9110 Brandywine Rd., Clinton, MD 20735
Founded: 1975
Dues: $5.00 per year ($100 lifetime)

Members: 700
Contact: Laurie Vege

Mary Surrat has the distinction of being the only woman ever tried, convicted and hung for helping to plan the assassination of a U.S. president. Can you guess which one? Abraham Lincoln. She was accused of aiding and abetting John Wilkes Booth. Booth did know Surratt and he did stay at the inn that her father owned, but Society members say that Mary got a raw deal from a Military Court that was looking for scapegoats, not justice!! Members receive a monthly newsletter filled with information on Civil War era social and cultural history. One of the most popular programs the Society runs, is a 12-hour bus tour over the escape route used by John Wikes Booth.

Titanic Historical Society

PO Box 53, Indian Orchard, MA 01151
Founded: 1963
Dues: Write for Details

(413) 543-4015
Members: 3000
Contact: Edward S. Kamuda

Perhaps two dozen survivors of the greatest sea disaster of all time are still alive today. April 15, 1987 marked the 75th anniversary of the sinking of the Titanic in which 1,522 of the 2,227 people on board lost their lives in the collision with an iceberg. The Titanic Historical Society meets each year and drops a wreath at the site of the sinking each year through the ice-patrol which looks out for icebergs and was started as a response to the Titanic disaster. At the most recent meeting, members got to take a close look at the recent underwater pictures that were taken by a mechanical robot. The society was instrumental in discovering the exact location of the ship's watery grave and helping to search it. The group hopes to start a Titanic museum filled with many of the artifacts that were found floating on the icy ocean surface after the ship had sunk.

<h1 style="text-align:center">GENEALOGICAL GROUPS</h1>

Alaska Yukon Pioneers

2725-71 E. Fir, Mt. Vernon, WA 98273 (206) 428-1912
Founded: 1923 Members: 360
Dues: Write for details Contact: Vera J. Sidars

Descendants of the Signers of the Declaration of Independence

50 Riverside Drive, New York, NY 10024 (212) 787-5595
Founded: 1907 Members: 1100
Dues: Write for details Contact: Mrs. Hans Bielenstein

International Sourdough Reunion

375 Dell Rd., Kelowna, BC, Canada, V1X 3P7 (614) 860-9817
Founded: 1931 Members: 1500
Dues: Write for details Contact: Nora Sinclair

Purpose: "To foster and perpetuate the true pioneer sourdough spirit of good fellowship and loyalty which prevailed in Alaska and the Yukon Territory." Membership is restricted to present or former residents of the Yukon or Alaska from the Gold Rush days.

Irish Family Names Society

Box 2095, La Mesa, CA 92041 (619) 466-8739
Founded: 1978 Members: 350
Dues: $12.00 per year Contact: William P. Durning

Researching the origins of the O'Henrys, O'Caseys, O'Malleys, McNamara, McGillicuddy, McKeon and other cherished names.

January 12th 1888 Blizzard Club

1201 Lincoln Mall, #611, Lincoln, NE 68508
Founded: 1940 Members: 60
  Contact: Doris Jenkins

"The Nebraska blizzard of 1888 was momentous because of the combination of three factors: the gale winds, the blinding snow and the extremely rapid drop in temperature from winter comfort levels to well below zero." More than forty people lost their lives in the storm. Many people confuse the January 12th blizzard that hit the Midwest with the March 1888 blizzard that hit New York---two completely different storms. This one was a cataclysmic blizzard. Hundreds of children were stranded in frigid school shanties, ranchers lost most of their cattle and went broke. "It was the wickedest thing I ever saw," said one observer. The prairie was newly-settled and the snow was crystal sharp and blinding in force. Heroic farmers burned hay and furniture for fuel. The January 12th, 1888 Blizzard Club will disband on January 12th, 1988, because there are no original members left who remember the storm. Today the members are either descendants of storm-rememberers or historians. For those who want to know more about the blizzard, Doris Jenkins wrote the book, *In All Its Fury*.

National Society Old Plymouth Colony Descendants

24 Watts Road, Londonderry, NH 03053
Founded: 1910
Dues: $50.00 for life   Contact: Melvin Edwin Watts

Preserving the history of the Pilgrims and early settlers and preserving historic spots.

Children of the Confederacy

328 North Blvd., Richmond, VA 23220   (814) 355-1636
Founded: 1954   Members: 3400

The South will rise again as this club teaches children about the "true history" of the South, the War Between the States and celebrates Confederate Memorial days. Members are young people from birth to 21 years of age who are descendants of soldiers for the Confederate Army, Navy, or civil service. Their parents may be members of United Daughters of the Confederacy or Sons of the Confederate Veterans.

Colonial Order of the Acorn

122 E. 58th St., New York, NY 10022   (212) 755-7082
Founded: 1894   Members: 200

"Those persons who were in the thirteen original states in 1776 could be called figuratively the Acorns from which grew the Tall Oak of the United States." Membership is limited to 200 descendants of those early Americans.

Descendants of the Illegitimate Sons and Daughters of the Kings of Britain....or...The Royal Bastards

107 Lake Lane Rock Creek, Jacksonville, NC 28540
Founded: 1950   Members: 180
Dues: $60.00 lifetime ($30 for application)   Contact: Herman Nickerson,

Jr.

Was your ancestor a "Royal Bastard?" If you can prove your lineage back to one of the original royal bastards---an illegitimate son or daughter of a king or queen of England, Scotland or Wales, then your membership is assured.
The king with the most "royal bastards" was Henry the First, with 22. (Charles the Second had 16 or 17.) These kings weren't as lecherous as it sounds though--in medieval times, the offspring were needed to take over land and marry other royalty into the family. The Royal Bastards have no meetings, but they do publish an annual report that includes the lineages of the new members.

Flagon and Trencher also known as Descendants of Colonial Tavern Keepers

421 Summit Ave., South Orange, NJ 07079
Founded: 1962
Contact: Dr. Kenn Stryker-Rodda

Members: 650
Dues: Write for details

Sure, the hospitality industry wasn't big before the American Revolution--of course, George Washington seemed to sleep everywhere, but there weren't any Holiday Inns or Motel 6's around. In any case, members of Flagon and Trencher are descendants of colonial tavern, hostelry or inn keepers. They collect genealogical records, and menus--anyone for a good manchet bread recipe?

National Society of Daughters of the Barons of Runnemede

1102 Westover Rd., Wilmington, DE 19807
Founded: 1921
Dues: Write for details

(302) 658-3958
Members: 600
Contact: Mrs. James A. Grady

Descendants of the barons who forced King John to sign the Magna Carta in 1215. (Author's note: I have trouble even tracing myself back to my father!)

National Society of the Daughters of Utah Pioneers

300 North Main Street, Salt Lake City, UT 84103 (801) 533-5759
Founded: 1901
Dues: $8.25 per year

Members: 22,500
Contact: Emma R. Olsen

Members are women over the age of 18 who are descendants of someone who came to Utah before the driving of the Golden Spike at Promontory Point, joining the railroad from East to West on May 10, 1869. Members work on placing historical markers around the state. The association's badge is an ox yoke surmounted by a beehive.

National Society of Sons and Daughters of the Pilgrims

1408 20th St., Arlington, VA 22202
Founded: 1908

Members: 750

Dues: Write for details

Contact: Barbara W. H. Loucks

Can you prove that an ancestor of yours was a Pilgrim (that is, someone who settled in the U.S. prior to 1700)? NSSDP tries to promote the principles and virtues of the Pilgrims, such as purity of the home, godly and temperate living, the free determination of men and political equality.

Russia Nobility Association in America

971 First Avenue, New York, NY 10022

(212) 755-7528

Founded: 1938

Members: 150

Dues: Write for details

Contact: Alexis Scherbaton

If you're listed in the Nobility Archives of the former Russian Imperial Senate...

Sons and Daughters of Pioneer Rivermen

121 River Avenue, Stickley, PA 15143

(412) 741-5395

Founded: 1941

Members: 2000

Dues: Write for details

Contact: Frederick Way, Jr.

At 81 years old, founder Frederick Way, Jr. remembers the days of steam-powered sternwheel paddleboats along the Mississippi. Way was a captain for 55 years, for sternwheelers, sidewheelers, packet boats, and modern diesel-powered boats. He'd originally left civil engineering study at Carnegie Mellon University to become a mud clerk on a packet boat. "You were the first one off and you had to jump out onto land. Sometimes you'd sink into mud over your ankles. That's why they called them mud clerks, " he said. Their quarterly magazine called *Reflector* goes to members as far away as Australia and Europe.

Sons and Daughters of the Soddies

Rte. 1, Box 225, Colby, KS 67701

(913) 462-6787

Founded: 1955

Members: 25,000

Dues: Write for Details

Contact: Vernon Englehardt

Did you ever live in a "sod" house? Members of Sons and Daughter of the Soddies have lived in or had relatives who lived in either grass-covered homes, adobe buildings or dugouts---all authentic dwelling types of early American pioneers on the prairie. The society maintains a museum in "Sod Town" near Colby, displaying several sod buildings and early American tools and weapons.

Sons of Sherman's March to the Sea

1725 Farmer Ave., Tempe, AZ 85281   (602) 967-5405
Founded: 1966   Members: 626
Dues: $3.00 Lifetime membership   Contact: Stan Schirmarcher

Sixty miles, as the Thunderbird flies, from Picacho Park, the westernmost Civil War battleground, sits Stan Schirmarcher, a retired shop teacher, helping people find their Civil War Ancestory through Veteran's Service Records and other resources. Sons of Sherman's March to the Sea is the only organization that specifically honors General Sherman. (Schirmarcher's grandfather was a drummer boy for General Sherman, on the route from Atlanta to Averysboro, NC. During the march, he was wounded in the heel as he stood near a cannon.) The organization has no regular meetings and as Stan says "we started the SSMS as the *only Civil War outfit open to Both sides* of the Mason Dixon Fence!." For $3.00, the quarterly "Bulletin," a membership card and picture of General Sherman will be sent.

In addition to being a civil war fanatic, Stan Schirmarcher is a bit of a religious fanatic and certainly a mail-order fanatic. Schirmarcher has sent about a dozen things that can be had for a dollar or two and a SASE. A membership to PADL (Polish Anti-Defamation League) is free...the membership card says "Don't touch that "Polock" Joke with a ten-foot Pole!." One hundred and eleven bible trivia questions are one dollar. A lifetime membership in "Sons of Santa Ana's Conquistadores" (Remember the Alamo!) is only $2.00. Twenty household hints and one amazing card trick goes for a buck. To become a charter member of "Suckers Anonymous" send two dollars and to become an official "Ding-a-linger" (an receive the Ding-a-linger "Oscar" for true screw-balls), one must be nominated by Ding-a-linger number 1, in Tempe Arizona.

Veterans of AEF Siberia

PO Box 518, Yountville, CA 94599   (707) 944-4244
Founded: 1940   Members: 9000
Dues: Write for details   Contact: Joseph Ahearn

Soldiers who served in Siberia from 1918 to 1920.

SCHOLARLY PURSUITS

School's never out for these inquiring minds, puzzling out some of life's great questions. (Like, "How to Talk Backward About Sex in Thai.")

American Association for Artificial Intelligence
445 Burgess Dr., Menlo Park, CA 94025   (415) 328-3123
Founded: 1979   Members: 15,000
Dues: Write for details   Contact: Claudia C. Mazzetti

2020 Update: ACTIVE

"The scientific goal of Artificial Intelligence is to understand minds by building them...we are still far from the depth of understanding required to build minds as complex as our own," starts the chairman's statement of the Sixth National Conference on Artificial Intelligence. Robots are no longer just the dreams of science fiction writers. Artificial Intelligence experts include technicians, scientists, engineers, professors and researchers. AAAI publishes *AI Magazine*, the oldest magazine devoted to the field.

American Name Society
7 E. 14th St., Apt. 17-U, New York, NY 10003(212) 929-8434
Founded: 1951   Members: 1100
Dues: $25.00 per year   Contact: Prof. Wayne H. Finke

2020 Update: ACTIVE

"What really *is* in a name? ANS is a group that researches names, real or imagined, believing that names are not given haphazardly, that they provide valuable cultural and historical insights. Articles in *Names*, the quarterly journal, have ranged from "The Name of the Comet" to "Reason for Reagan." Annual meeting.

American Pain Society
1615 L Street, NW, Washington, DC 20036   (202) 296-9200
Founded: 1977   Members: 1000
Dues: $20.00 per year and up   Contact: Marie W. Klemann

2020 Update: ACTIVE

(A National Chapter of the International Association for the Study of Pain) Doctors and dentists try to understand pain (Author's note: I had a friend in high school whose dentist used to say, "This is going to *hurt!*...and leer evilly...R.R.)

American Society of Papyrologists

Department of Classics
Stanford University, Stanford, CA 94305   (415) 497-0808
Founded: 1961   Members: 400
                                                 Contact: Susan A. Stephens

Scientists and others study ancient Egyptian paper, called papyrus (it's made from the papyrus plant), and study the manuscripts themselves.

Association for the Study of Dreams

Department of Psychology
University of Northern Iowa, Cedar Falls, IO 50614
Founded: 1985   Members: 300
Dues: $50.00 per year   Contact: Jayne Gackenbach,
PhD

Dream specialists, sleep physiologists, dream researchers, sociologists, artists, educators and individual dreamers promote the recognition, study and research, of the relevance and interpretation of dreams. The annual convention includes such highlights as the "Share a Dream" breakfast, and the "Dream Ball." Speakers' topics include "Dreamwork and Spirituality," "Dream Theorists of Antiquity, Middle Ages and the Renaissance" and "Dreams of Death."

Desert Fishes Council

407 W. Line St., Bishop, CA 93514   (619) 872-1171
Founded: 1970   Members: 400
Dues: $10.00 per year   Contact: E. P. Pister

Scientists and others helping to preserve the desert ecology.

Foundation for Research on the Nature of Man

Box 6847, College Station, Durham, NC 27708   (919) 688-8241
Founded: 1962   Members:
Dues: Write for details   Contact: Dr. K. Ramakrishna
Rao

What makes a man, a man? This foundation is devoted to understanding the human individual, offering summer study programs.

Gypsy Lore Society, North American Chapter

2104 Dexter Ave., #203, Silver Spring, MD 20902   (301) 681-3123

Founded: 1977   Members: 250
Dues: $15.00 per year   Contact: Sheila Salo

Members are scholars or students in anthropology, sociology, history, linguistics,
folklore, dance, music, literature and art, who are interested in the culture of
Gypsies. Quarterly newsletter and annual meeting.

Hankes Foundation
1768 Cofax Ave., S., Minneapolis, MN 55403   (612) 374-2453
Founded: 1982   Contact: Elmer J. Hankes

Foundation members speak a language called Emsighay invented by Elmer
Hankes, based on an abstract binary logic. Hankes invented it for use in
international communications--(didn't anyone tell him that communication and
languages have nothing to do with logic?)

Institute for the Encyclopedia of Human Ideas on Ultimate Reality and Meaning

15 St. Mary St., Toronto, ON, Canada M4Y 2R5   (416) 922-2476
Founded: 1970   Members: 200+
Dues: $25(Canadian)/ year   Contact: Prof. Tibor Horvath

Housewives, scientists, professors, teachers, lawyers and priests come together to
explore the same question, "What is reality and its ultimate aspects and how do
we find meaning in our lives?" The founder, Tibor Horvath--or Mr. Reality, as he
is referred to by his peers--is a soft-spoken elderly professor who speaks several
languages. Horvath says his favorite type of person is the Intellectual Democrat--
the person who says he or she can learn from everyone else. He believes the name
of the organization has worked in their favor. "People don't know what it means.
So they ask, 'What is this?' And we smile and say, 'Exactly. What is this? What is
this?'" Members receive the *Ultimate Reality Newsletter*; Reality Conferences with
members attending from around the world are held every two years.

International Maledicta Society
331 S. Greenfield Ave., Waukesha, WI 53186   (414) 542-5853
Founded: 1976   Members: 3,000
Dues: $20.00 per year   Contact: Reinhold A. Aman

&!@#*$!?#! Reinhold A. Aman swears that he knows how to curse in over 200
languages. Americans have brought cursing to an all-time low, he claims, since
"The Dirty Dozen" words, once taboo, are now commonplace. The result is that
American cursing has lost its sting, its ability to let off steam, so Americans resort

to physical violence. Aman's study of cursing got him fired from the University of
Wisconsin, an action he fought in Federal Court. When he saw the department
chairman for the last time, he tossed him a traditional Thai insult: "Talking to you
is like playing violin to a water buffalo."

Aman began his study of "dirty words" after translating a list of German insults
from 1876. One insult meant, "I'm going to knock you on the ear with a cooking
spoon, you monkey." He wondered, "Why call a human being a monkey?" From
that start, he used his fluency in six languages (with the help of a dictionary, he's
good for 25) to study "cursing." It hasn't paid well over the years (he's no stranger
to the welfare office), but he doesn't skimp on the journal, *Maledicta: International
Journal of Verbal Aggression*. The journal with its scholarly approach has tackled such
articles as "The Sexual Side of Rhyming Slang," How to Hate Thy Neighbor: A
Guide to Racist Maledicta" and "Talking Backward about Sex in Thai."

The Maledicta (which means "bad words" in Latin) Society, has members in all
U.S. states and 65 foreign countries. It specializes in uncensored studies and
glossaries of offensive and negatively-valued words and expressions from all
languages, cultures, past and present. Swearwords, Curses, Slurs, Stereotypes,
Terminology of Body Parts, and Insults are some of the categories studied. The
present long-term project of Maledicta is the Dictionary of Regional Anatomical
Terms...an uncensored worldwide survey of the contemporary vocabulary of sex,
excretions and offensive exclamations. The dictionary is expected to have over 1.5
million entries.

Aman says that the best insults are in Yiddish, because its speakers have had three
languages to draw from (German, Slavic and Hebrew) and "for 2,000 years the
Jews have been on the dirty end of the stick, persecuted and pushed around with
no way to fight back physically, so they've had to resort to words." His favorite
Yiddish expression: "May all your teeth fall out except one, so you can have a
toothache."

International Society for the History of Ideas
Department of Philosophy, HB 739
Temple University, Philadelphia, PA 19122   (215) 787-8591
Founded: 1959   Members: 45
Dues: Write for details   Contact: John Fisher

International Society for the History of Rhetoric
University of California Press
2120 Berkeley Way, Berkeley, CA 94740
Founded: 1975   Members: 500
Dues: Write for details   Contact: JJ. Murphy, Ph.D.

International Society for the Study of Time

PO Box 815, Westport, CT 06881   (203) 226-0686
Founded: 1966   Members: 200
Dues: Write for details   Contact: Dr. J. T. Fraser

A scholarly organization, that holds a convention every 6 years--like clockwork.

Mend our Tongues Society

2119 College Street, Cedar Falls, IA 50613   (319) 266-8669
Founded: 1982   Contact: Gerald Baker

"Zyzzonony," the process of inventing words, was invented by MOTS to be the last word...in the dictionary. Mend our Tongues Society was formed as a parody of the "Save our Tongues" Society, a group founded to criticize grammatical errors in print. (Of course *they* were unaware that "SOTS" means "fools" in French.) MOTS (meaning "words" in French) purpose is linguistic research and the invention of new words: "Vultch," to watch or follow like a vulture; "sheeple," people who exhibit sheeplike behavior; and "chlorophory," the wearing of green as on St. Patrick's Day.

Place Name Survey of the United States

Elleneer Library, Nicholl State University
Thibodaux, TX 70310   (504) 446-3300
Founded: 1969   Members: 150
Dues: Write for details   Contact: Dr. Randall A. Detro

Scholars and individuals interested in the geographical, historical and linguistic history of U.S. place names.

Science Frontiers

2119 College Street, Cedar Falls, IA 50613   (319) 266-8669
Contact: Gerald Baker

Why does the ratio of human births in May to human births in November vary as a direct function of geographical latitude? Science Frontiers is an organization that studies such anomalies, or facts that aren't explainable by current theories. Science Frontiers researcher Gerald Baker, who explained the invention of videotaped images years before it was patented, says that though there are lots of hypotheses on the answer to the May baby and other unanswered questions, they are still just speculation.

Society for the History of Discoveries

45 Mill Rock Rd., Hamden, CT 06511
Founded: 1960
Dues: Write for details

(203) 436-8638
Members: 300
Contact: Barbara B. McCorkle

College professors and others who are interested in the history of geographical explorations and discoveries--the discovery of the New World, Balboa, Columbus, Hudson and the rest of those fellows.

Society for the Protection of Old Fishes (SPOOF)

College of Fisheries, WH-10, University of Washington, Seattle, WA 98195
Founded: 1952
Dues: Write for details

Members: 200
Contact: Dr. George Brown

In 1938, a fisherman on Lake Michigan reeled in a coelacanth....a fish thought to be extinct for 60 or 70 million years! Fourteen years later, Professor J. L. B. Smith caught another one, and now these extinct fish are caught regularly. And thus, a society was hatched. S.P.O.O.F. is *not* a spoof, but rather a gathering of biochemists, ichthyologists and others (including the curator of the Museum of Natural History) who are interested in ancient life forms. S.P.O.O.F. studies and investigates frozen, live or preserved fishes, from lung fishes, to sharks to sturgeons.

Society of Tympanuchus Cupido Pinnatus, Ltd.

740 N. Plankinton Avenue, Milwaukee, WI 53203 (414) 276-3003
Founded: 1961
Dues: $35.00 per year

Members: 1,200
Contact: Bernard J. Westphall

"To save the Prairie Chicken from Extinction." Of course.

Tree-Ring Society

Tree-Ring Laboratory, University of Arizona
Tucson, AZ 85721
Founded: 1935
Dues: $15.00 per issue of journal

(602) 621-2191
Members: 389
Contact: Jeffrey S. Dean

If you ever wondered where all the dendrochronologists were hanging out...if you ever wondered what a dendrochronologist did--they study tree-rings. The club publishes the *Tree-Ring Bulletin.*

SPEAKING OUT!

Thanks to the First Amendment, this colorful crowd gets to champion their worthy causes, like mushrooms, the evils of rock music, sensible tipping...and more.

Adabuse

71-34 Austin St., Forest Hills, NY 11375   (718) 520-1515
Founded: 1980   Contact: Jeffrey L. Blask

Founded to keep the New York yellow Pages in one book! Splitting the books into business and consumer volumes meant more money for big advertisers and was just a way for the phone company to reap bigger profits. Well, Adabuse didn't succeed in taking the phone company to court. They are now planning their next move.

American Association of Dental Victims

3320 East 7th Street, Long Beach, CA 90804   (213) 433-9649
Founded: 1976   Members: 80 regional reps.
Fees: None   Contact: Faye L. Willard

After being duped into spending $125,000 on unnecessary dental work, Faye Willard decided to bite back. The American Association of Dental Victims is not *against* dentists but is pro-information, with a board to help patients with dental complaints. The logo of the organization, the cracked Liberty Bell, symbolizes the crack in the integrity of the once-noble dental profession. The association publishes *How to Sue a Dentist and other Impossible Feats*.

American Vegan Society

PO Box H, Malaga, NJ 08328   (609) 694-2887
Founded: 1960
Dues: Write for details   Contact: H. Jay Dinshah

Veganism is the reverence for all life, avoiding cruelty and exploitation of animals, maintenance of a totally vegetarian diet and the use of non-animal clothing.

American Vegetarian, Inc.

PO Box 5333, Takoma Park, MD 20912   (301) 270-3444

Founded: 1967
Dues: Write for details   Contact: Nellie Shriver

Promoting a world without suffering, for humans, animals, insects and plants, they also coordinate the Boycott McDonald's Coalition (see separate entry) and are involved in lawsuits against schools that require vivisection (killing animals...like those frogs in Biology 101) in the classroom.

Better Education Thru Simplified Spelling

2340 E. Hammond Lake Dr., Bloomfield Hills, MI 48013   (313) 334-6061
Founded: 1978   Members: 140
Dues: Write for details   Contact: Dr. Abraham E. Citron

It takes over 650 rules to spell just 95% of the 20,000 most frequently used English words! BETSS believes that by gradually changing spelling to reflect the way words sound, illiteracy could be reduced. BETTS recommends dropping the final 'E' on words where it doesn't matter like "giv" and "hav," dropping the silent 'B' on words like "crum," "dum" and "thum." "Donkey" and "Whiskey" would change to' "Donky" and "Whisky." "Phone" would become "Fone" and "League and Catalogue" would become "Leag and Catalog." The group contends that its an uphill battle to change the rules that have been haphazardly created over so many years.

Boycott McDonalds Coalition

PO Box 1836, Boston, MA 02205   (617) 734-4068
Founded: 1981   Contact: Heather Schofield

Formerly the "Boycott Burger King Coalition," they changed direction after Burger King met their demands of withdrawing veal from the menu and installing salad bars. The boycott McDonalds Coalition wants Mickey Dees to offer a non-meat sandwich--something in the way of a nut-burger or a tofu sandwich, or at least a baked potato!! The Boycott McDonald's Coalition has a couple of major beefs with the chain. They cite McDonald's use of rain forest beef in Central America (encouraging destruction of forests for raising cattle), racist hiring practices, and the lack of information about how their food is prepared...(do vegetarians who eat the fries know that the potatoes are preprocessed by soaking them in sheep lard, or that the Golden Arches buys these tubers from a farm next to the nation's only nuclear weapons processing plant?)

Brothers United for Future Foreskins

PO Box 26377, Tempe, AZ 85282
Founded: 1972   Members: 75

Dues: Write for details

A "social welfare organization for persons interested in foreskin reconstruction."
They distributed information on the way of reconstructing foreskins to men who
had been circumcised and wanted "to be natural again."

Committee for Do-It-Yourself Household Moving

PO Box 2662, Phoenix, AZ 85002   (602) 263-6815
Founded: 1974   Contact: Paul J. Kelley

U-Haul and Ryder are just two of the members of this organization, trying to
change tax incentives on Capitol Hill for do-it-yourself movers.

Committee to Eliminate Legal-Size Files

c/o Assn. of Records Managers and Administrators
42000 Somerset Dr. Ste. 215, Prairie Village, KS 66208   (913) 341-3808
Founded: 1980   Members: 8,500
Dues: Write for details   Contact: Walter S. Mullarky

The committee, or ELF, as it's called, is a project of the Association of Record
Managers and Administrators. The ELFs contend that everyone pays for wasted
legal file space. Legal-sized file cabinets take up 17% more space than a regular
file cabinet! This is a situation that real-estate developers and landlords might
enjoy, but working stiffs are the ones who get stuck with the bill for the extra floor
space in the end. The costs don't end with the extra floor space. Business owners
must pay for larger carbon paper, a double stock of paper, stationery, binders,
folders and envelopes to fit the larger-size paper. ELFs have started a nationwide
campaign to stop the wasteful practice, vowing not to rest until the last legal-size
paper mill stops producing. So far, they've changed the shape of file cabinets at
the General Service Administration and Federal Courts System, but the record-
keeping departments of legal firms are not budging. Still, a 25% savings in office
supplies is a mighty attractive motive for change.

Committee for National Arbor Day

640 Eagle Rock Ave., West Orange, NJ 07052   (201) 731-0594
Founded: 1936   Members: 50
Dues: Write for details   Contact: Harry J. Banker

Tree experts who want the last Friday of April to be declared "National Arbor
Day," as a way of saying that trees are very important to you and me!

Conference on Peace Research in History

University College
Adelphi University, Garden City, NY 11530   (516) 663-1047
Founded: 1963   Members: 290
Tax deductible gifts accepted   Contact: Glen Zeitzer

Seeks to "clarify the causes of international peace and difficulties in creating it." Members are pacifists and peace researchers.

Council to Save the Postcard

1819 H. St. NW, Suite 630, Washington, DC 20006
Contact: Harry J. Lambeth

It used to cost just a couple of pennies to send a postcard; now these picture-postcard manufacturers complain that the cost of postage is putting them out of business. Nobody can afford to send a dozen postcards to everyone back home when they go on vacation anymore.

Coupon Exchange Club

PO Box 13708, Wauwatosa, WI 53213   Founded: 1972
Dues: $17.50 per year   Contact: Becky Thompson

Clip those coupons! For $2.50, this club will send you $8.00 in coupons! And if you're lucky enough to live in a double-coupon region...why that's $16.00 in savings for just $2.50!! Best of all, you can choose exactly what you want...25¢ off those Oreos or 15¢ off White Cloud toilet tissue or whatever your store-bound heart desires. Ain't this country grand?

Daylight Savings Time Coalition

1000 Connecticut Ave., NW #304, Washington   DC 20036
Founded: 1984   Contact: James C. Benfield

A group of candy makers, sporting goods manufacturers and others who would benefit from more daylight during later hours. They helped pass a bill extending daylight savings time by one month in April and October.

Fat Lip Readers Theater

1448 Willard St., San Francisco, CA 94117   (415) 664-6842
Contact: Laura Bock

This activist group speaks out to prohibit discrimination on the basis of size. They perform scripts on growing up fat in America, with meetings afterwards.

Fundamentalists Anonymous

PO Box 20324, Greeley Square Station, New York, NY 10001 (212) 696-0420
Founded: 1985   Members: 30,000
Dues: Call for information   Contact: Richard Yao

Disillusioned people, some who have given substantial portions of their life savings to Fundamentalist churches, now have a place to turn. "I sent every cent I could get my hands on to Jimmy Swaggart, the PTL Club and the 700 Club," said one caller. "When I ran out of money, I cut back on my food budget. I ate popcorn for two weeks so I could send more." Those who call the hotline receive a newsletter and are referred to one of the 41 local chapters across the country.

Gray Panthers

311 S. Juniper Street, Philadelphia, PA 19107   (215) 545-6555
Founded: 1970   Members: 10,000
Dues: $12.00 per year   Contact: Christina Long

What do older people want? Health care for all, regardless of income, a stop to age discrimination in housing, no mandatory retirement age, and an end to media's depiction of the elderly as helpless, useless and uninformed, for starters, and they're organizing to get it! Gray Panthers was founded by Maggie Kuhn and six friends when they were forced to retire at 65. Maggie says, "There's no disgrace or shame in growing old--we're all doing it." With almost 120 local chapters in 40 states, the Gray Panthers are growling against many of the "ageist" policies that the oldest President in American history has supported.

Group Against Smoker's Pollution...or....GASP of America

PO Box 632, College Park, MD 20740   (301) 577-6427
Founded: 1971   Members: 10,000
Dues: Write for details   Contact: Clara L. Gouin

Over a hundred local groups around the country fighting to change the laws so that non-smokers need not have to breathe second-hand smoke. Presents the "Ventilator Award" to the person who's done the most each year to regulate smoking.

Holiday Institute of Yonkers

Box 1354, Bronx, NY 10475
Founded: 1969   Contact: William Bickel

Working to persuade New York Governor Rockefeller to proclaim July 20th as Moon Landing Day, they're currently working for an international holiday on December 10th, called Humanities Day. Members receive the monthly

International Smart Shoppers Club
11394 James Watt #313, El Paso, TX 79936
Contact: Gil Lewis

Another coupon-clipping club.

Men's Rights Association
17854 Lyons, Forest Lake, MN 55025   (612) 464-7887
Founded: 1973   Members: 5000
Dues: $20.00 membership fee   Contact: Richard F. Doyle

Founder Rich Doyle had returned from the Korean War to find his wife living
with another man. The ensuing divorce was painful and traumatic, and his
children were "condemned to live in an atmosphere I considered to be
deplorable." Finding so many other men in the same straits, he founded the
MRA, a group of "Male Boosters and Divorce Racket Busters." The club helps
men win fair divorce settlements, by providing advice and support. "We are not
'anti-women'," they claim, although they "have uncovered proof that maternal
custody is the leading cause of juvenile delinquency and that most child abuse
involves children placed in maternal custody." Members receive instructional
materials, referrals and a free bumper sticker to demonstrate their loyalty to the
male sex.

Mothers-In-Law Club International
420 Adelberg Ln., Cedarhurst, NY 11516   (516) 295-4744
Founded: 1970   Members: 5000
Dues: Write for details   Contact: Sylvia Parker

Trying to change the "false and unkind image of the mother-in-law," they are
trying to establish a "mother-in-law day" on the second Sunday in August.
Ultimately, Mothers-in-Law Club International tries to foster a happy intra-family
relationship.

Mushroom Caucus
2201 Rayburn House Bldg., Washington, DC 20515   (202) 225-5761
Founded: 1978   Members: 50
                                             Contact: Rep. Richard Schulze

Promoting the U.S. mushroom industry. Members are congressmen from the

mushroom-growing states, trying to control the onslaught of cheap foreign
mushrooms.

National Alliance of Supermarket Shoppers

2 Broadlawn Avenue, Great Neck, NY 11023   (516) 328-6222
Founded: 1980   Members: 50,000
Dues: Write for details   Contact: Carolyn R. Palzer

Standing up for the rights of supermarket shoppers, the National Alliance acts on
complaints of shoppers negotiating with supermarkets. They lobby the
government for changes in supermarket laws that will benefit the customer, like
mandatory price labels on all products. The Alliance bestows the Golden
Shopping Cart Award to legislators, supermarkets, manufacturers, and others.

National Arbor Day Foundation

100 Arbor Ave., Nebraska City, NE 68410   (402) 475-5655
Founded: 1972   Contact: John Rosenow

Promoting the observance of Arbor Day each year.

National Association to Aid Fat Americans

PO Box 43, Bellrose, NY 11426   (516) 352-3120
Founded: 1969   Members: 1500
Dues: 35.00 per year   Contact: William J. Fabrey

"How *dare* you presume I'd rather be thin" reads a button on the front of the
NAAFA brochure. Thirty million heavier-than-average Americans exist in a
society geared towards slimness as an ideal, but NAAFA helps fat people lead
happier lives by dealing with discrimination and unsympathetic treatment from
those around them. NAAFA says that the word "overweight" doesn't make sense,
since there is no such thing as an ideal weight for everyone. The thin ideal is so
persuasive that "up to 20% of young women are so afraid of becoming fat that
they develop anorexia or bulimia." Members meet regularly in local chapters, and
participate in computer dating, penpal and other social programs. Committees
study different problems fat people have, and lobby for better treatment in the
media, in the workplace and in the marketplace. The Fatabilia museum has a
collection of biographical information on "Famous Fats," plus the association
sponsors special interest groups on "Feminists, Women Size 48 and Larger" and
"Fat Admirers."

National Association of Railroad Passengers
236 Massachusetts Ave., NE, Washington, DC 20002
Founded: 1966   Dues: $15.00 per year

Fighting on Capitol Hill for faster and better train service in America, they also publish the *NARP News* --11 times per year.

National Council for the Observance of Grandparent's Day
PO Box 490022, Atlanta, GA 30349   (404) 455-1616
Founded: 1978   Contact: Mike Goldgar

Trying to generate support and publicity for the observance of a national holiday honoring grandparents.

National Father's Day Committee...and...
National Mother's Day Committee
47 W. 34th St., New York, NY 10001
Founded: 1937   Contact: Theodore M.
Kaufman

Sponsors an award banquet each year to acknowledge "Fathers of the Year" and "Mothers of the Year" in the categories of literature, stage, screen, sports, television and radio.

National Neighbors
815 15th St. NW, #611, Washington, DC 20005   (202) 347-6501
Founded: 1970   Members: 2500

Promotes the development of interracial neighborhoods.

National Organization for Changing Men
Address Unknown, Washington, DC
Members: 555   Contact: Bob Brannon

"Our cause is to give up power," said one member from California. At a time when women are vying for more power, the National Organization of Changing Men is telling men to step off the ladder of success, to be weak and fearful and to nurture. They denounce competition and violence as a "contemptible outgrowth of the traditional masculine ethic." The primary purpose of NOCM, said leader Bob Brannon, is to lend men's support to feminist ideals to be non-sexist males. The membership is about 30% gay.

National Organization of Circumcision Information Resource Centers

731 Sir Francis Drake Blvd., San Anselmo, CA 94960 (415) 454-5669

The United States is the only country to continue routine circumcision for non-religious, non-medical reasons. "To remove the foreskin for hygiene is no more logical than pulling teeth instead of cleaning them." Though he regards this as no laughing matter, Jeffrey Wood, former director of Intact Educational Foundation, also sent along a copy of the anti-circumcision song, "What Have They Done to My Schlong, Ma."

Phonemic Spelling Council

144 Lake Miriam Rd., SE, Winter Haven,. FL 33880 (813) 324-4096
Founded: 1971   Contact: Dr. Emmett A. Betts

Promoting a simpler spelling of our complex language.

People for Global Understanding

Global Understanding Day
1125 Jordan Lane, Grand Blanc, MI 48439
Paul H. Jordan MD

People for peace, "preservation and sound functioning of the planet."

Perhaps...Kids Meeting Kids Can Make a Difference

380 Riverside Dr., New York, NY 10025   (212) 662-2327
Founded: 1982   Contact: Marvin Sochet
Tax deductible gifts accepted

According to a Harvard Medical School study, the threat of nuclear war is the biggest worry of American and Russian kids alike. Kids Meeting Kids helps American and Soviet children to find ways to meet and talk to each other. In 1982, the organization organized the first public meeting of Soviet and American children. Later they negotiated the first exchange of children's visits between the countries, instituted a pen-pal program between the superpowers and held a "Kids Summit Conference." Marvin Sochet says that the point of the group is for kids not to feel helpless in a world where nuclear war is a grave possibility. By giving a face and name to the so-called "enemy," perhaps...Kids Meeting Kids Can Make A Difference.

Redeem Our Country (ROC)

1110 S. Pomona Ave., Fullerton, CA 92632   (714) 871-2952
Founded: 1981   Members: 35,000
Membership Fee: $10.00   Contact: Jim Townsend

- "Nothing for those already broke"

"Abolish the Federal Reserve" is the ROC's cry. With Howard Jarvis listed as their
National Honorary Chairman, ROC presents the case that the Reserve is
controlled by foreigners and swindling power brokers who lend money to
America's enemies and have their own interests in mind. Reads the membership
coupon: "Dear Mr. Townsend: I'm sick of working six months out of each year to
pay the Federal Reserve Bankers their profits. Without the Federal Reserve there
would be no need for the Internal Revenue Service. I'm with you and ROC...sign
me up."

Rock is Stoning Kids

c/o Summit Ministries
PO Box 207, Manitou Springs, CO 80829   (303) 685-9103
Founded: 1984   Contact: David A. Noebel

Making people aware of the "evil of the rock' n' roll music subculture."

S.C.R.O.O.G.E.
The Society to Curtail Ridiculous, Outrageous and Ostentatious Gift Exchanges

1447 Westwood Road, Charlottesville, VA 22901 (804) 997-4648
Founded: 1979   Members: 800
Dues: $2.00 lifetime membership   Contact: Charles G. Langham

This SCROOGE isn't anti-Christmas...it's just the over-commercialization of the
holiday that upsets these folks.. The SCROOGE principles:
--avoid giving and receiving expensive gifts that are not really useful
--make every effort to pay for gifts with cash, not credit cards
--emphasize gifts that involve thought and originality
Try to continue gift-giving mainly to young children, they suggest. For others on
your gift list, consider contributions to charity in their names, or presents that
require creative thought on your part. Other suggestions include a gift certificate
for a weekend of babysitting and an evergreen house plant. Good gift ideas for
children might be homemade gift projects: printing stamps made from potatoes or
old erasers, cardboard-box dollhouses and "stained glass" cookies to eat or hang
on the Christmas tree. Members receive a newsletter each year before Christmas.
One issue advised them of the 18-month law,an observation that your Christmas
gifts end up in your lawn sale 18 months later. Apparently, most folks feel too

guilty to offer these items the first spring or summer, and keep them for another year...until the guilt wears off.

Soldiers for Peace

46 Union St., Peterborough, NH 03458	(603) 924-6811
Founded: 1980	Members: 500
Dues: Write for Details	Contact: Taylor Morris

Group advocates having 100,000 young Americans exchange places with 100,000 young Russians in an effort towards world peace.

Tippers Anonymous

PO Box 178, Cochituate, MA 01778	(617) 653-8256
Founded: 1960	Members: 14,000
Dues: $2.00 for 30 tippers cards	Contact: Robert S. Farrington

"I often found myself subject to the whims of the waiter," says Robert Farrington. He felt that waiters and waitresses had forgotten the meaning of TIPS--To Insure Prompt Service. After being ill-served too many times, Farrington started Tippers Anonymous and devised the Tippers Report Card. The Report Card, a small card to be left with your tip (or non-tip), rates service on a scale from poor to excellent, providing, as Farrington puts it, "chastisement or a little praise." Farrington feels that excellent restaurant service deserves a 25% tip and poor service deserves 5% to nothing at all. Farrington publishes *Up Your Tips*, a guide for restaurant owners and servers.

Tippers International

PO Box 1934, Wausau, WI 54401	(414) 231-5852
Founded: 1970	Members: 30,000
Dues: Write for details	Contact: John E. Schein

"Let the tip do the talking" is this group's motto. "Pocket Guide for Tipping" and "The Art of Tipping: Customs and Controversies" are books available to help members "come to grips with tips." Proponents of freedom of choice in tipping, they offer such tipping tools as comment cards to leave behind for rating service and a pocket-size tipping computer to calculate the exact gratuity.

Typographic Council for Spelling Reform

c/o Photo-Lettering

216 E. 45th St., New York, NY 10017	(914) 271-3294
Founded: 1973	Contact:Dr. Edward

Rondthaller

If u can reed this, ur red-ee for speling reeform. One in ten Americans are functional
illiterates, says Dr. Edward Rondthaller. Rondthaller is a proponent of spelling
words as they are pronounced. He calls this new spelling "American." The idea of
phonetic spelling has been around for over one hundred years, but with the use of
computers, phonetic translations could be made easily and would make reading
English a much easier task for those who have trouble. As Rondthaller says,
"Some of our best thinkers are our worst spellers. Unlike other languages, English
is very short on logic." Rondthaller tells the story of the English professor at Yale
who saw a sign in a restaurant near the college, reading "Lam Chops." He went in
and explained that 'Lam' needed a 'B' at the end. The next week he went by the
same restaurant...and saw a sign that said "Clamb Chowder."

U.S.-U.S.S.R. Bridges for Peace
The Norwich Center, Inc., Box 710, Norwich, VT 05055   (802) 649-1000
Founded: 1981   Members: 300
Tax deductible contributions accepted   Contact: Clinton Gardner

They've been successful in initiating exchange programs in which Americans have
really gotten to know Russians and vice versa. Their purpose is to end the arms
race and free the money spent on the military for global development needs, like
feeding the hungry.

Viewers for Quality Television
PO Box 195, Fairfax Station, VA 22039   (703) 425-0075
Dues: $15.00 per year   Contact: Dorothy Swanson

VQT was formed as an alternative voice to the Neilsens--rating a show on its
quality, not on the quantity of viewers it has. They endorse a dozen shows per
season, helping to inform and educate viewers. They also educate viewers on how
to write an effective letter to the networks to keep their favorite shows on the air.
Recently VQT endorsed "Newhart," "The Cosby Show," "Murder She Wrote,"
"Moonlighting," "The Golden Girls," "Cheers" and others. Members receive a
newsletter, and a convention is planned.

Walking Association
Box 37228, Tucson, AZ, 85740   (602) 742-9589
Founded: 1976
Dues: $12.00 per year   Contact: Robert B. Sleight,
Ph.D.

Works towards more and better sidewalks around America.

FOR A SMILE

The Loyal and Benevolent Order of Pessimists may not approve, but we thought you'd have fun with the bananas, potatoes, tomatoes, turtles and other good eggs in this smorgasbord of silliness.

American Association of Aardvark Aficionados

12 Banghart Pl., Mt. Tabor, NJ 07878	(201) 586-9393
Founded: 1975	Members: 600
	Contact: Robert L. Bogart

"Bent for the unusual," enhancing the image of the aardvark, National Aardvark Week, the first week in March, Holds Miss American Aardvark Contest. Newsletter is called *Hark-Vark*.

American Humor Studies Association

American Studies Dept.	
University of Maryland, College Park, MD 20742	(301) 454-4661
Founded: 1974	Members: 200
Dues: Write for details	Contact: Lawrence E. Mintz

Professors and comedians studying American Humor--doesn't sound very funny.

American Zit Farmers Association

Grodeegifts
304 N. Second, Kure Beach, NC 28449
Dues: $10.00

Members receive a certificate, almanac, sticker, cap and fertilizer---(a bag of potato chips???) Mostly a gimmick, but good fun.

American Zombie Association

RR #1, Box 103A, Menlo, IA 50164	(515) 524-5414
Founded: 1980	Members: 200+
Dues: None	Contact: Donna Schildberg

After a boring session of the National Limestone Association's convention (now known as the Crushed Stone Association), John Schildberg and two friends went down to Trader Vic's bar and started downing zombies (check with your local bartender for the recipe--they're lethal!) "After about five or six of them, your tongue gets pretty loose," says John, who started tying the stem of a maraschino cherry with his tongue. Thus was born the American Zombie Association. Members are required to drink three zombies in an hour, tie the cherry stem in their mouth in less than 15 seconds and then walk back to their hotel room unaided. John's wife, Donna, was immediately handed the presidency when she was able to tie the cherry stem with the cherry still attached! The AZA meets in conjunction with the Crushed Stone Convention, giving "stoned" a whole new meaning. The only dues members pay are during the morning after...but the action happens at Trader Vic's, where the club drinks $500-$600 worth of zombies. Members can enroll other members...one member on a trip to China claims to have signed up an entire province.

Association for the Promotion of Humor in International Affairs

PO Box 18418, Asheville, NC 28814   (704) 253-5383
Founded: 1973   Members: 400
Dues: $2.00 to $10.00   Contact: Alfred E. Davidson

Where are the Mark Twains, James Thurbers and Chaucers of today, APHIA bemoans? The founders say that in a world where "political leaders fumble uncertainly with ever greater governmental power, humor is a vital necessity." Humor is useful in "containing men whose sense of proportion and reality are distorted."

APHIA was started by three Americans living in Paris. The main function of the group is the luncheon party held every year in Paris where the NOBLE prize is awarded to a humorist "of world stature." Two of the NOBLE prize winners have been Art Buchwald who received 100,000 pennies and Peter Ustinov who was awarded a Time Capsule. In addition to the Noble prize, APHIA also awards the Booby Prize for unconscious contributions to humor. Chief of Staff Donald Regan received the Booby Prize in 1986. The prize remembers August 1986, when Regan was pleading with Congress not to pass anti-apartheid sanctions. Regan asked if "American women were prepared to give up all their diamonds." "Indignant American women replied that, on the contrary, they were prepared to give up Mr. Regan." The prize was a glittering piece of fool's gold. Other Booby Prize winners have been Defense Secretary Caspar Weinberger, who was awarded a cap pistol for "disclaiming that his defense policy was limited to limited nuclear war--in fact, most of the Booby Prize winners have been Americans (Billy Carter, Senator Proxmire and Milton Friedman.) APHIA is open to anyone with a sense of humor.

Benevolent and Loyal Order of Pessimists

PO Box 1945, Iowa City, IA 52244   (319) 351-2973
Founded: 1975   Members: 120

Dues: Write for details   Contact: Jack Duvall

"Pessimism is still misunderstood in this country," says Jack Duvall. BLOOP tries to screen applicants with care, but too often, a happy applicant slips through who turns out to be an Amway salesmen, or even worse in Iowa, "someone who is about to begin farming."

Located in Iowa City, coincidentally the home of the president of Optimists International, pessimists say that they are not necessarily unhappy people. On the contrary, they have the satisfaction of being right 90 percent of the time and pleasantly surprised the other 10. While the president of Optimists International says that "We always look to the bright side of things," the pessimists counter that the effects of optimism are sinister: "crushed hopes, dashed illusions and a constant sense of unfulfillment."

When planning a recent BLOOP convention, the first choice for dinner was the "Ming Garden" restaurant. Unfortunately, it burned down two months before the convention date. They picked a second restaurant, staying away from the fortune cookies and sweet dessert called the "lucky roll." They then started the task of picking the Outstanding Pessimist of the year, with its coveted trophy--a plastic statue of a horse's rear end.

Jack Duvall expressed concern over the publicity that BLOOP would receive from appearing in *Join the Club*. "Our organization has helped thousands to accept themselves as pessimists, to look at the brighter side of being a pessimist--in short, to learn how to cope in a cruelly optimistic society. For those people, the threat of publicity that your book poses could set their recovery back months, even years." Yet, the BLOOP board of directors did consent, even with fears of political reprisals. Spokesperson Duvall says that pessimist-baiting has been a theme of the Reagan administration. He is starting to hear stories of "pessimists being rounded up, held without due process, and forced to watch game shows and sitcoms featuring optimistic single parents having a whale of a time with their zany kids and lovers."
Or it could be worse.

Bonehead Club of Dallas
7770 Goforth Circle, Dallas, TX 75238
Founded: 1919   Members: Limited to 57
                                                Contact: Brad Angers

The Bonehead Club motto vows "to learn more and more about less and less, until we eventually know everything about nothing." The club awards the annual "Bonehead of the Year" award to a person or organization which has committed some monumental goof. In recent years, it has gone to a sports or political figure for a dubious distinction. (The Hunt brothers won in 1981 for their silver-buying

fiasco.) It also has been awarded to some early pioneers in aviation: one year to
Brodbeck, who built a spring-powered airship (forgetting that a spring cannot be
rewound while recharging) in 1865, and another year to Larry Walters who was
lifted 16,000 feet in his lawn chair tethered to helium balloons (neither of the
honorees were killed in the ensuing crashes.)

The Bonehead Club claims to be the oldest continually active club in the United
States, meeting every Friday since it was founded. Officer titles are: Big Chief,
Little Chief, Scribbler and Money-Grabber. Other (more fictional)
accomplishments of The Bonehead Club include the creation of Bonehead
University-- the only educational institution in the world devoted solely to
teaching of the non-essential (some students I know would dispute that Bonehead
University is the *only* one!) Also celebrated is the Bonehead Building- - a 56-floor
architectural marvel (actually it was supposed to have 57 floors but the first floor is
still under construction.) The club's newsletter is called *Pithyosseous*.

The Boring Institute
PO Box 40, Maplewood, NJ 07040   (201) 763-6392
Founded: 1984
Dues: $10.00 one-time fee   Contact: Alan Caruba

What do Joan Rivers, Robin Leach and Don Johnson have in common? Yes, they
won The Boring Institute's Most Boring Celebrities of the Year award. The
Institute is also famous for its picks of the Most Boring Film Awards (1986
brought us "The Clan of Cave Bear" and "Shanghai Surprise") and The Most
Boring News Stories of the Year.

Founder Alan Caruba says there is a serious side of boredom. "Boredom is
virtually epidemic in America these days. It is a significant contributing factor to
school drop-outs, a sign of potential teen suicide, a factor in the job burn-out
syndrome, and plays a large role in marital failures." Caruba says boredom starts
at an early age, as a reaction to a barrage of media distractions." People need to
learn to end the boredom in their lives. To this end, Caruba has written *Boring
Stuff: How to Spot It & Avoid It*--$7.45 in softcover. Another self-help tool for the
bored is the Boring Poster, "Twenty-five ways to avoid boredom" (number 25 on
the list is **Turn off the TV!**) Caruba said, "I think half of the insurance industry
wrote to me wanting a poster."

The Institute sponsors "National Anti-Boredom Month" each July and has its own
political *in*action committee, The Boring Party (gearing up to do as little as
possible about the 1988 Presidential elections.) As the official Boring candidate,
Caruba says, "I am the candidate for people who just want to be left alone,"
adding, "I have never let ignorance of the issues ever stand in the way of
commenting on them."

As an Associate Member, one receives "A Boring Certificate" of Associate Membership, a membership card in "The Boring Party" and a "Boring Bumpersticker."

Burlington Liars Club

c/o Donald Reed,149 Oakland Ave., Burlington, WI 53105 (414) 763-3341
Founded: 1929   Members: 50,000
Dues: $1.00 for life   Contact: John Soeth

Purpose: to perpetuate the art of telling tall tales. Members send in a lie and a dollar to receive a membership card for life. Each year, the three officers meet and a champion liar is picked. Last year, with 306 entries from 23 states and 16 countries (6 lies from India and one from Japan), the winner was Clarence Klott of Herman, Missouri. Donald Reed says that his all-time favorite lie comes from a man from Ecklumb, Missouri who said that he saw a politician standing on the street corner with his hands in his *own* pockets. The group was founded when newspaper reporter Otis Hulett (now 89 years old) wrote that the oldtimers sat around the Burlington Police Station telling lies to each other. Hulett picked the first champion liar and the story was picked up by the newswire and carried around the country. Of course the whole newspaper story was a fabrication, but picking the champion liar became a tradition.

Couch Potatoes

PO Box 249, Dixon, CA 95620   (916) 678-2955
Founded: 1976   Members: 8,000 worldwide
Dues: $6.00   Contact: Robert Armstrong

Do you enjoy excessive amounts of TV viewing?
Were some of the most enjoyable times of your life experienced in front of your TV set?
Were your formative years nurtured by the "electronic babysitter?
Do the people on TV seem more real to you than your friends and family?

Then you're ready for "The Couch Potatoes"…sometimes called "The International Order of the Couch Potatoes." Membership requirements are an "undying love of television viewing," plus a list of five of one's all-time favorite TV programs. Among the questions on the application form: "If I do anything at all during commercials, I usually ___________" and "When I really want to lose myself I watch________." The $6.00 membership fee entitles one to full membership privileges: a membership card and four issues of *The Tuber's Voice* (written during commercials.) Goals of the group are to watch as much television as possible, defend the name of television against its enemies, and abolish the guilt about watching "too much TV." Or for $20.00, prospective members can get the membership card, the newsletter, an official Couch Potato T-Shirt (indicate Potato style for boys or Couch Tomato style for girls), a copy of *The Official Couch Potato Handbook*, a Couch Potato membership button, and a Couch Potato Rabbit-Ear Antenna Pennant.

Slogans:
•If it's on TV, it must be good
•There's no such thing as a bad TV show!
•Art may imitate life, but life imitates television.

Theme song:
"Is there room on the couch for me?"

Darwin University
The Church of Universal Confusion
Box 2326, Evanston, WY 82930   (307) 789-0828
Founded: 1982
Dues: $15.00 per degree   Contact: David Lemire, Th.D.

The Darwin University awards honorary degrees at the bargain price of $15.00 each!! Choose from the Associate's, Bachelor's, or Master's Degree in Thinkology. Or go for the big one with the highly coveted Doctor of Philosophy in Thinkology (Ph.T.) and Doctor of Thinkology (Th.D.) Lemire says that the history of giving out honorary Th.D. degrees began "in 1939 when the Wizard of Oz awarded the first Th.D. to the Scarecrow."

Darwin University also offers a MBWA--or Management by Wandering Around (first awarded by Tom Powers of *In Search of Excellence*.)

The Church of Universal Confusion says that if you're sick and tired of trying to buy your way to heaven, listening to "bible-thumping phonies," the C.U.C. will send you an honorary Doctorate of Universal Confusion. (Just show it to St. Peter on the way in.)

DeadfromtheNeckup, Inc.
PO Box 57141, Washington, DC 20037
Dues: Write for details   Contact: Chuck Shepard

Members receive a newsletter called *View from the Ledge*. Their motto is: "You're only young once, but you can always be immature."

Densa
PO Box 23584, Rochester, NY 14692   (716) 724-2270
Founded: 1983   Members: 750

Dues: Write for details   Contact: J. D. Stewart

Rejected by Mensa?(see separate entry) Have an I.Q. of under 134? J.D. Stewart
says Mensa only has 70,000 members----that leaves most of the world as Dense.
He "believes the bottom 98% of the world's 5 billion people who are not geniuses
deserve a place to get together and show their lack of brainpower." DENSA
which is not Latin, stands for Diversely Educated Not Seriously Affected. An
outgrowth of the International Dull Folks, Stewart started DENSA for those
people who didn't have their SAT scores tattooed to their forehead for everyone to
read. Test questions for entry- What sport is the hockey puck used in? Who's
buried in grant's tomb? (Bonus point question: Why?)

Motto: "Do you dare to be dense?"

Diastema Club of America
21247 S. Crestmont Drive, Moses Lake, WA 98837   (509) 765-1577
Founded: 1982   Members: 350
Dues: $5.00 lifetime membership fee   Contact: Dale Hempel

What do model Lauren Hutton, Supreme Court Justice Sandra Day O'Conner,
Chaucer's Wife of Bath, and Cleopatra have in common? They are all potential
members of the Diastema Club of America. Diastema is a technical term
meaning a gap between the front two teeth, but diastema members are not
admitted with any old gap--no, their gap must measure in at a spacious two
millimeters wide!

The Diastema Code of Ethics states:
"Never try to hide gap with hand or other appendages."
"Enter all spitting contests, liquid or seed."
"Remember that what [you] have is God-given and that no orthodontist should
ever take it away"

Furthermore, members must smile at least once a day and say, "I am a
DIASTEMATIC" and must be totally dedicated to spending the rest of their lives
being DIASTEMATIC! Founder and school superintendent Dale Hempel says as
the club gets bigger, so does his gap. He used to be able to spit watermelon seeds
through his gap...now he can spot peach seeds! Meetings are held in Union Gap,
Washington, where members can preview the new movie from filmmaker Les
Blank called "Gap-Toothed Women"--an interview with over 100 women with
gap-teeth ranging from 18 months to 88 years old, to find out how the space
between their teeth has affected their lives.

Eat Cheese or Die (Cheese Heads Anonymous)
The Udderly Cool Club
The Royal Bovinosaurus Society
The Cow Cart
PO Box 281, Madison, WI 53701

Contact: Dennis DeNure

DeNure's Factory, a cheese store in Madison Wisconsin sells T-Shirts through a brochure called "Cowsmopolitan." The Bovinosaur is a prehistoric cow-like creature that roamed the hills and valleys of Wisconsin. Other T-Shirt slogans: "To Err is Human, To Moo--Bovine," "Wisconsin, Land of fine Dairy-aires," and "Any Town Called Moscow Can't Be All Bad." Good for a laugh but we wonder how active these so-called clubs really are

Humor Correspondence Club
G.PO Box 3341, Brooklyn, NY 11202   (718) 855-5057
Founded: 1978   Members: 80
Dues: $4.00 per year   Contact: Robert Makinson

Think you're funny? You can make friends with other people who love humor by exchanging letters. Other services available are "The Comedy Writers Association," "The Songwriters & Lyricists Club," "The Humor Stamp Club" and "The Comedy Performers Association." Bob Makinson also writes and sells a series of jokes to help performers. For $18.00 a year, you can receive the bi-monthly *Latest Jokes*, with 40 up-to-date jokes. From the latest issue:

I hear Ruth Westheimer and Henry Block may do a TV Special...because there are only two things in life you can be sure of...Sex and Taxes.

Politicians talk too much. So how about a Poindexter-North ticket?

Now they're beginning to advertise contraceptives on TV. And actually my TV set is so small it could actually fit into one of those things.

Humor Project
110 Spring St., Saratoga Springs, NY 12866   (518) 587-8
Founded: 1977   Members: 5000
Dues: $15.00 for *Laughing Matters*   Contact: Dr. Joel Goodman

Dr. Joel Goodman helps people take themselves lightly. Described as the "only full-time humor educator in the country," he has given courses to over 80,000 people on the value of humor in managing stress and making life more enjoyable. Goodman, who looks a little like his hero Woody Allen, edits the yearly *Laughing Matters*, which takes a light and serious look at the positive power of humor in everyday life and work. The project sponsors the national conference on "The Positive Power of Humor and Creativity" is geared to managers, nurses, therapists, social workers, teachers, physicians, dentists and the clergy and an annual "Humor, Creativity and Magic Workshop." So, as Goodman says, "Jest for the health of it."

Hypernium Society

200 East Montgomery Ave. Apt. J-0, Ardmore, PA 19003 (215) 964-7183
Founded: 1983   Members: 25 and growing!
Dues: Free   Contact: David Karo

Hyperniums are a type of lawn ornament consisting of a basketball-sized mirror-plated glass ball resting atop a concrete pedestal two to three feet high. There are also called gazing globes, sun balls and reflecting balls. The purpose of the club is to promote the hypernium and increase public awareness of them, with members submitting photographs of unusual hyperniums they have sighted. Recently the club has expanded to document other unusual lawn ornaments, as well as studying ornamaniacs (homeowners compelled to display upwards of 500 lawn ornaments on their front lawn) Club publications include an annual calendar plus the *Hypernium Hotline* newsletter.

I Hate Filing Club

Pendaflex
71 Clinton Rd., Garden City, NY 11530

                                                     Members: 45,000
Dues: Free   Contact: Helen Michaels

Sure, this club is a gimmick to sell Pendaflex folders, but it really is quite funny. People can send in their filing ideas and win prizes.

International Association of Turtles

643 W. Barry #2C, Chicago, IL, 60657
Founded: 1935?   Members: 100,000+
Dues: None   Contact: Maurice Feldman

To become an official Turtle, you must first solve the following riddles:
> 1. What is it a man can do standing up, a woman sitting down, and a dog on three legs? (Answer: Shake hands)
> 2. What is it that a cow has four of and a woman has only two of? (Answer: Legs)
> 3. What is a four-letter word ending in k that means that same as intercourse? (Answer: Talk)
> 4. What is it on a man that is round, hard, and sticks so far out of his

pajamas you can hang a hat on it? (Answer: His head)

The International Association of Turtles was popular among FDR's
"experimental" troops during WWII, because the "Imperial Turtle" was C.P.
Raymond, Harbor Master at the port of embarkation in New York--he would
hand Green Turtle cards out to all the new soldiers. "We were just raw
greenhorns," remembers Mr. Feldman, "visualizing war as spear-helmeted men
firing at other guys' pie-shaped helmets, in trenches stretching out forever." One
of the assumptions that is made of prospective Turtles is that they own a jackass.
All through the war years, a club member could walk into any bar and yell "Are
you a Turtle?" and the password would be replied by dozens of soldiers, sailors,
airmen, WACs, WAVES, or BAMs: "You bet your sweet ass I am." Those who
didn't answer correctly would have to buy the asker a drink of his choice--club
rules.

International Banana Club

2524 N. El Molino Ave., Altadena, CA 91001   (818) 798-2272
Founded: 1973   Members: 7,012
Dues: $15.00 lifetime membership   Contact: Ken Bannister

It all started when Ken Bannister started sticking Chiquita Banana Stickers on
people's lapels at a local convention. The reaction was a smile and "What's this
for?" Bannister said, "Don't worry. You're just one of the bunch." With that he
earned the name "Bananister" and he started the International Banana Club,
with himself as the T.B. or Top Banana. Club rules: just make someone laugh
each day!

Members have their own handshake, their own titles and even their own password
("Woddis." It means whatever you want it to mean.) There is the 12,000 item
yellow-and-brown banana museum, with a banana mirror, petrified banana, brass
banana...even a well-balanced banana putter that was handed to honorary
bananas, Johnny Carson and Bob Hope. Every year, banana fans gather in
Arcadia for the annual picnic, where they sing the banana song, pick Mr. and
Mrs. Banana International, play "Draw and Peel" (their own game) and Banana
Checkers.

Ambitious members earn banana merits for making people laugh and for sending
items to the museum. (Off-color items are worthy of demerits.) With these merits
you can earn a M.B. (Master of Bananastry) or P.H.B. (Doctor of Bananastry.)
Bannister is married and the father of three children. "It does the same thing for
me as it does for other people," he says, "It gets your mind off your silly business."
On occasion, a newsletter called *Woodis News* will appear, alerting members to
trips and events. Sound appealing...?

International Dull Folks, Unlimited

PO Box 23584, Rochester, NY 14692   (716) 334-3398
Founded: 1983   Members: 800
Dues: $5.00   Contact: J. D. "Dull" Stewart

If you're content with your brown suit, aluminum-sided house, and low charisma, you've got plenty of company. Says Chairman of the Bored, J. D. "Dull" Stewart, "We know there are hundreds of others like us, ravishing meatloaf, drinking generic beer and eating jello or planning to spend a big weekend playing with the kids, painting a bookcase or working over the compost pile...we're out of it and proud of it." Maybe the most exciting thing they ever did was break away from the male-only Dull Men's Club (see the "Gone But Not Forgotten" chapter.) Aside from that, it's been strictly dullsville.

Stewart names the "10 Dullest Americans" yearly, whose ranks have included Joan Collins, Ed McMahon, Frank Perdue and NYC mayor Ed Koch (ever notice how the two look alike?), Rodney Dangerfield, Bo Derek and even Sesame Street's Bert (who was so excited that "Gosh, there are other people like *me!*")

If you haven't been picked by *Who's Who* in this or any other year, you're eligible for *Who's Nobody in America*, a register open to all, club members or not. And this year also marks the unveiling of the Dull Folks' Hall of Fame, a 19 1/2" "thighscraper" located in the town of Henrietta, NY, on the site of the former compost pile in a far corner of J.D.'s backyard.

Your annual dues entitle you to a membership card, a dull person's nametag (with a generic bar code for the namespace), a two-page list of dull people's platitudes, "The Case for Dullness" (which traces the history of the Dullness Movement), and a newsletter, the irregularly-published *The Snooze News*.

International Hort! Club

c/o The Imperial Debubba
1523 McGillivray Drive, Spingfield, OH 45503
Founded: 1964   Members: Countless
Dues: $5.00 for 100 years   Contact: Dick Hatfield

"Never have so many done so little for nobody"

The motto sums up the International HORT! society. Even the club calling card says, "23 years of pioneering nothingness." Imperial Debubba Dick Hatfield made up the club with no particular purpose in mind...it's a nonsense organization for people who are "cool," invented in the "cool" generation when dropping meaningless words into everyday conversation was evidence of how really "cool" you were. Members are called "debubbas." The President of the United States is called the Noble Hort of the Better Sort, and membership jackets are Debubba-blazers. Of course, HORT! has no meaning, but must be used as a greeting and farewell word by members. Dick Hatfield says, "Meetings are held every Tuesday night anywhere. So no matter where you are, you can have a meeting there." For five bucks, you receive credentials, membership card, Pant-of-Legs crest (instead of a coat-of-arms) and the HORT! club history.

International Laughter Society

16000 Glen Una Drive, Los Gatos, CA 95030   (408) 395-LAFF
Founded: 1983   Members: 1,222
Dues: $49.95 lifetime membership   Contact: L. Katherine Ferrari

"How's your laugh life?" asks Katherine Ferrari: Ms. Ferrari, formerly a successful architect, started the group after going through some difficult, stressful times in her own life. One day she went to the record shop and bought a whole bunch of Bill Cosby tapes. After listening to them in her car tape deck, tears of laughter started rolling down her face. If stress can cause illness, she decided, then perhaps laughter can cure or help decrease stress, depression and burnout. The club motto: "Laughter is contagious. Let's start an epidemic!

The ILS is forming chapters around the country and plans to offer laughter fitness classes, which Ferrari calls "sedentary jogging." Like a health club for laughter, workshops bring its healing power to corporations, medical associations and others. (Production at one large insurance company increased by 44 percent in three months, after it sent its middle management staff to a laughter therapy session.) Members do not have to go through the Society's courses to better their "laugh life," though. Lifetime members are sent aThe Humor First + Aid Kit. The kit comes equipped with Jiffy Jokes, Mental Snacks (Motivational Quotes), One Share of Laughing-Stock (suitable for framing), Hug Coupons, Stress Strategies and how-to information on getting more laughter out of life and on telling better jokes...plus the quarterly newsletter, entitled the *Laff-Letter*. Famous members of the Society: Norman Cousins, Bill Cosby, George Burns, "Laugh-in"'s Ruth Buzzi, plus Erma Bombeck, and Phyllis Diller. "Laugh for the Health of it!" T-shirts are available, too. The club's mascot is a seven-foot stuffed gorilla named Sam Simeon--because only gorillas, orangutans and chimpanzees are the only *non*humans with the capacity to laugh. Says Phyllis Diller: "A smile is a curve that sets everything straight."

International Order of the Armadillo

PO Box 1522, Gainesville, FL 32602   (904) 376-4477
Founded: 1982   Members: 1000
Dues: $6.00 lifetime membership   Contact: R. L. Graessle

Mixing history with business-(A Giant Armadillo which may reach four feet in length and weigh up to 140 pounds!) you can buy Armadillo shirts, slippers, golf club cover, and almost anything else. Membership includes a laminated membership card and an armadillo decal. Founder Robert Graessle says that wearing an armadillo on your shirt is the antithesis of wearing an alligator--- Armadillos are the underdogs in life--they're kind of ugly, (their armor shell likens them to a "pocket-sized dinosaur) and they have the unfortunate habit of winding up under the tires of trucks and cars. While there are no meetings or rules, members are encouraged to wildly wave their arms when trying to cross a street.

International Organization of Nerds

PO Box 118555, Cincinnati, OH 45211   (513) 941-2624
Founded: 1984   Members: 5,000
Dues: $4.95--or $5.00   Contact: Bruce L. Chapman

Are your socks red, your pants four inches above your shoes, is your shirt buttoned up to the top? Do you have a calculator hanging from your belt and a pen holder in your shirt pocket? ION wants you. Bruce L. Chapman, Supreme Archnerd, considers Pee-Wee's Big Adventure, the wearing of tortoise-shell glasses and fashions by Ralph Lauren to be endorsements of nerddom. Uncoordinated clothing is "most necessary"(the litmus test for nerddom is in the details.) Notable nerds include Prince Charles, Mayor Koch, Woody Allen, Howard Cosell, Doc Severinson of the Tonight Show and Walter Mondale. During puberty, nerds hide copies of *Popular Mechanics* under their beds.

Nerds are now losing their stigma after "Revenge of the Nerds" and the advent of the microchip revolution. Girls want a guy who knows his way around the computer room--even if his eyeglasses are held together by a Band-Aid.

One funny incident happened in 1985 when one B.L. Chapman, as she is listed in the Cincinnati telephone book, started getting dozens of phone calls asking if she was a nerd. At first she was taken aback, and answered that, in fact she was a nerd. But when the caller asked if she was the Supreme Archnerd, she said "I guess I am a nerd, but I'm not the head one." Anyway, by the end of the first week, she had the routine down pat and could anticipate the questions. These wrong numbers from around the country didn't anger her, only make her curious. She turned to the local newspaper, who helped her find *Mr.* B.L. Chapman, the Supreme Archnerd. The meeting was very nerdy indeed, with Mr. B.L. giving Ms. B.L. a complimentary membership and a "IF U R A NERD HONK" bumper sticker. He handed her a copy of *Big Nerd News*, taught her the "drenami" greeting (think a minute) and apologized for the telephone mix-up.

Eighty-five percent of the members were nominated as nerds by someone else-- but members must be signed up by other nerds. Members can order a real "nerdy" clock, with the numbers on the face reversed so that it can only be read by looking into a mirror. There are nerd rubber stamps and nerd T-Shirts. The soon-to-be-a-hit-single "You Big Nerd" has been released for members' perusal, too. Note that ten percent of all ION sales are donated to the Muscular Dystrophy Association--after all, Jerry Lewis was the original nerd . By the way, DRENMAI is the "Secret" code word of all "official" nerds! Unofficial Nerds can be placed under Nerd arrest if they use DRENAMAI and can't prove their identity by showing their ID Card.

International Save the Pun Foundation
PO Box 5040, Station A., Toronto, ON, Canada M5W 1N4   (416) 486-1282
Founded: 1979   Members: 1000
Dues: $19.00 per year   Contact: John S. Crosbie

Founded by John S. Crosbie to "battle functional illiteracy with the sharp schtick of humor." *The Pundit* is published each month (even President Reagan receives one) and each January, the "10 best-stressed puns of the year" are announced. They respectfully submit the following:

A string walked into a bar one night and order a drink. The bartender looked at him and said, "We don't serve strings here."

Offended, the string left. Then a second string came in and asked for a drink. "Get lost!" the bartender cried, "We don't serve strings here!"

As the second string was leaving, a third showed up. The second paused to warn him, but the third was very thirsty, so he tied himself onto a knot and ruffled his hair before he approached the bar.

When the bartender glared at him and asked "Are you a string?," he replied, "No, I'm a frayed knot!"

and...

It is a little-known fact that when the renowned Bishop Tutu from Africa toured the United States last spring, he visited his relatives in Tennessee. Apparently, until then no one had been aware that he was a Chattanooga Tutu!

The group's motto is: "A Day Without Puns is like a Day Without Sunshine-- There is Gloom for Improvement!"

Joygerms Unlimited
PO Box 219, Eastwood Station, Syracuse, NY 13206   (315) 472-2779
Founded: 1981   Members: 30,000
Dues: No dues, just do..   Contact: Joan White

Founded to spread happiness, optimism and kindness. A Joygerm is any sincere man, woman or child who believes positively that the "bright side is the right side"; "there's no time like the pleasant"; "if you can't lick 'em-JOYdom; and "Antibody that's Antibody is a Joygerm!"

Joygerm Joan says, "learning that though the germ of joy, life holds hope and can be ah so wonderful and exhilarating. Happiness is in spite of, not because of; life's a blessing, not a burden and yes, Joy Begins when it dwells within."

Members range from an Abbey of nuns in Wales to an entire school of American Native children in Arizona. Joan says that "too many people look at the world through 'woes-colored' glasses and we want to change all that." She started the group after reading a funny article about a couple who were running a "woes and worries" club--people would buy the hour to have someone else do the worrying for them. Joan thought the idea too negative. As she said, "Joygerms Unlimited" was her own "Sulk Vaccine" for the grumps of the world.

Every July the Joygerm Parade is held in downtown Syracuse. The club has its own songs, flags, t-shirts, buttons, bumper stickers, and the club dance is the "Joygerm Jerk."

By sending a stamped self-addressed envelope, prospective members receive a membership card and literature infused with such upbeat messages as :
Catch Joygerm Fever: The Highly-Contagious, Wonderfully Incurable Disease Reaching Epidemic Proportion. Prescribed treatment: Large Daily Doses of Kindness and Courtesy.

One of the groups goals happens on January 8th -- National Joygerm Day. On this day:- Hug, Grin, Smile & Win Over at least one Gruff & Grumpy Grouch to the Joygerm Generation! Joygerm Mania Forever!

Lazy Bones Club
PO Box 467, Morrisville, NC 27560
Founded: 1986   Contact: Otis Broadwell
Dues: $5.00 lifetime membership   (King Boner)

They claim to be so lazy that they didn't get around to opening a bank account to deposit the membership checks...so they returned them. That's just one the surprises members might receive in this club. They've sent out Christmas cards in February with their motto: "I'll do it tomorrow." When these financial wizards can afford to, they would like to start a newsletter called *The Wish Bone*. Members receive a membership card and a certificate.

Limerick Special Interest Group
Box 365, Moffett, CA 94035
Founded: 1981   Members: 60
Dues: $15.00 per year   Contact: Arthur Deex

A collector or reader or writer,
Might find his day a bit brighter,
If he wrote to these folks,
He could try out his jokes,
In verses increasingly lighter.

National Association for the Advancement of Aardvarks in America
947 Perkins Ave., Waukesha, WI 53186
Founded: 1978   Members: 172
Dues: Write for details   Contact: Biff B. Byrne

"To present a fair and accurate picture of the aardvark" and to replace the bald
eagle as our national symbol with the aardvark.

National Knock-Knock Joke Club
205 Prune Tree Drive, Healdsburg, CA 95448   (707) 433-6259
Founded: 1979   Members: 10,000
Dues: $1.00 and a joke   Contact: Charles Orr

"Knock-Knock. Who's there?" Mr. Knock-Knock, as he is known in the *Guinness
Book of World Records*, has written and catalogued over 150,000 knock-knock jokes,
appeared on television and been heard on over 100 radio shows. He's planning
not only a national convention but also a contest for the best knock-knock of the
year. (Did you know that at one time knock-knock jokes were so popular that they
were given away in packets of 10 at the gas station as a premium for filling up
one's tank?)

Among Orr's gems:

Knock Knock. Who's there?
Marcus Welby. Marcus Welby who?
Marcus Welby dead for all you care!

Knock Knock. Who's there?
Truffles. Truffles who?
Nobody knows the Truffles I've had.

Knock Knock. Who's there?
Despair. Despair who?
Despair tire is flat.

Knock Knock. Who's there?
Lipset. Lipset who?
Lipset taste wine will
never taste mine.

Nurses for Laughter
3401 S.W. Illinois, Portland, OR 97201   (503) 225-7709
Founded: 1982   Members: 1000
Dues: $10.00 per year   Contact: Deborah Leiber

Putting humor into the health care system---lord knows it needs a laugh.

Pals of the Museum of Bad Art
PO Box 1009, Cedar Hill, TX 75104   (214) 827-3855
Founded: 1986   Members:
Dues: $15.00 per year   Contact: James "Big Bucks" Burnett

Tacky is the word here. The Museum of Bad Art is dedicated to displaying the very worst in modern kitsch. Originally the museum was only going to display bad record cover art (like *Tennessee Ernie Ford and the San Quentin Prison Choir* and *How to Decorate Your House with Utica Sheets and Towels*. But the cover art idea was too limiting. "We really felt there was a void out there," said co-founder Greta Poulsen. So, the curators opened the museum to other wonders of the modern world, such as 3-D Jesuses, black velveteen paintings and life-sized statues of Elvis, the King (at 200 pounds.) Housed in a 12' by 8' room at 6315 Prospect Street in Dallas, the museum is open to the public once a month.

Porlock Society
Department of English
University of Missouri, Columbia, MO 65211 (314) 882-3766
Founded: 1977   Members: 230
Dues: Write for details   Contact: Russell J. Meyer

You're sound asleep on your English homework--you open one eye and groan--"Only 500 more boring pages of this--why didn't anyone interrupt this guy and tell him?"

The Porlock Society interrupts to bring you this special announcement. As a public service to society and bored students everywhere, scholarly members (possibly wearing a cape with a big red E on it) have come to the rescue, picking out overlong, over-boring papers and literary works from the past, present and future, interrupting them as often and as loudly as possible. Members receive the journal, *Cogito Interruptus*.

Possum Admiration League
PO Box 2572, Owensboro, KY 42302   (502) 683-5481
Founded: 1984   Members: 8000

Dues: $5.00   Contact: Poor Ol' George

Cuntrary to poplar be-leaf...Possums ARE NOT born dead along the side of the road. Poor Ol' George knows lot bout dem critters. As founder of the Possum Admiration League, editor of the Possum Country News and the "Poor Ol' George" Calendur--he's made possums and the hillbilly twang his pastime. George says that since the United States has the eagle as its official bird...our next project will be to go to Warshington and get the Possum adopted as the Official National Marsupial of the United States. According to The Possum Calandur, "National Possum Week" has been declared, falling in Ok-tobur. And as for eating them, Poor Ol' George says that Possum is brain food. "Once you eat a possum, you'll never forget it."

The Poor Ol' George calandur also feeturs recipees, folklore, fav-o-rite towns, weatherlore and lotza other useless stuff. There's lotza special days, liek "the city slicker learns to cut firewood day," and "the start your own airline day." The calandur has a page of Krazy Laws: (supposedly real) "You must have a hunting license to set a trap for a mouse in California" and "It is i-legal to drive more than two thousand sheep down Hollywood Boulevard at one time."

Fer $4.95, you kin becum a Kaintucky Moonshiner. Fer $5.00, you kin get the next six issues of the ginny-wine, won'n'only *Possum County News. Possum County News* is Published Sprang, Simmer, Fawl and Winner. Its "All the News Taht's Fit to Print...and then Some!"

Puns Corps

3108 Dashiell Rd., Falls Church, VA 22042   (703) 533-3668
Founded: 1977   Members: 1000
Dues: Write for details   Contact: Robert L. Birch

Return form W-1016 and fill in S-1940 in triplicate.

Improvement of government jargon and the elimination of unintended ambiguities in writing, especially in Federal Government prose. Albatross Award for the "most uncatalogable and unfindable publication" and the Pedro Award for the "burro-crat" who helps people not find information. "One-Tooth Rhee Day (one-two-three) on January 23 (1/23) to "celebrate the creation of the confusionist branch of American government"

Punsters Unlimited (PU)

The Unicorn Hunters
Lake Superior State College, Sault Ste. Marie, MI 49783   (906) 635-2315
Founded: 1970   Contact: Earle Harris

Assesses puns as Certified true puns, groaners, or no pun at all. All puns are assigned a number, over the years more than 3,500 puns have been assigned series numbers. Send your pun for examination in a self-addressed envelope and PU will examine it. If it's not a pun, there is a checklist for what it may be. (e.g., a funny joke, a not very funny joke, a spoonerism, a limerick, an epigram, a smile, a gag, a wisecrack, a "We don't know what it is you sent us, but it is very funny, or a "We don't know what it is you sent us, and are sorry your sent it to us, and don't know what to do about it.") November 8th is the annual Aid and Abet Punsters Day-- purpose is to encourage punsters to make puns with elan; and to train upcoming generations in the fine art of punning; and to encourage the registration of new puns.

Punsters Unlimited says the following is "the greatest pun of all time: Though he's not very humble, there's no police like Holmes....A groaner variation on the same theme: Nero, watching Rome burn and noticing that the buildings were beginning to fall apart in most of the city, observed: Though it's beginning to crumble, there's no blaze like Rome."

Salvation and Laughter Together (SALT)

Box 6928, Fort Worth, TX 76115   (817) 923-1921
Founded: 1983   Members: 156
Dues: $7.00 per year   Contact: Robert J. Larremore

Religion and humor--some might wonder if they belong together. Theologins of SALT are seeking to develop a theology of humor that can be incorporated into everyday life. They conduct church training programs and seminars on religion and humor, as well as interviews with comedians. *L.I.G.H.T. (Laughter In God, History and Theology)* is the bi-annual journal.

Sarcastics Anonymous...and...Laugh Lovers

PO Box 1495., Pleasanton, CA 94566   (415) 462-3470
Founded: 1983   Members: 200
Dues: $15.00 per year   Contact: Dr. Virginia O. Tooper

"Please send me information immediately, so that I may become a member quickly before I lose the very small amount of interest I have in your organization," wrote one member to the Laugh Professor, Dr. Virginia O. Tooper. Tooper says that for years, she, too, was a victim of "sarcasm abuse." She learned at an early age to fight back with a sharp barb, but later she realized that SHE couldn't control her sarcasm, and she was down to only one friend--and HE wasn't calling! "Now, if I think of a searing, witty remark, I think, 'Oh, I'm so proud of myself.' But I don't say it. I run straight to the ladies' room. I write it down. I'm saving things for a book." Sarcastics Anonymous is for people who realize they are sarcastic and want to get it under control or are sarcastic and want to get better at it while enjoying the company of others of like mind and wit. Then there is a third category, Sarcanon, for those who must live or work with sarcastics. Members receive a year's subscription to *Laugh Lovers News* (many S.A.'s belong to Laugh Lovers, a group that has grown out of courses that Tooper gives on the value of humor.) The Laugh Professor says that the world needs to be able to control sarcasm, as it is impossible to get rid of it. Besides she said, "If we got rid of sarcasm, Don Rickles would have to go on food stamps."

As a quick lesson, Tooper says that when you are the victim of a sarcastic remark by a "friend" or office associate, you can: (a) play dumb, (b) deflect it, or (c) attack back. As an example:

The Sarcastic says to you, "I see you make all your own clothes."
You respond:
(Playing Dumb): "Yes," (smile) "this is one of the best, don't you think?"
(Deflecting It): "Yes, and what talent it takes when you don't have a sewing machine."
(Attacking Back): "Yes, I studied with your mother."

The Society of Victor Invictus

1346 Connecticut Avenue, NW, Washington, DC 20036
Founded: 1977   Members: 500+
Dues: $10.00 for life   Contact: Don McLaughlin

It all started with one of the most publicized tragedies of modern times to befall a giraffe---yes, a giraffe named Victor. It all started in 1977 when 15-year-old Victor "lost his footing and spread-eagled himself while attempting to be "of service" to Arabesque, one his three female giraffe friends at the Marwell Park Zoo," 70 miles from London. When Victor hit the ground, the world stopped. "'Winch him, float him, excavate him, do any damned thing, at any cost, but get him to his feet,' cried strong men in their anguish." Finally on the fourth day he made it, "inspired by the nudging nose of Arabesque and assisted by a crane operated by Her Majesty's Navy." Unfortunately, Victor did not live through the ordeal, and The Society of Victor Invictus was then formed to honor this fallen lover. At the first annual meeting, giraffe lovers packed in wall-to-wall, many in costume--sheep garb was popular, too. New members can join and receive the Victor emblem.
Motto: SURUM SEMPER (Ever Upwards)

Whimsical Alternatives Coalition Political Action Committee-- WACPAC

PO Box 53131, Washington, DC 20009   (202) 328-0199
Founded: April 1, 1982   Members: 1000
Dues: Donations accepted   Contact: Michael Grant

Are you a closet dictator? Know the seven warning signals.
Formed because politicians were taking themselves too seriously, WACPAC puts
laughs back into the political system. WACPAC's semi-annual event in D.C.
themes have included a fundraiser for deposed dictators---on April Fool's Day.
They've honored "Slime Man" of the year and presented the "Congressional
Medal de Marcos" for the best *fabricated* war record. (You might have noticed
them giving out "Leave it to Deaver" buttons on Capitol Hill.)

WACPAC invites you to participate in a new fundraising idea for the CIA's war in
Central America--**Buy Covert Bonds!**. "Reap enormous tax benefits which
heretofore were available only to drug dealers and organized crime." "At maturity,
we will redeem your bonds in the foreign nation and foreign currency of your
choice Or, if you prefer, you can rollover your bonds *and invest in whatever revolutions
are going on at the time.*"

World Humor and Irony Membership (WHIM)
English Department
Arizona State University, Tempe, AZ 85287   (602) 965-7592
Founded: 1980   Members: 1000
Dues: $25.00 membership/conference fee   Contact: Don L. F. Nilsen

The main function of WHIM is the presentation of the yearly International
Humor Conference, held over the weekend of April Fool's Day at Arizona State
University. Special events include the annual Larry Wilde Joke Telling Contest, a
Humor-in-Music Concert, presentations by humor writers and performers.

Unicorn, Ltd. Conglomerate
Unicorn Ltd. Conglomerate, Lake Superior State College
Office of College Relations, Sault Ste. Marie, MI 49783   (906) 635-2315
Dues: $3.00 per year   Contact: W. T. Rabe

"The Unicorn Hunters firmly believe that every man has a unicorn he is
predestined to hunt. It is not necessary actually to track, find and slay this beaste,
but only that the Quest be most diligently pursued."

The conglomerate is a truly American idea, embodying a wide range of activities.
See elsewhere for The World Sauntering Society, Punsters Unlimited, Friends of
Lizzie Borden, Old Soldiers of Baker Street of Two Saults and The Stone
Skipping and Gerplunking Club. Other activities include "Silent Record Week,"
promoting the virtues of silence in a world of cacophony and the Unicorn's
celebration of spring with the annual snowman burning . November 8th marks
"Aid and Abet Punsters Day," encouraging punmaker to make puns and June 1st
to 7th marks "Teacher "Thank You" Week, encouraging people to visit or call a
teacher or professor who influenced your life and send them a big red apple.

Lots of other fun stuff, too. *The Woods Runner* is the magazine of the Unicorn Hunters.

Up Uranus Society
PO Box 1369, Carmel, IN 46032
Write for more information

Uranus has a club too!! Members can receive the *Up Uranus* newsletter, t-shirts, bumper stickers etc. (From the newsletter) "The narrow shaft of knowledge penetrating Uranus should not be broken off." Uranus--"Not a place where the Sun never shines, but certainly a place where the Sun Shines faintly."

FROM THE BEYOND

Far-out is nearby, compared with this otherworldly crew.

Aerial Phenomena Research Organization

3597 West Grape Drive, Tucson, AZ 85741   (602) 323-1825
Founded: 1952   Members: 1200
Dues: $20.00 per year   Contact: Jim Lorenzen

What are UFOs?
Why are they here?
and Where do they come from?

The Aerial Phenomena Research Organization is trying to find scientifically acceptable explanations to the phenomena of Unidentified Flying Objects. UFOs have been spotted in almost every country on earth, in urban and rural areas, on the ground as well as in the air. UFOs have been mentioned many time in the Bible, in cave drawings in France and in the ancient sculptures of Japan. There are thousands of witnesses each year, including ex-President Carter, astronauts, airplane pilots, military personnel and others. The Aerial Phenomena Research Organization claims that the reason for government secrecy on UFOs is obvious-- any country that could possess even **one** of the powers of n UFO (the ability to disappear from radar screens, the ability to speed up to 5000 miles per hour and abruptly change direction or the ability to disrupt electric power transmission) could rule the earth.

Amalgamated Flying Saucer Clubs of America

PO Box 39, Yucca Valley, CA 92284   (619) 365-1141
Founded: 1959   Members: 5600
Dues: $1.00 per year   Contact: Gabriel Green

Gabriel Green wears his message attached to the lapel of his polyester suit: "Flying Saucers are real." Green, founder and president of the Amalgamated Flying Saucer Clubs of America, says of UFOs that "hundreds of people have not only seen them, but have actually ridden in these craft and personally met their occupants. These 'contactees' discovered that the pilots and other crew members of these interplanetary spaceships were NOT grotesque beings, but were, instead, highly intelligent, friendly, men and women from civilizations evolved far in advance of our own." Green says that the "Space People" have come to show us the way out of our problems. "Some of the many amazing benefits of the knowledge already received from the Space People--or promised by them if we will welcome them in a friendly manner-- are: elimination of disease, poverty and smog...and for many living today, personal journeys to other planets beyond the stars."

The club's information sheet explains that the Space People "are humanoid, and they can and do pass among us unnoticed...Their height varies from about 3 to 10 feet, depending upon their environmental and racial backgrounds. They are often quite good-looking and usually retain a youthful appearance, despite life spans that extend over several hundred years." We are told that these space people come from planets much like our own, which is why they look like us. Furthermore, "underground bases with artificial gravity and air supply are maintained on our Moon, and on other Moons."

The information sheet is a wonderful wealth of information on the questions you've been asking most: "How do Saucers Disappear Instantaneously?" (Answer:electromagnetics); "What is the purpose of the Space People in coming to Earth?" (Answer: they want to save us from destroying ourselves), and "What is the nature of the economic system on other advanced planets?" (Answer: no taxation and insurance is free!.) Finally, the group's newsletter, *Flying Saucer International*, says that if the end of the world comes, spaceships will swoop out of the sky and evacuate up to 10% of the world's population.

Members can get copies of reports from people who have contacted aliens, as well as "tape-recorded messages from space people." The club even offers a language course in the universal tongue that is spoken by all the members of the "Universal Alliance of Planets."

American Association of Electronic Voice Phenomena

726 Dill Rd., Severna Park, MD 21146   (301) 647-8742
Founded: 1982   Members: 200
Dues: $20.00 per year   Contact: Sarah Estep

"Established to Investigate Evidence as a Result of the Electronic Voice that we Survive Death," the AAEVP is interested in the evidence of post-mortem survival, particularly verbal communication from the deceased, or electronic voice phenomena. While investigating evidence that suggests individual consciousness survives death, members tape record the voices, and hold workshops in places like Egypt, which is a "favored" location for EVP transmission. They publish a quarterly newsletter and hold a yearly convention. The society's *Taped Survival Project* is a chance for members to record a short message on a cassette containing information he or she will communicate to the Society's survival board after death.

American Association of Meta-Science

PO Box 1182, Huntsville, AL 35807   (205) 881-7165

Founded: 1977   Members: 200
Dues: Write for details   Contact: William F. Sowder

Explorers and observers of the paranormal as well as UFOs, members have developed and use special instruments to measure, detect and stimulate "subtle, unseen energies." Helps members develop their psychic and spiritual abilities.

American Society for Psychical Research

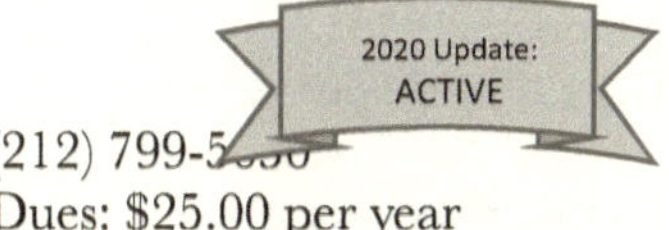

5 West 73 St., New York, NY 10023   (212) 799-5050
Founded: 1885   Dues: $25.00 per year

The ASPR was formed to advance the understanding of phenomena alleged to be paranormal: telepathy, clairvoyance, precognition, psychokinesis and related occurrences. The organization works on research, investigating reports of spontaneous occurrences, telepathic or precognitive dreams, apparitions, poltergeists, hauntings and the like. Members receive the quarterly newsletter and journal.

American Society of Dowsers

Danville, VT 05828   (802) 684-3417
Founded: 1961   Members: 3500
Dues: $20.00 per year ($200 lifetime)   Contact: Barbara H. Roberts

Members learn how to find water with (or without) a forked stick, pendulums and rods. These water witches, or diviners, can locate mineral deposits, oil and various other objects through these extrasensory techniques. Dowsing was routinely used in past centuries to locate wells. American colonists apparently used dowsers to locate thousands of wells in early America. The American Society of Dowsers estimates that nearly a quarter-million water wells sunk on the Atlantic seaboard since Colonial times have been located by "witching."

Today 25,000 practice the arcane art in the United States, but The American Society of Dowsers says that anyone can learn to dowse. A professional dowser can tell you exactly where to find water, at what depth, how many gallons per minute the well will produce and whether the water will be drinkable. Some dowsers insist on using a cherry branch or branch from a hazel bush. Others carry plastic "Y" rods--but dowsers insist that it is not the tool but the dowser that does the work: the tool is just a means of turning subconscious ability into visible action. A couple of years ago, a well-drilling company would flatly refuse to dig a well at a location that had been doused, but the "weird" stigma is not as strong today, with some well companies actually employing dowsers. The American Society of Dowsers believes that dowsing is a skill that can be learned, and shared by anyone and everyone. They offer beginners' courses, with beginners' divining rods. There are 64 regional chapters all over the country, with people who are

using their unconscious brainpower to do what they thought was impossible.
Members receive *The American Dowser*, and the yearly convention is held in
Danville in mid-September.

Ancient Astronaut Society

1921 St. Johns Ave., Highland Park, IL 60035   (312) 295-8899
Founded: 1973   Members: 4000
Dues: $10.00 per year   Contact: Gene M. Phillips

Members believe that the earth might have been visited by aliens who created
advanced civilizations in prehistoric times. Founder Gene Phillips has traveled the
earth to prove that "a highly-developed, technological civilization existed on Earth
before our recorded history, and that intelligent beings from outer space visited
our planet many thousands of years ago."

Members claim that the ancient astronaut theory can explain such questions as:
•The beginnings of life on Earth
•The emergence of intelligence on Earth
•The difference between the ape species and intelligent human beings (the missing
link)
•The original core of global mythology
•The origins of the giant figures carved or drawn on the earth as if to be seen
only from the air.

Membership is open to everyone, and members receive the bi-monthly
publication *Ancient Skies* and a membership certificate. The society also conducts
field trips around to world to sites in Egypt, Mexico, Malta, Bolivia, Peru or
wherever the signs of Ancient Astronauts have appeared.

Associated Readers of Tarot International

PO Box 803, Dubois, PA 15801
Founded: 1972   Members: 900
Dues: Write for details   Contact: Alex Aspinall

A "new age" group of Tarot readers, who wish to learn the arts of divination and
meditation using Tarot. Members learn how to use the allegorical representations
of the Tarot cards.

Astro Musical Research

PO Box 118, New York, NY 10033
Founded: 1980   Members: 350
Dues: Write for details   Contact: Gerald Jay Markoe

Astromusic is "the music of the spheres," "a translation of the planets at your birth into music on cassette." A translation of one's computerized birth chart or horoscope into a musical composition, when listened to, will result in enhanced meditation, claims founder Gerald Markoe. . "We are all born with certain 'notes'--how we 'play' them is up to us," he says. One member said that the Astromusic "contains many of the same tunes I used to improvise on the piano years ago! I can recognize the music as coming out of my own psyche." Anyone who purchases an Astromusic cassette is automatically a member.

Awareness Research Foundation
DeSoto Square, #29, 35 Ritter Rd., Hayesville, NC   (704) 389-8672
Founded: 1969
Dues: Write for details   Contact: Helen I. Hoag

Speaking of metaphysics, space ships, reincarnation and the "cosmic truths," The Awareness Research Foundation says that there are seven universes, each with a "governing lord." Another notion is that each person experiences many different "stages of evolution" before joining the human race. Helen Hoag says that while the group is not a religious organization, they are spiritual. They publish *Meet the Lords* monthly and a number of books including *My Visits to Other Planets*, *Technique of Past Lives Recall*, *My Lives on Atlantis*, and *The Three Missing Planets*.

Borderline Sciences Research Foundation
PO Box 429, Garberville, CA 95440   (619) 724-2043
Founded: 1945   Members: 600
Dues: $20.00 per year   Contact: Thomas Joseph
Brown

The borderline is the region between the visible and the invisible, between fantasy and reality. BSRF's subjects of inquiry include hollow earth theories, research into the borderline of the mind, dowsing, flying saucers and telepathy, UFOs, Tesla technology, and photography of the invisible. Members receive a bi-monthly journal.

Center for Borderline History
PO Box 1792, Station "E," Victoria, BC, Canada V8W 2Y3
Founded: 1984   Members: Write for details
Dues: $12.00 per year   Contact: Robert Velick

Members are interested in the study of the influences of occult forces upon the evolution of the world. The center publishes the *International Conspiracy Digest* quarterly, as well as the book *International Conspiracies and Their Occult Origins* with reports of the inner workings of "the Rosicrucians," "The Druids Cult of the All-Seeing Eye" "the Golden Dawn," "The Great White Brotherhood" and other occult groups. Lots of super-strange occult stuff here.

Center for UFO Studies

PO Box 1621, Lima, OH 45802 (419) 222-4324
Founded: 1973 Members: 2000
Dues: $25.00 per year Contact: John P. Timmerman

Collects and studies UFO sighting reports and publishes findings. Members receive the Center's journal.

Central Premonitions Registry

PO Box 482, Times Sq. Station, New York, NY 10036
Founded: 1968 Members: 8
Dues: Write for details Contact: Robert D. Nelson

Got a funny feeling? This registry is the first private agency in the US dedicated to the "scientific evaluation of premonitions and their use as an early warning system for assassinations, plane crashes, floods, fires and other catastrophes." People who experience dreams and premonitions of impending disasters relating to state, national or international disasters are asked to send them to the registry. The premonitions are coded and put into categories, such as the death of personalities, war, disasters, the outcome of elections, and messages and visitations." Psychically gifted individuals are encouraged to participate in dream and telepathy studies at local dream labs.

Collectors of Unusual Data- International (COUD-I)

2313 Shields Ave., Jennings, MO 63136 (314) 388-0087
Founded: 1985 Members: 25
Dues: None Contact: Raymond Nelke

COUD-I members are collectors of unusual facts, information and trivia. Strange aspects of JFK's assassination, unusually meteorological events (like frogs falling out of the sky), and perpetual motion devices are just some of the oddities they get into.

Committee for the Scientific Investigation of the Paranormal

PO Box 229, Central Park Station, Buffalo, NY 14215 (716) 834-3222
Founded: 1976 Members: 200
Dues: Write for details Contact: Paul Kurtz

Paranormal events, UFOs, astrology and psychic phenomena are examined encouraging scientific skepticism on these issues and provides a "dissenting scientific point of view." Awards the "Responsibility in Journalism Award" for fair reporting of paranormal claims.

Dolphin Society

PO Box 2271, Wilmington, CA 90748   (213) 328-2032
Founded: 1975
Dues: $8.00 per year for newsletter   Contact: Jerry Doran

About .004% of the world's population are "merfolk," dolphins who have temporarily shifted to human form in order to lead humans to higher consciousness, claims the Dolphin Society. Among the group's goals: to help humans reclaim their heritage as Gods through integration with the advanced civilization of the Sea; to establish diplomatic relations with dolphins, whales, elephants and the Earth; and to increase human intelligence, health, lifespan and psychic powers through underwater birth and dolphin midwives.

Founder Jerry Doran was one of three crew members of an unarmed ship to avenge whale hunting by ramming and destroying the Sierra, an infamous "pirate" whaling ship which had killed over 20,000 whales. (True to his reverence for life, no one was hurt in the incident.) An experimenter in human/dolphin communication, Doran maintains that all that's really needed is a device to raise human speech by 8 octaves, and to lower dolphin speech by 8 octaves. The gentle dolphin's word for love, Doran says, is "TePuu-Hii."

The society is accepting applications for a planned interspecies community in the South Pacific, where human, elephants, whales, apes and dolphins will be equals. Children will grow up in the ocean, attending daycare centers staffed by dolphins and "non-threatening humans." Its spirit of cooperation and gentleness will "avoid child abuse, bullying and other negative factors of human culture." (They have land in Hawaii and practical plans for an artificial island in international waters.) Once people have gained dolphin consciousness, says Doran, dolphin starships will land, and we will be teleported to other star systems and dimensions.

The Dolphin Society was incorporated as a church in 1985. Training in out-of-body travel with dolphin and whale avatars is available. The newsletter, *Wetimes,* is quarterly and transcripts of conversations with Mermaids cost $5.00.

Dozenal Society of America

Math Department
Nassau Community College, Garden City, NY 11530 (516) 669-0273
Founded: 1944   Members: 144
Dues: $12.00 per year ($144 lifetime)   Contact: Gene Zirkel

The advantages of using Base 12 in mathematics, counting, musical notation, computers, weights and measures are clear to this group. President Gene Zirkel says "practical people almost never measure in tens: Bakers use dozens, carpenters divide the foot into 12 inches, Grocers (gross-ers) use 12 dozens and druggists and jewelers divide the pound into 12 ounces." They have a 144-volume library of Base Twelve books, publish the *Duodecimal Bulletin* and well as a number of books of the subject of 12 in counting. (True to form, their dues are $12 and they limit membership to 144.)

Dracula World Enterprises

Penthouse North, 29 Washington Square W., New York, NY 10011
Founded: 1980   Contact: Shelley Leigh-Hunt

"Concerned with the many aspects of vampirism."

ESP Research Associates Foundation

Union National Plaza, Suite 1660, Little Rock, AR 72201   (501) 375-5377
Founded: 1962   Members: 450
Dues: Write for details   Contact: Al Pollard

Members believe that they have extrasensory perception and explore its possible uses.

Fair Witness Project

4219 W. Olive St., Suite 247, Burbank, CA 91505 (818) 506-8365
Founded: 1984   Members: 150
Dues: $20.00 per year   Contact: William L. Moore

"When a paranormal event makes headlines, truth is often the last thing to be examined." Fair Witness is a group of scientists and journalists who investigate what they call cases of "high-strange singularity" involving the paranormal phenomena. Such cases include UFO abductions, or discoveries about the Great Pyramids. They report the facts--and only the facts--back to the public, thereby acting as a "fair witness" to the event. Members receive the monthly *Focus* newsletter, as well as a listing of books and publications on the paranormal.

Ghost Research Society

PO Box 205, Oak Lawn, IL 60454   (312) 425-5163
Founded: 1978   Members: 200
Dues: $10 per year ($250 lifetime)   Contact: Dale Kaczmarek

Dale Kaczmarek is the original "Ghostbuster." Kaczmarek, who's president of the Ghost Research Society, investigates claims of hauntings, with field trips to "haunted sites" (which Dale calls "excursions into the unknown.") Kaczmarek has worked with psychics and mediums to successfully "clear" or "deghost" dozens of homes in past years. Members try to prove that man exists after death and that ghosts inhabit the earth. "Ghosts cannot understand why nobody can see or talk to them and many times this can lead to emotional problems connected with the ghost as well," says Kaczmarek. "The ghost may then attempt to communicate with the living in various ways: in the form of psychic scents, footsteps, slamming doors, voices, the movement of objects, etc." Dale says that the ghost hunter, with the help of a psychic, acts as a sort of therapist for the ghost, communicating through a trance and helping the ghost to evolve spiritually and leave everyone on earth alone. Kaczamarek sponsors lectures and "ghost tours." Members receive *Ghost Trackers* newsletter.

Ground Saucer Watch

13238 N. Seventh Dr., Phoenix, AZ 85029	(602) 942-7216
Founded: 1957	Members: 500
Dues: Write for details	Contact: William H. Spaulding

Attention: Scientists and engineers who want to set the record straight on UFOs once and for all! Their objectives are to provide a safe forum for anyone to come forth with a claim of aerial phenomena, without fear of being ridiculed or made the front cover story of the *National Enquirer*. Also to give the media, some sane information on the subject. They do what they can to use honest-to-goodness measuring devices in their work.

Haunt Hunters

c/o Goodwilling	
963 Clayton Rd., Ballwin, MO 63011	(314) 831-1379
Founded: 1965	Members: 300
Dues: Write for details	Contact: Gordon J. Hoener

They don't seem to actually *hunt* ghosts, but act as a clearinghouse for experiences and information of ghosts, haunted houses and other unexplainable goodies.

International Association for Near-death Studies

University of Connecticut, Storrs, CT 06268	(203) 486-4172
Founded: 1981	Members: 800
Dues: Write for details	Contact: John Alexander

"Hey, you died? So did I!" Members have all passed into the temporary and fuzzy state of "clinical death," or have passed very near to death. The group supports and promotes scientific study into the subject of near-death experiences. Members record their experiences on paper or audiotape. The most popular account is of temporarily leaving one's body for a quick float above--the typical "out-of-the-body experience." Members receive *Vital Signs* newsletter.

International Imagery Association

PO Box 1046, Bronx, NY 10471
Founded: 1979
Dues: $50.00 per year   Contact: Judith Marks

Dedicated to studying mental imagery, the source of our creativity. Members conduct ongoing dialogues on how imagery aids in fulfilling human potential. Conferences and journal for members.

International Tesla Society

Box 150, 330-A W. Uintah, Suite 215, Colorado Springs, CO 80901
(303) 570-0876
Founded: 1984
Dues: $18.00 per year   Contact: Ted S. McKee

It's hard to believe, but one of the most brilliant men of modern times fed the pigeons in the park each morning without fail, cleaned the silverware and crystal in fancy restaurants with *exactly* 18 napkins and claimed to have received signals from distant planets. And he died penniless on the docks of New York City.

Only since his death has Nikola Tesla has been honored for the invention of the radio (long before Marconi), the polyphase electric motor and the radio-guided torpedo. After coming to the US from Austria-Hungry, Tesla went to work briefly for Edison. He didn't stay long, though, because of the famous "war of the currents" between them. Edison believed that direct current was the way of the future, while Tesla saw that alternating current could be transmitted over long distances without loss of power. The argument kept them apart, kept Tesla from winning a Nobel Prize in 1915 ...but in the end, Tesla won the "war of the currents."

Tesla's ideas ran from the practical to the very far-out. He devised a high-energy generator in his lab in Colorado that shot out millions of volts of electricity into the sky...simulating lightning bolts. He carried an electric vibrator in his pocket that he claimed could split the earth in two...because it mirrored the frequency of the earth (not until 1960 were scientists able to confirm that his calculation of that frequency was indeed correct.) Tesla conceived of death rays that could melt an airplane 250 miles away, "Star Wars" systems, and ways to send telegraphic messages to the stars.

The Society started with a Tesla Symposium in 1984 (another is planned for 1988.) The goals today are the formation of a Tesla museum, establishing the Tesla Research Laboratories and acquiring a Tesla bust. A newsletter is published and a number of interesting publications are sold through *High Energy Enterprises*. One book is on how to build your own high-energy Tesla Coil (and make artificial lightning in your own backyard!) Other books are on anti-gravity and about lost civilizations on Mars.

Metascience Foundation

c/o MetaScience Annual
Box 32, Kingston, RI 02881   (401) 294-2414
Founded: 1976   Members: 2000
Dues: $25 per year   Contact: Marc Seifer

Remote viewing, dream telepathy, psychic photography, precognition, psychokinesis, life after death, ghosts, astral travel, and the multidimensionality of time--these are just some of the otherworldly subjects that the Metascience Foundation conducts research on. The quarterly journal has included articles on "Attempts at Photographing the Human Aura with Infra-Red," "Poltergeists" and much, much more!

Michigan/Canadian Bigfoot Information Center

152 W. Sherman, Caro, MI 48723   (517) 673-2715
Founded: 1970   Members: 4
Dues: Write for details   Contact: Wayne W. King

Gather information about the "Sasquatch" or "Bigfoot," those large, hairy, scary manlike creatures. They're trying to obtain a Sasquatch specimen, conducting overnight vigils in areas where the nocturnal creature has been spotted, with assistance from anthropologists and wildlife pathologists. The group has been offered hundreds of thousands of dollars to catch Bigfoot...by a foreign government (Wayne King won't tell us which one, though. Your guess?) Mr. King and others have made plaster footprint casts of Bigfoot, but are still searching for hard proof of the furry fellow's existence.

Mind Science Foundation

8301 Broadway, Suite 100, San Antonio, TX   78209   (512) 821-6094
Founded: 1958
Dues: Write for details   Contact: Tom Slick

Does research on extrasensory perception and altered states of consciousness.

Mutual UFO Network (MUFON)

103 Oldtowne Rd., Seguin, TX 78155   (512) 379-9216
Founded: 1969   Members: 1500
Dues: $25.00 per year   Contact: Walter H. Andrus, Jr.

The Mutual UFO Network was formed to continue the scientific investigation of UFOs when the U.S. Air Force was planning to close *Project Blue Book*, their official investigation into UFO activity. MUFON is now the world's largest UFO membership organization. Members include pilots, doctors, psychologists, military personnel, engineers, and other interested people, investigating the unresolved enigma of UFOs. Operates Amateur Radio Networks which quickly receive and disseminate UFO sighting reports and current info on the little green men. Members receive the *MUFON UFO Journal* and they meet at the yearly convention.

National Council for Geocosmic Research

28 Sustuehanna Ave., Towson, MD 21204   (301) 828-NCGR
Founded: 1957   Members: 3000
Dues: $25.00 per year ($5.00 initiation fee)   Contact: Linda Martin

The brightest stars in the world of astrology come together at the National Counsel for Geocosmic Research. NCGR was formed as a cooperative venture between psychologists and astrologers to explore the "interaction between the earth and cosmos." While most people are interested in the psychological aspects of astrology, many members are scientifically or mathematically inclined. Special interest groups include financial (member Arch Crawford has a newsletter on stock market analysis, and another expert has written on gold cycles and astrology), heliocentric astrology, and meditation techniques in astrology. Members receive the twice-yearly journal, *Geocosmic News*, plus a monthly member letter and bi-annual directory of members. They hold conferences three times a year.

National Investigations Committee on UFOs

PO Box 5, Van Nuys, CA 91408   (818) 989-5942
Founded: 1967   Members: 2000
Dues: $20.00 per year   Contact: Dr. Frank E. Stranges

What is the *truth* concerning UFOs and associated phenomena? Members receive the confidential *Space-Link Letter*. Also, an audio tape series is available for members with some compelling titles like: "How to Become an Interplanetary Traveler" (we want to know if the budget travel version is available yet), "The Hollow Earth Mystery" and "The Day You Vanish from this Planet" (Is this finally the secret to where Jim Morrison and Jimmy Hoffa are?)

Network of Kindred Spirits

7005 Florida St., Chevy Chase, MD 20815   (301) 654-2353
Founded: 1980   Contact: Charles H. Simpkinson

These therapists meet to talk about the relationship between spirituality and psychology, and how it affects their lives.

New York FORTEAN Society

PO Box 20024, New York, NY 10025
Dues: Write for details   Contact: John A. Keel

Members meet for lectures and field trips to sites of weird unexplained happenings in the New York Area.

Occidental Society of Metempiric Analysis

Box 308, Simla, CO 80835   (303) 541-2544
Founded: 1977   Members: 20
Dues: Write for details   Contact: Robert J. Everhart

Robert J. Everhart has been tracking the unexplained for over 40 years. He said of the strangest experiences he's had, twice his things were "turned every which way but loose in the office due to poltergeists!!" (Author's note: My wife has used *that* excuse before.) Members receive *The Beacon* every once in a while. Mr. Everhart's goal is to one day open a museum of metempiric phenomena--including the occult, ESP and everything else.

Pennsylvania Association for the Study of the Unexplained

6 Oakhill Avenue, Greensburg, PA 15601   (412) 838-7768
Founded: 1981   Members: 80
Dues: $3.00 per month   Contact: Stan Gordon

"Taking a serious, scientific look into UFOs, Bigfoot and other Phenomena, " their perusals include unexplained animal mutilations, religious miracles, strange geological formations, unexplainable artifacts, and "out-of-place" animal sightings of panthers, monkeys and lions. "UFOs and creatures such as Bigfoot, black panthers and the Eastern cougar are all reported yearly in Pennsylvania," says founder Stan Gordon, who has been interested in the unexplained since the age of 10. He says that all PASU members are volunteers who spend their time and money to help investigate reports that are phoned in on the "hotline."

Planetary Society

65 N. Catalina Ave., Pasadena, CA 91106   (818) 793-5100
Founded: 1980   Members: 110,000
Dues: Write for details   Contact: Dr. Louis Friedman

"Devoted to a realistic continuing program of planetary exploration and the search for extraterrestrial life."

Project Starlight International

PO Box 599, College Park, MD 20740
Founded: 1964   Contact: Ray Stanford

Getting the hard facts on UFOs, Project Starlight International uses measuring devices such as manetometers, gravimeters, spectrometers, radar, and lasers to prove or disprove the existence of UFOs.

Project VISIT - Vehicle Internal Systems Investigative Team

PO Box 877, Friendswood, TX 77546   (713) 488-2884
Founded: 1976   Members: 50
Dues: Write for details   Contact: John F. Schnessler

These engineers and scientists are asking questions like: How do UFOs work? Are the engine systems similar in different sightings? One of the VISIT committees is responsible for hypothesizing advanced propulsion concepts.

Psychic Detective Bureau

Aries, Inc., PO 24571, Creve Couer, MO 63141
Contact: B.C. Jaegers

These psychics volunteer to solve crimes, working with the police and the FBI.

Psychic Science International Special Interest Group..or...PSI SIG

7514 Belleplain Dr., Huber Heights, OH 45424   (513) 236-0361
Founded: 1976   Members: 200
Dues: $14.00 per year   Contact: Richard Allen Strong

Psychic Science International is a special interest group of Mensa (see separate entry), holding discussions on theories of existence and reality, human auras, clairvoyance, mental and thought projection, telepathy, dowsing, psychokinesis, survival after death, and other topics. Members receive the *PSI SIG* newsletter and are invited to the yearly conference.

Psychical Research Foundation

Psychology Department
West Georgia College, Carrollton, GA 30118   (919) 968-4956
Founded: 1960
Dues: Write for details   Contact: William G. Roll

This educational research center investigates the possibilities of continuation of consciousness after death of the physical body--with research on out-of-body experiences, hauntings, poltergeist activity and mediumship.

Sasquatch Investigations of Mid-America

PO Box 441, Edmond, OK 73083   (405) 947-1332
Dues: Write for details   Contact: Hayden C. Hewes

Sasquatch or Bigfoot is large, hairy and nocturnal, usually sighted in thickly-wooded regions. (Doesn't hang out in the 7-11 much.) He's about eight feet tall, walks upright, intelligent and allegedly peaceful. The group has a thousand reports of sightings.

Shroud of Turin Research Project

PO Box 7, Amston, CT 06231   (203) 537-2387
Founded: 1978   Members: 35
Dues: Write for details   Contact: Thomas F. D'Muhala

The Shroud of Turin is a linen cloth, with an image of a man's face on it that first turned up nearly seven centuries ago, belonging to a French knight. Many believe it to be the burial cloth of Christ, with the face being his. The purpose of the research project is to determine the chemistry of the cloth and the image on it, to verify or refute the authenticity of the Shroud. Non-destructive testing is being completed to analyze the images and stains on the Shroud.

Skynet

257 Sycamore Glen, Pasadena, CA 91105   (213) 256-8655
Founded: 1965   Members: 100
Dues: Write for details   Contact: Ann Druffel

SKYNET is a network of UFO spotters and documenters in Southern California. Members have some of the most advanced equipment--telescopes, photographic, electromagnetic and tracking equipment. Members act as an alert team, ready to verify UFOs from different locations around Southern California. After a sighting call comes in to the SKYNET center, members are alerted and they contact other members who live in the line-of-sight where the UFO is traveling. The heart of SKYNET is the membership list and its large maps, sprinkled with colored dots representing the locations of members. Members include professional astronomers, physicists, an aerospace engineer and others. Coordinator and author Ann Druffel says, "Fear of ridicule keeps many UFO witnesses from speaking out as freely as they should." Druffel feels that when people are more willing to share their sightings of UFOs, then verifying their existence will become easier. Skynet is affiliated with MUFON (see separate entry.)

Society for the Investigation of the Unexplained...or SITU

Box 265, Little Silver, NJ 07739   (201) 842-5229
Founded: 1965   Members: 1500
Dues: $12.00 per year   Contact: Robert C. Warth

They're here...dozens of file cabinets chock-full of information on **everything** from Loch Ness monster type creatures spotted in North America, to reports of living frogs and toads found entombed in rock...manufactured objects found in chucks of coal...giant, red-haired mummies...reports on the discovery of Atlantis...reports of giant winged creatures from various areas of the world, larger than any known birds...rainmaking...travel in the fourth dimension...**anything** that traditional scientists won't touch. SITU uses this information for articles in the society's quarterly journal, *Pursuit.*

Space and Unexplained Celestial Events Research Society

PO Box D, Jane Lew, WV 26378   (304) 269-2719
Founded: 1954   Members: 6000
Dues: Write for details   Contact: Gray Barker

People interested in flying saucers.

Tesla Memorial Society

453 Martin Rd., Lackawanna, NY 14218   (716) 822-0281
Founded: 1979   Members: 1200+
Dues: Write for details   Contact: Nicholas Kosanovich

Triskaidekaphobia Illuminatus Society

938 Westminister St., NW, Washington, DC 20001   (202) 232-0269
Founded: 1984
Dues: Write for details   Contact: Malcolm Riviera

These people believe the number 13 has the ability to affect the balance of world power and political structures through the Illuminati--the *enlightened* people. They seek to isolate seeming unconnected events caused by the numerical forces inherent in the number 13, correlating the meanings of these events. The group has a task force to eliminate triskaidekaphobia (fear of the number 13) from society. Members receive *The 13th Illuminated Stratum* newsletter.

Vampire Research Center

PO Box 252, Elmhurst, NY 11373
Founded: 1972 — Members: 20
Dues: Write for details — Contact: Dr. Stephen Kaplan

Vampirologists, sociologists, anthropologists and hematologists are conducting a demographic study of vampires. They distribute questionnaires to gather info on individuals who believe that they or people they know are vampires ("Here ya go, Vlad...fill it out. Need a sharp pencil?") Come visit the Vampirology Hall of Fame.

Vampire Studies Society

PO Box 205, Oak Lawn, IL 60454 — (312) 749-7697
Founded: 1977
Dues: Write for details — Contact: Marin V. Riccardo

They study vampires in folklore, legends, and literature, and hold "psychic rap sessions."

Vestigia

56 Brookwood Rd., Stanhope, NJ 07874 — (201) 347-3638
Founded: 1976 — Members: 150
Dues: Write for details — Contact: Robert E. Jones

Vestigia is a Latin word meaning "footprint." This group of scientists, engineers and others conducts research into the unexplained.

PEERING INTO THE FUTURE....

Earthrise

PO Box 120, Annex Sta., Providence, RI 02901 — (401) 272-7145
Founded: 1972 — Contact: Thomas Carleton

Researchers and educators interested in long term global trends. Distributors of the "Global Futures Game," a simulation on the world for the next 50 years.

Future Problem Solving Program

Coe College, Cedar Rapids, IA 52402
Founded: 1974

(319) 399-8688
Members: 100,000
Contact: Anne B. Crabbe

Training students to think creatively about their future. Problems on robotics, UFOs, nuclear waste, nuclear war, ocean communities and others are chosen by teams of students building problem solving, research and teamwork skills.

Futures Information Network

Mental Health Research Institute, University of Michigan
Ann Arbor, MI 48104
Founded: 1971

(313) 764-2585
Contact: Manfred Kochen

Compiling trends, into forecasts and proposals on the future.

Institute for Alternative Futures

1405 King St., Alexandria, VA 22314
Founded: 1977

(703) 960-7855
Contact: Clement Bezold

Founded by Clement Bezold and Alvin Toffler, author of *Future Shock*, Bezold says that everyone is a futurist and people choose their own future: "Each of us carries models of the future around in our heads." Bezold says that the job of the Institute for Alternative Futures is to make the future more conscious. The Institute works in the range of 10 to 50 years in the future (usually 10 to 25 years.) Many projects deal with projections on the shape of the workplace of the future and the role that technology will play. Books and reports available include *Pharmacy in the 21st Century*, *The Future of Florida* and *Blood Services in 1995*.

Institute for Twenty-First Century Studies

108 Robinson St., Chinchilla, PA 18410
Founded: 1959
Dues: Write for details

(717) 587-5719
Members: 225
Contact:Prof. Theodore
Cogswell

Professional authors, editors and artists in the science fiction and fantasy genre. With many well-known members (Arthur C. Clarke) from countries around the world, and meeting once a year.

L5 Society

1060 E. Elm Street, Tucson, AZ 85719
Founded: 1975

(602) 622-6351
Members: 6000

Dues: $30.00 per year   Contact: Phillip K. Chapman

"To create a spacefaring civilization that will establish communities beyond the
Earth" is the stated purpose of L5. The group's name refers to a point in the
Earth-Moon system where little or no energy would be required to keep an object
in a stationary position, relative to Earth and Moon's orbit. L5'ers lobby their
elected officials as well as the National Commission on Space to make settlements
in space a priority and a reality. L5 believes that space civilizations are
scientifically feasible today. Members from around the world receive the *L5*
newsletter nine times per year and *Space Frontier* magazine quarterly. Starting in
1987, L5 will merge with the National Space Society.

World Future Society

4916 St. Elmo St., Bethesda, MD 20814   (301) 656-8274
Founded: 1966   Members: 25,000
Dues: Write for details   Contact: Edward Cornish

World Futurists believe that we *can* shape our future. "No one knows exactly what
will happen in the future, but by studying the many possible things that might
happen, people can more rationally decide on the sort of future that would be
most desirable and then work to achieve it." Members from over 80 countries join
to discuss such topics as "Family Life in a Computerized Home" and
"Electronically-Delivered Education" The society has published over 30 books,
and issues *The Futurist* magazine each month. The futurists are best known for
their yearly forecasts of the future...these are not predications, they explain, but
possibilities. Some of these "Futurables" (as they've Been coined) :

- Cars will last almost a quarter of a century, on the average, by the year 2000,
  eliminating the word "clunker" from our language.

- Society's most dangerous criminals will be sent away to other planets or to
  underwater prisons guarded by robots.

- Marticulture, food farmed on the ocean, will surpass agriculture as the source
  of the planet's food.

- The bathroom will become the center of family life, with bathtub sizes
  increasing to fit a family for recreational purposes.

YOU'RE KIDDING !!

Somebody's pulling your leg just beyond the reach of reality...

Association to Save Madonna From Nuclear War
228 McCormick #3, Cincinnati, OH 45219
Write for more information

Let's declare a "nuclear-free zone" within a 200-mile radius of any place that the rock singer is. And if each and every person declared *their* own "nuclear-free zone," then we could halt the arms race.

Association of Tongue Depressors
4424 N. Washington Blvd., Arlington, VA 22201   (703) 525-1017
Founded: 1978   Members: 28
Dues: Write for details   Contact: Matthew Schorr

Striving for safe, sturdy, sterile sticks is this group's objective. This is a hot meeting ground for health care companies, researchers and manufacturers. Members receive *Wooden Stick Monthly*.

California Depopulation Commission
PO Box 964, Ross, CA 94957   (415) 456-5881
Founded: 1965   Members: 2000
Dues: None   Contact: David C. Camp

If you're on the freeway and you see a bumper sticker that says "Go Back- You Are Going the Wrong Way," "It's In to Be Out," or "Progress, Smogress," you'll know that the driver is a member of the California Depopulation Commission. Members hope to stop further migration into California by persuading non-natives to move back to their home states. The Commission initiated the "Elsewhere is Beautiful" campaign, handing out promotional literature from other states, and designated August as "Florida Appreciation Month." (Thanks to Florida, California isn't even more crowded!.) The Commission humorously suggests that air pollution and population can be reduced by eliminating all off-ramps on interstate freeways, giving California the distinction of having the longest dead-end streets in the country.

CALDEPOP bestows the "The Blessing of San Andreas" to those who have contributed to the cause; winners include Dean Martin for his beautiful and moving rendition of the song "Goin' Back to Houston." An equal non-opportunity group, they "do not target any ethnic or national group; we feel that the California problem is one of warm bodies (too many.)"

While CALDEPOP is serious about its mission, they believe that their tongue-in-cheek approach is much more effective in stopping or reversing what is fast becoming "America's most awesome wasteland." Preferring to operate "slightly in the red," they caution "do not send money; we can't be trusted."

Church of Beaver Cleaver

122 East Benson St., Decatur, GA 30030
Dues: $1.00

A divine spoof starring the holy trinity of "Beaver," "Eddie," and "Ward."

Church of Lateral Religion

22 Hyde Park Terrace, Leeds LS6 1BJ, England
Dues: Write for details   Contact: Rev. M. Baker

Motto: "I Believe Everything"--"I Believe Nothing"

What is the connection between Ronald Reagan and the Devil? The Church of Lateral Religion doesn't know. Send them a SASE for lots of arcane stuff on nothing in particular---great "RONALD WILSON REAGAN = 666" t-shirts, buttons and posters.

Church of the SubGenius

PO Box 140306, Dallas, TX 75214   (214) 823-8534
Founded: 1979   Members: 6,000
Dues: $20.00(includes ordainment materials) Contact: Rev. Ivan Stang

ARE YOU ABNORMAL?? (Then you're probably BETTER than most people) reads the invitation to become a follower of Bob Dobbs. "Quit your job and Praise Bob!"

Of all the clubs in this book, The Church of the SubGenius almost defies description. It is possibly one of the best and sharpest spoofs of all time on weird cults and religions. Bob Dobbs, the pipe-smoking half-tone face is the Church's leader--- He is super-salesman allegedly with mystical powers--and he will save the planet through salesmanship. Bob Dobbs basic message is he needs money and you need slack. Getting "slack" is having absolutely 'free' time, devoid of all stress, to do whatever you damn well please for 'eternity'. Church members tend to be the "non-joining" types--too young to be hippies and too young to be punks, people who disdain clubs, cults and religions.

Rev. Ivan Stang and his gang of cartoonists, artists, and writers have mastered making clip-art look like it's come straight from the lunatic fringe. For example, "The Book of Subgenius: Lunatic Prophecies for the Coming Weird Times" has over 5,000 pictures of Bob Dobbs crammed into it. Church of SubGenius has started to branch out, working on film projects and church "devivals," which are multi-media extravaganzas. At one devival called "The Night of Slack" in San Francisco, Bob Dobbs, who had never been seen in person before, was shot on stage--did he live?? did he die?? Will he come back to earth as a sea monkey?? Church officials won't say for sure--but the "IS BOB DEAD?" controversy lives on. Member get *The Stark Fist of Removal,* published quarterly. Lots of stuff is available for members-- of course the usual propaganda stickers, posters of Bob, rubber stamps and t-shirts but also sacred audio tapes from "The Hour of Slack Radio Show"-- Where does the money go??? Right into Bob's pocket, a virtual profit center to help Bob achieve his eternal goal of eternal slack.

Motto: You'll Pay To Know What You Really Think.

Committee for Immediate Nuclear War

PO Box 290451, 2732 S. University Dr., Davie, FL 33328
Founded: 1979   Members: 30
Dues: None   Contact: Richard Grayson

"Nuclear war would end such problems as boredom, soap operas and street peddlers," says Richard Grayson. After all, says this Floridian wisecracker, isn't "the anticipation of a frightening event always worse than the event itself?" He cites visits to grandma and oral surgery as examples. "Then isn't the anticipation of nuclear war worse than the war itself?" Grayson thinks that Reagan has done a pretty good job of moving us towards nuclear war but he just hasn't moved quickly enough. He says that politicians just aren't farsighted enough to start the atomic ball rolling. If people can have PC's with the power of yesteryear's supercomputers, why can't people have PNW's--personal nuclear weapons? A nuclear winter would add a little variety to the climate in South Florida...and Personal Nuclear Weapons would really take care of traffic jams. Senior citizens wouldn't feel so bad about going bald---after all, they wouldn't be alone.

The Committee for Immediate Nuclear War was formed as a PAC (Political Action Committee) really as a joke (if you didn't figure that out already.) Richard Grayson registered it to see if the government would allow a PAC as off-colored as his to exist. In the process, he also formed the "Antarctica Freeze Committee," the "Steering Committee for American Motorists," "Numismatics for Change," the "People Who Think Nancy Reagan Should Eat More," "Absent-Minded Professors for Something or Other" and "Future Fetuses of America." Committee for Immediate Nuclear War has been the most popular of all his PACs, though.

Members consist mostly of weird teenagers, says Grayson--he gets lots of letters from kids who are assigned to write about an organization for a class report. Then there are a couple of gung-ho Americans--"This will definitely stop the Communists," one Florida man wrote. We're afraid he's right.

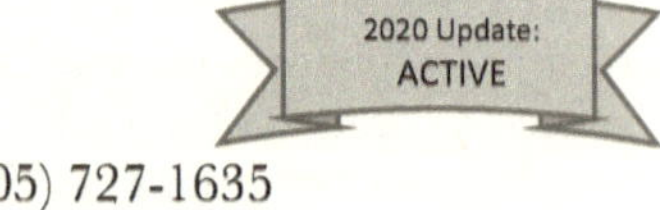

Flat Earth Research Society International

Box 2533, Lancaster, CA 93539   (805) 727-1635
Founded: 1972   Members: 3300
Dues: $10.00 per year   Contact: Charles K. Johnson

NASA is run by "professional criminals," explains Charles Johnson. The take-offs, the outer space televised shuttle happenings and landings are all done in television studios. "One thing we know for sure about this world...the known inhabited world is Flat, Level, *a Plane World*." The Flat Earth Society aims to replace the "science religion…" with Sanity! It's not a new idea...no, the International Flat Earth Society is the oldest continuous Society existing on the world today. Johnson says it began with Creation...er, yes...well, they can safely trace it back to the Universal Zetetic Society of America and Great Britain in the 1800s. This bunk called science is the fault of The Church of England--Luther and his followers like Newton invented the hoax called Gravity. "We maintain that what is called 'Science' today and 'scientists' consist of the same old gang of witch doctors, sorcerers, tellers of tales, the 'Poets-Entertainers' for the common people." As the Wright brothers said, "Science theory held us up for years. When we threw out all science, started from experiment and experience, then we invented the airplane" By the way, airplanes all fly on the same level above this *Plane* Earth. Johnson says that the sun and moon **do** move, but...**Earth does not move, whirl spin or gyrate**. Australians do not hang by their feet under the world...*this is a fact, not a theory*!!

Members are "the thinking classes--lawyers and MD's--airplane pilots and navigators---yes there are a lot of closet flat earthers who waiting to come out. Some have said of IFES members that "they are the last pocket of individual thinkers in the English-speaking world" They are trying to right the lunacy of science which makes the whole Biblical foundation of our world invalid...if the earth is round then how can the U.S. be "one nation *under* God?" Meetings are now secret...but soon great changes will occur and large public meetings will be held. There, people will discover that the sun is only 32 miles wide. Behold...Heaven is just a little farther away than the sun, which is 3,000 miles above the earth. (about the distance from Burbank to Newark) *This is fact, not theory!* The earth is a flat disk that remains still...*fact, not theory!* Johnson says Columbus knew the earth was flat because the Nina, Pinta and Santa Maria didn't start sailing downhill as soon as they were out of sight of Iberia.

Members receive the quarterly *Flat Earth News* and membership card and Certificate. For $6.00, members can receive the Flat Earth Map. But first you must, in writing, swear allegiance to the society---that you will not harm or defame the society---so help you under God over this Flat Earth.

Foreign Car Haters Club of America

PO Box 31610, Phoenix, AZ 85046   (602) 254-4140
Founded: 1983   Members: 400
Dues: Write for details   Contact: Kate Bortells

A white 1972 Datsun 510 was the victim of the First National Car Bash in 1984, as bloodthirsty members paid $1 each to wield a sledgehammer, turning the foreigner into a heap of mangled metal. Club president (and former male stripper) John Rosen wrote, "We're going to rev it up until it croaks. We're going to torture it before we kill it and when we're done, Americans everywhere will stand tall and breathe free." Rosen, who drives the club car, a black, three-ton 1971 Chrysler Imperial, said, "We need a safety valve for the frustration we feel about foreign cars. When we see people buying foreign cars, they're sabotaging America."

For entertainment, club members like to cruise the highway at 45 mph, keeping the foreigners boxed in, while letting the American cars pass. Members can choose from bumper stickers reading "Hungry? Out of work? Eat your foreign car" and "I don't brake for foreign cars." The club membership card reads "We promise to harass foreign cars (while having a good laugh.) We promise to be polite and courteous to American car-owners and devilishly rude to foreign car-owners."

One member, an owner of a Rent-a-Wreck Franchise, said, "To hell with gas! Life is too short. If it gets over 17 m.p.g., it's not worth driving anyway! I'm proud to say I've never had a car that weighs less than two tons." Rosen, who is planning the next foreign car bash this spring, says, "We are everybody's hero - or everybody's villain. You either hate us, or you love us."

Hollow Earth Society...or...
International Society for a Complete Earth

PO Box 103, Houston, MO 65483
Founded: 1977   Members: 4000
Dues: Write for details   Contact: W. Shoush

Our earth is as hollow as a tennis ball...a super-race of people inhabit the inner-earth...there is a conspiracy to keep knowledge of our "hollow earth" a secret....ARE THESE PEOPLE SERIOUS???

The Hollow Earth Society believes that polar explorer Admiral Richard Evelyn Byrd entered the world of the "inner-earth" in 1947 through a sea channel. The group has now launched an expedition to the underworld with a small submarine called "Omega." "When forces allow the truth of the hollow earth to be told, and we are joined with the more advanced civilization below us, then we shall have a 'complete earth.'" (It's okay with us.)

Institute of Scientific Santa Clausism

PO Box 70829, New Orleans, LA 70172

Dues: $2 per year   Contact: Rev. Dan Meyer

Santa Claus exists! Members send eyewitness accounts that are published in the quarterly *Journal of the Institute of Scientific Santa Clausism*. They claim to have found the actual Shroud of Santa.

International Brotherhood of Old Bastards

2330 S. Brentwood Blvd., Suite 666, St. Louis, MO   63144 (314) 544-3311

Founded: 1813   Members: 307,421

Dues: $5.00 voluntary   Contact: Cozen P. Bantling
                                                     (Supreme Archbastard)

With the motto: "Illegitimus Non Carborundum," Archbastard Cozen P. Bantling says IBOB has "no dues, no meetings, no charity drives, no axes to grind, no committees, no responsibilities - only a few laughs." For $25.00, you, too, can become an archbastard. Some of these "laughs" are really new business ideas: opening up a "Cat Ranch" to sell catskin capes, cat fur coats, and cat fur rings. They would get the cats (because everyone wants to get rid of cats anyway) by running an ad in the paper saying, "Cats Wanted for New Business." They would feed the cats by opening up a "Rat Ranch" next door. Another "new idea" comes from Brother Abe Cohen of St. Louis, MO, who says he's developed a rubber stamp that will adequately answer 64% of all interoffice memos and up to 79% of other correspondence. The short simple, direct message is: HORSE MANURE. The IBOB creed is as follows:

Age Limits: approaching, at or past 39, but feel and act 39 (or less.) Or old enough to know better, but young enough to try.

Drinking Habits: Hearty.

Greeting: When meeting a brother or sister Old Bastard, loudly shout, "Hi, You Old Bastard!"

Conduct: Firmly establish reputation so that everyone will say, "There is the Biggest, Baddest, Meanest Old Bastard in Town.

Sex: Frequently.

Pledge: To continue bastardly deeds in solemn hope of someday achieving the highest honor of them all--the title of Supreme Archbastard (Selected each year on April 1st, Founders Day.)

Song: 'Making Whoopee'

Cozen said that IBOB has allowed women to join recognizing the fact that "some of the biggest OB's around are women."

International Stop Continental Drift Society

Star Rte., Box 38, Winthrop, WA 98862   (509) 996-2576
Founded: 1976   Members: 758
Dues: $5.00   Contact: John C. Holden

ISCDS asks: "If Plate Tectonics is so hot--why can't anyone explain what makes it work?" The goals of the organization are:
1. Immediate cessation of sea-floor spreading
2. Cooling of orogenic magmas
3. Quiescence of large volcanos
4. Damping of seisms greater than 4.0 on the Richter Scale
5. End of subduction and other crustal discriminations.

They want it--and they want it now! (give or take a million years)

The International Stop Continental Drift Society plans a "Continental Drift Hit List," that will debunk all so-called scientists who are responsible for promoting the theories of plate tectonics.

Members who are technical people as well as laypersons receive a bumper sticker, an official Stop Continental Drift certificate and an occasional newsletter. Members can also get their hands on the official "Drift Globe"--continents can be placed in any configuration, attached with Velcro attachments--Yes, friends, a veritable trip in time --230 million years of drift at your fingertips!

John Dillinger Died for You Society

PO Box 409490, Chicago, IL 60640
Founded: 1966   Contact: Horace Naismith
Dues: Write for details

A group of graduate students in Austin, Texas founded the Society to celebrate the first time a major American university agreed to accept a thesis on the submachine gun, towards a master's degree in history. The group is headed by the mysterious Horace Naismith (Doctor Naismith for short), reputedly one of the famed bank robber's illegitimate sons.

The objectives of the society are threefold. First is to correct the misconceptions about Dillinger as a common criminal...he was merely an economic reformer, a "Robin Hood" of the people, using unorthodox banking methods. If it weren't for him, the U.S. Justice Department might never have been transformed into the

mighty FBI. Second, the group serves as a clearinghouse for Dillinger research
and information, which is forwarded to the John Dillinger Museum in Indiana
(not officially connected with them.) Third and most importantly, the society vows
to locate and resolve questions concerning "Dillinger's allegedly oversized private
part, which both the Smithsonian Institute and the National Medical Museum
persist in denying they have ever possessed or displayed...his amputated member
pickled in a bottle has allegedly been on public view at one place or the other at
one time or another." Millions of people have claimed to have seen this *piece* of
American folklore.

Those inducted into the society include Joe Pinksto, director of the John Dillinger
Museum in Nasville, Indiana and posthumously, FBI Director, J. Edgar Hoover,
the man who chased Dillinger to an early grave. Members get a "credit card"
designed to be hung from the end of a rifle, a cap and a bumper sticker that says,
cryptically, DEATH TO VIOLENCE.

Official Adage: "Never trust a women or an automatic pistol." (Dillinger said this
to a gangmember in 1933)

Official Slogan: "Keep calm and lie down on the floor." (Dillinger said this to
bank customers and employees from 1933-34)

Official Song: "The Ballad of John Dillinger"

Ladies Against Women

1600 Woolsey, No. 7, Berkeley, CA 94703 (415) 841-6500
Founded: 1980 Members: 12,000
Dues: $15.00 per year Contact: Mrs. T. Bill Banks
  (Lady Chair-Man)

Back to the days when men were gentlemen and women were ladies. Ladies
Against Women is a group of "decent ladies with a moral imperative to return to
the Good Old Days"! They sponsor Consciousness Lowering Sessions for females
who insist they are women, and workshops for "uppity women" on stress
reduction through apathy. Ladies Against Women say that what real Ladies need
are more strong male authority figures, a return to the days of strong dress codes
and a repeal of the women's vote! They been known to disrupt "women's events"
with a "picket-reception line" for real ladies. Their daughters belong to "Younger
Ladies Against Younger Women, their men belong to "For Ladies Against
Women" (FLAW) and their mothers to "Another Mother for World Domination."

Ladies Against Women will stand up for a man's world of war and destruction--
showing their support with bake sales for the Pentagon--"ban books, not bombs,"
they yell. And finally, back to the age when a women could walk with something
furry and warm on her shoulders without being sneered at, their "Save the Stoles"

fashion show for endangered accessories has been a sell-out. Members receive *National Embroiderer* and can pin buttons to their lapel reading, "Ban the Poor!," "Make America a Man Again---Invade Abroad!," "Abolish the Environment!---It Takes Up too Much Space!," "Protect the Unconceived---Sperms Are People Too!," "You're Nobody 'Till You're Mrs. Somebody!," "Procreation, Not Recreation!"

A wonderful spoof on the "ladies auxiliary," hitting the submissive housewife over the head until she cries out, "ERA!" Ladies Against Women are quite a brave bunch, mimicking groups as serious and powerful as the Moral Majority (they stayed "in character" while being physically attacked by a group of fundamentalists outside the Reagan-Falwell Prayer Breakfast at the Republican Convention in Dallas.)

Slogans: "Tupperware Preserves the Family" and "I'd Rather Be Ironing"

Man Will Never Fly Memorial Society
PO Box 1903, Kill Devil Hills, NC 27948   (919) 441-7482
Founded: 1959   Members: 5000
Dues: $2.00 lifetime membership   Contact: Ed North, Jr.

Their Solemn Pledge: Given the choice, I will never fly; but given no choice, I will never fly sober.

In 1903, the editor of a Dayton newspaper said, when informed of the mythical first plane flight, "Man will never fly. And if he does he will never come from Dayton." The society's members disbelieve that a machine made of a couple tons of metal will actually lift off the ground. They contend that taking a plane flight is nothing more than boarding a large Greyhound bus with wings, where expensive backdrops and scenery of clouds are moved passed the windows. Surely they believe that balloons fly, but planes? No!

Each year on the eve of the anniversary of the first "imaginary" flight of those great illusionaries from Dayton (December 16th), the group meets at Kitty Hawk and presents the Aviation Hall of Infamy Award to some aviation goof-off who has done the least for aviation. Recent recipients have included Senator John Glenn, Mr. "Right Stuff" Chuck Yeager (who apologized for being so clumsy as to break the sound barrier), and Snoopy. Present projects of the organization include the building of an Invisible Museum for UFOs. Local chapters have their own projects: the Fly Wrights of Dayton continue to recycle airplanes into beer cans, and the White Knuckle Chapter of Austin is researching the octane rating of chili gas, in case someone *does* invent the airplane.

The Man Will Never Fly Memorial Society--in an effort to promote sensible forms of travel--dedicated 1987 as The Year of the Bus.

Their theme song (to the tune of "The Man on the Flying Trapeze")

First Verse:
NOW BACK IN DECEMBER OF NINETEEN-O-THREE
THE WRIGHT BROTHERS CAME TO DARE COUNTY TO SEE
IF THEY COULD DEFY THE LAW OF GRAV-I-TY
BY TRYING TO MAKE LIKE A BIRD

THEY HAD LOOKED THE WORLD OVER FOR JUST THE RIGHT
SPOT
WITH BREEZES AND SUNSHINE AND SAND
WHERE IT WASN'T TOO COLD AND IT WASN'T TOO HOT
AND THERE'S ALWAYS A SOFT SPOT TO LAND

Chorus:
OH--FILL UP YOUR GLASSES AND LET'S HAVE A ROUND
FOR WILBUR AND ORVILLE THOSE MEN OF REKNOWN
WHO TAUGHT US TO FLY WITHOUT LEAVING THE GROUND
AND THAT'S WHAT WE'RE DOING TONIGHT!

Members receive a certificate and membership card, both emblazoned with the society's motto: "Birds Fly...Men Drink." (See "The First Flight Society" for more on remembering the boys from Dayton)

N.O.T. S.A.F.E. (National Organization Taunting Safety and Fairness Everywhere)

Box 5743, Montecito, CA 93108   (805) 969-6217
Founded: 1980   Members: 1000
Dues: $15.00 per year ($75 lifetime)   Contact: Dale Lowdermilk

Warning: This book may be hazardous to your health--- The authors and publisher assume no responsibility for paper cuts or other injuries that this book may cause.

NOT SAFE calls itself "the world's most sarcastic organization." Founder Dale Lowdermilk believes that government "stupidity" can be attacked with wit, satire and overkill. His mission: "help abolish everything." NOT SAFE suggests that 99% of all airline accidents could be avoided if planes were required to remove their wings and taxi to their destination, or if only one plane was allowed to fly over the U.S. at a time, reducing the chance of mid-airs---Lowdermilk loves this suggestion, since he's an air traffic controller. Other suggestions include mandatory wearing of lightning rods by anyone walking in a thunderstorm, and a mandatory "fat warning" label on all food containing calories. A ban on aspirin, "which kills 900 people a year." A 25 mph national speed limit, "which would not only save human lives by reducing accidents, but reduce the slaughter of insect life on our highways." Warning labels on banana peels--people have slipped and hurt themselves--could be big trouble for Chiquita. Outlaw the smelling of flowers--"Do you realize that when you smell a flower you are putting your nose near the sexual organ of another species?" says Lowdermilk. NOT SAFE suggests that to be really Safe people should stay in bed, but get plenty of exercise. (Yippee!)

NOT SAFE has a serious side--they want people to be allowed to give $1.00 of their tax return to the governmental agency of their choice, limit the number of laws that are introduced, and add "none of the above" to the ballot. Members, who are the creative source of most of NOT SAFE's ideas, receive *Quagmire*, the club's official newsletter---members never meet though because of the danger of spreading contagious disease.

Motto: If it's worth doing right...it's worth overdoing....and...
Protect everyone from everything at all costs.

LIVELLAFOTOOREHTSITNEMNREVOG
(Read Backwards)

New First Arachnid Church
4249 30th Avenue South, Minneapolis, MN 55406
Write for more information

They believe with utmost conviction that the Great Spider created himself on a whim, and the Universe out of boredom. "He used to roar with laughter at the wars and break into tears during the famines and plagues." Warning: When you get to heaven, you'll be met by a Huge Black Thing! Believe in him or he'll eat you.

Society of Dirty Old Men
Box 18202, Indianapolis, IN 46218
Founded: 1973   Members: 21,000
Dues: Write for details   Contact: Donald M. Butler

Bringing up the rear, snicker award to the ten women who contribute the least toward female subservience to the "male race" and annual Most Quotable Dirty Old Men of the Year Award to quotable men based on the brass, bluff, bravado and basic American baloney of their remarks. Speakers bureau on the subject of "A Women's Place" and "ERA- A Communistic Trick." SDOM publishes "Every Males Guide to Chauvinism"

Society to Promote Respect and Recognition of Millard Fillmore
3507 Stoneybrook Rd., Randallstown, MD 21133

Founded: 1967

Dues: Write for details

Members: 50

Contact: Rae Rossen

With the creed "Millard who?" they celebrate the birthday of hapless Millard Fillmore, the country's *13th* president. President for only two years from 1850 to 1852, filling in after Zachary Taylor died, Fillmore failed to get re-elected. He tried to run again in 1856 as a member of the "Know Nothing" party, but only carried one state, Maryland. (Society president Rossen says, "What he lacked in charisma, he made up for in mediocrity.") Actually, Fillmore was the Rodney Dangerfield of his day and a master of misinformation, and, speaking of misinformation, President Reagan recently mentioned Fillmore in a speech...probably the first president in a hundred years to mention Fillmore publicly. Reagan said that Fillmore's life was "a superb example of the American dream," but true to form, misstated Millard's anniversary.

Each year at the Fillmore birthday celebration, the society has its "moment of discovery"--some trivial thing printed about usually turns out to be wrong. They call it the "Flukes of Fillmore." Baltimore author H.L. Mencken started a rumor that Fillmore was the first president to install a bathtub in the White House...actually not true (some say Mrs. Fillmore, but historians say all she ever installed was the White House Library.) Currently, Fillmore is credited with installing the first cast-iron stove in the White House which he called "that temple of inconveniences." Born in a log cabin in Buffalo, New York, young Millard taught himself to read from a dictionary. On a positive note, he did conduct open relations with Japan and Hawaii during his presidency, inaugurate railway service between New York and Chicago and reduce postage rates from 5 cents to 3 cents.

The club was founded as an outgrowth of "The Students' Committee for the Glorification of Millard Fillmore," founded by Jeff Amdur, an 11th grader, who said he had nothing better to do. One year they staged a re-inauguration party, where everyone sang "The Ballad of Millard Fillmore," and held a news conference, with Millard himself played by the husband of the society's president.

Society of Screwed Americans

496 LaGuardia Place, Suite No. 123, New York, NY 10012

Do you have marital Problems, landlord harassment?
Is the IRS and your lawyer calling? For $9.95 you too can show that you've been ripped off by the system. Members receive a t-shirt, certificate and membership card.

EVERYTHING AND ANYTHING

If you find a thread, a trend, or a train of thought in this group of clubs, it's news to us. Here are just zillions of fun things to do, be, have or...?

American Council of Spotted Asses

2126 Fairview Pl., Billings, MT 59102   (406) 259-4926
Founded: 1969   Members: 150
Dues: $12.00 per year   Contact: John Conter

Tammy Hoem, 12 years old, from Billings, Montana, showed her Spotted Ass in the Eastern Montana Fair and won third place. Tammy says, "Next year I'm going to enter and get first place. I don't like those horse people sneering at my Donkey." The SAPS Club (Spotted Ass Promoters Club) was formed for people who don't own a Spotted Ass but are interested in promoting the breed. There are only 365 registered Spotted Asses in the world (one ass for every day of the year.) The newsletter offers "Spotted Asses For Sale," and Spotted Ass caps.

Spotted Ass Promoter (SAPS) Club Toast:

May your friends never leave you,
May your spurs never rust.
May your spotted ass never stumble,
May your cinch never bust.
May your boots never pinch,
May your crops never fail.
May you always have plenty to eat and drink,
May you never go to jail.

American Driving Society

PO Box 160, Metamora, MI 48455   (800) 233-9806
Dues: $35.00 per year

Publishes *The Whip* for member horse lovers.

American Homebrewers Association

Box 287, Boulder, CO 80306   (303) 447-0816
Founded: 1978   Members: 5,000
Dues: $17.00 per year   Contact: Charles N. Papazian

Beermakers, microbrewers and beer lovers come together for homebrewing classes, festivals and tastings. Members receive *Zymurgy*.

American Museum of Magic
107 East Michigan, Marshall, MI 49068
Dues: Write for details   Contact: Robert Lund

Houdini and other masters of illusion are immortalized here. Members receive free admission.

American Sunbathing Association
1703 N. Main Street, Kissimee, FL 32743   (305) 933-2064
Founded: 1931   Members: 25,000
Dues: $12.50 per year   Contact: Arne Eriksen

Motto: Nudism... the foundation for a better life!
Comprising over 150 clubs nationwide promoting "Social Nudism." While we've been conditioned to associate nudism with sex, nudists are able to keep the two as separate issues. "Nudists do not advocate a clothesless social order in the twentieth century...subway, elevated and railroad travel make such a mode undesirable...even the thought of it is ridiculous." The society helps to establish nudist parks, resorts and camps (the first one in the country was founded in 1930 in Spring Valley, NY.) T-shirts, visors and towels are available to members...as is a newsletter.

Astrologer's Guild of America
PO Box 75, New York, NY 10011
Founded: 1927
Dues: Write for details   Contact: Joehe Mahoney

Those interested in horoscopes and the planets come together.

Brotherhood of the Knights of the Vine
PO Box 13285, Sacramento, CA 95813   (916) 269-1021
Founded: 1971   Members: 1500
Dues: $150.00 initiation, $75.00 each year   Contact: Norman E. Gates

With the slogan, "Water separates the people of the world; wine unites them," The Brotherhood is an association of individuals who share an appreciation in the Vines and Wines of America. Sixteen chapters exist around the country-- members are knighted, with the highest title of Supreme Knight and Supreme Lady to a select few who have crusaded the cause of America's wines.

By Hand and Foot: Tools Dependent on Human Energy

PO Box 611, Brattleboro, VT 5301   (802) 254-2388
Founded: 1976
Dues: Write for details   Contact: Dennis Ward

With a little body English and elbow grease, they establish and research efficient tools--for homeowners, gardeners and farmers--that don't need electricity or gasoline to be used.

Central Bureau for Astronomical Telegrams

Smithsonian Astrophysical Observatory
60 Garden St., Cambridge, MA 02138   (617) 495-7244
Founded: 1920   Members: 15
Dues: Depends on type of service   Contact: Dr. Brian G. Marsden

An information service for astronomers, CBAT tells what's hot in the sky. Receive a postcard, telegram or computer up-date on the latest "minor planets" to watch for or special attractions like novas and supernovas. Comets get top billing, too. Every couple of months, the *Minor Planets Circulars* are sent to nocturnal space-watchers.

Chili Appreciation Society International

c/o Tolbert's Texas Chili Parlor
4533 McKinney, Dallas, TX 75205   (214) 522-4340
Founded: 1939   Contact: Kathleen Tolbert
Ryan

These "tough-mouthed gourmets called chili heads" meet each year for the Terlingua International Frank Tolbert Memorial Chili Cook-off," held the first Saturday in November. Chili cooks the world over compete for the title of international chili cook champion, producing the best Texas-style chili.

Chili-USA (Chili-Heads Interacting for Legislative Initiative in the U.S.A.)

1919 Pennsylvania Ave., NW, Suite 300, Washington, DC 20006   (202) 333-3901
Founded: 1983   Contact: R. N. Dunagan

These chili eaters are working towards the passage of a House-Senate joint resolution that would proclaim chili as America's official food. The group also awards the Will Rogers Chili Humanitarian Award to someone who has "significantly increased public knowledge of chili's exceptional gastronomic properties and of the warm camaraderie it so often inspires."

Circus Model Builders, International

347 Lonsdale Ave., Dayton, OH 45419

(513) 299-0515

Founded: 1936

Members: 1800

Dues: $16.50 per year

Contact: Sally Conover

Miniature model builders from a dozen countries. The *Little Circus Wagon* newsletter is bi-monthly.

Clowns of America International

1342 Sylvan Way, West Bend, WI 53095

(414) 338-3569

Founded: 1968

Members: 4,100

Dues: $15.00 per year, $5 initiation fee

Contact: Hunter Stevens

"Why not expand on your funology and become a Clownologist?" Dedicated to the art of Clowning and to bringing joy and happiness to everyone, COAI is open to both professional and hobbyist clowns. "Clowning is one of the oldest professions in the world," they report, "having roots deep in history." One member, Albert Sikorsky (formerly an IRS investigator), says that clowning "goes back to the cavemen. There's always been somebody around who was funny." Clowns livened up ancient Egypt--one pharaoh supposedly performed incognito for many years as a clown until he was able to attain the throne. *The New Calliope* is published six times a year, with tips on costumes, tricks, make-up and props. One of their COA "clown alleys" (as fish are to schools and birds are to flocks, clowns are to alleys) hosts an annual convention each spring.

Continental Confederation of Adopted Indians

2420 Zollinger Road, Columbus, OH 43221

Founded: 1950

Members: 150

Dues: Write for details

Contact: Lt. Col. Daniel F. Clancy

A worldwide group of "non-blooded Indians," they're an Honorary tribe around the world. Big Crosby was the "Continental War Chanter." A few people with real Indian blood have gained tribal membership. The tribe is concerned with Indian welfare--demanding that the bones of Indian Princess Pocahontas be returned to her native land--the bones of the famous wife of explorer John Rolfe have been buried at Gravesend, England for more than 300 years--but the British had no interest in complying.

Crab Apple

14 Eleanor Place, Monsey, NY 10952

Founded: 1980

Members: 150 families

Dues: $20.00 per year

Contact: Stephen Wulfson

A network of Apple II Computer owners.

The Don's Club

Phoenix, AZ   (602) 264-2611
Founded: 1934
Dues: Write for details   Contact: Dick Totman

Somewhere in the Superstition Mountains of Arizona, the Lost Dutchman Mine waits. The mine yielded high grade gold ore for its discoverer, Miguel Peralta, in the 1840's but its location was lost until Jacob "the Dutchman" Waltz found it in the 1880's. Waltz would go into the mountains and come back to Phoenix with bags loaded with gold. He reportedly drew a map of the location before he died, and in 1931, Adolph Ruth claimed to have found the map. Ruth left home with map in hand only to be found six months later with two bullet holes in his skull. Many more have been killed in the search, but the Don's Club sets out each year, braving desert temperatures of over 110 degrees to find the mine. One hopeful, Bob Corbin (attorney general of Arizona), has been looking for 40 years. "The fun's in the looking," he says.

Far and Wide Recording Club

PO Box 51, Lively, ON, Canada POM 2EO   (705) 692-3374
Founded: 1967   Members:
Dues: $8.00 per year   Contact: Ross V. Smith

Instead of pen pals, this is a club for tape-pals. There was a time when there were at least 20 major tape trading clubs, but today, because of television and video cameras, only four are active (though for the visually handicapped, who can join for a reduced membership, tape correspondence is perfect.) At least one Far and Wide Recording Club member met her fiancé by tape. He was from New Zealand and she was from Ohio. He proposed to her on tape, and then backed it up by a phone call. At last report, they were happily married living in New Zealand, with one child.

Flanged Wheel Society

1301 Thatcher Avenue, Dellwood, MO
Founded: 1955   Contact: William J. Clouser

Railroad enthusiasts, be it transcontinental or on city streets. The named was proposed because it was noted that be it a streetcar, rail car, or locomotive, each has a flanged wheel.

Freeway Singles Club
Huntington Beach, CA
Founded: 1983   Members: 4,000
Dues: Write for details   Contact: Ruth Guillou

Truly a Southern California invention, the Freeway Singles club allows people to
window shop for dates while driving around in the privacy of their car. Members
get a numbered decal for their rear window, that can be recorded by an interested
driver-by. The club was started by Ruth Guillou, a 50-year-old widow who felt
helpless at the opportunity to meet a handsome older gentlemen who was driving
a cream-colored Cadillac. "We both kept looking at each other, smiling," Ruth
said. "It's a dumb thing to do. You can't shake hands. You can't say hello." She
vowed not to let the chance slip away again. Though the club doesn't introduce
people directly, members can write to the Porsche or pick-up truck driver of their
dreams through the club's post-office box system. Clubs just like the Freeway
Singles Club have started popping up all over the country.

Friends of the Origami Center of America
15 W. 77th St., New York, NY 10024   (212) 496-1890
Founded: 1980   Members: 650
Dues: $15.00 per year   Contact: Alice Gray

"The Origami Center is the hub and clearinghouse for paper folding in America."
(In Japanese, "ori" means folding and "kami" means paper.) The art of paper
folding was probably first practiced by magicians, but now many people of many
ages enjoy it. Members receive *The Origamian* with articles, instructions on new
models and profiles of folders.

Goose and Gander
Society for Preservation of 1st Wives & Husbands
155 Mildred Circle, Concord, MA 01742-3723
Founded: 1982   Members: 300
Dues: Write for details   Contact: Anne Branscomb

Just like the goose, these club members mate for life. Members are required to
have been married at least 25 years to the same spouse, with no previous
marriages. Furthermore, members are dedicated to mutual lifelong support,
loyalty to friends, devotion to each other, and a dedication to public service. Hey,
these people are bucking a trend!

International Brotherhood of Magicians

28 N. Main St., Kenton, OH 43326   (419) 675-7150
Founded: 1923   Members: 11,000
Dues: Write for details   Contact: Theresa Zoeller

Magicians, assistants, agents, and others interested in magic work toward ending the misleading advertising of tricks. They oppose disclosure of the principles of illusions, except in the proper books and magazines, and they encourage the humane treatment of animals that are used in acts.

International Jugglers Association

203 Crosby Ave., Kenmore, NY 14217   (716) 876-5331
Founded: 1947   Members: 3,000
Dues: $15.00 per year ($3.00 initiation fee)   Contact: Richard J.
Chamberlin

"As a part of his act in the first decade of this century, the world-renowned German "gentleman juggler" Kara sat on a chair and balanced a full wine glass on three straws on his forehead, at the same time spinning a tray with the index finger of his left hand and juggling a plate and bottle with this right hand!

President Reagan was shown juggling three plates...not in the White House...but in a 1947 issue of *Movie Life* magazine.

Juggling is considered by circus performers to be the riskiest kind of act because it's so hard to do flawlessly, performance after performance. Most good jugglers are adept at covering up mistakes though. There is no sex discrimination in the juggling world, with some of the most famous jugglers of all time being women.

The International Jugglers Association's main event has always been the annual six-day convention, held the third week of July with hundreds of juggling performers. The convention's highlights are 24-hour open juggling, international competitions and parade, all open to the general public. With members in 21 countries, IJA is open to top professionals, avid hobbyists and enthusiastic beginning jugglers. IJA's *Juggler's World* magazine is probably the best publication on juggling available.

Love Project

PO Box 7601, San Diego, CA 92107   (619) 225-0133
Founded: 1972   Members: 600
Dues: $15.00 per year   Contact: Arleen Lorrance

"The Love Project principles...enable us to express finer frequencies of

consciousness while functioning in universal love." Three Love Project principles
are "Problems are opportunities," "Have no expectations, but rather, abundant
expectancy," and "Provide others with opportunities to give." The Love Project is
rather unstructured and members receive the *Seeker Magazine*.

Morse Telegraph Club, Inc.

712 South 49, Lincoln, NE 68510
Founded: 1942   Members: 2500
Dues: Write for details   Contact: WK Dunbar

One of the last groups of telegraph operators using Morse code still existing. On
their yearly meeting, the fourth Saturday in April, Western Union and Canadian
Telecom provide a free circuit, connecting all the clubs in the U.S. and Canada.
Dots and Dashes newsletter is published quarterly.

North American Association of Ventriloquists

Maher Studios, Box 420, Littleton, CO 80160   (303) 798-6830
Founded: 1944   Members: 2,000
Dues: $8.00 per year   Contact: Clinton Detweiler

You say you want to make your dummy talk? NAAV offers the Maher Home
Course of Ventriloquism. NAAV members receive the bi-monthly newsletter,
Newsy Vents, with articles on famous dummies, reviews on new dummies for sale
and dialogues and scripts to feed your dummy.

International Beer Tasting Society

1800 E. First St., Santa Ana, CA 92701   (714) 973-1345
Founded: 1956   Contact: Martin J. Lockney

"Beer lover who want to enjoy beer in the company of other beer lovers"---they
try and "taste" as many beers as possible.

International Chili Society

PO Box 2966, Newport Beach, CA 92663   (714) 631-1780
Founded: 1978   Members: 10,000
Dues: $15.00 per year   Contact: Jim West

It all started in 1967 when New York humorist H. Allen Smith declared himself
the country's greatest chili cook and authority, writing an article in *Holiday*
magazine titled, "Nobody Knows More About Chili Than I Do." Some Texans
took this as a challenge and enlisted race car driver and designer Carroll Shelby

into organizing it. From this first small event, Shelby, a chili lover all his life, helped start the International Chili Society. The purpose of the Society is to develop and improve the preparation and appreciation of *true* chili and to determine each year the World Champion Chili Cook. The organization sanctions over 300 cookoffs, involving 10,000 cooks in 44 states and 11 foreign countries, last year raising over $8 million for charity. The 1986 winner, Jim Beatty, won $25,000. A bimonthly newsletter lists upcoming cookoffs as well as such fun features as the personal chili recipes of the stars. (Their response to the authors' request for a club song? "None--nobody can sing.")

International Connoisseurs of Green & Red Chile

World Headquarters,
Box 3467, New Mexico State University, Las Cruces, NM 88003
(505) 646-1939

Members: 3000

Dues: $10.00   Contact: Jeanne B. Croft

To educate the uninformed of the world to the joys of the chile mystique and culture is their goal. Members are chile chefs, chile growers and chile gourmets who distinguish one chile from another. They offer chile seeds, growing information and a chile newsletter. Originally spelled "Chili," these New Mexicans have taken a bold step away from the standard brown chili of Texas. Ordered red or green, the Texas fruit is always brown. The spelling issue was even taken up by the U.S. Senate, with the Senator from New Mexico setting the record straight on which state produces and spells Chile correctly.

International Training in Communication (Toastmistress)

2519 Woodland Dr., Anaheim, CA 92801   (714) 995-3660
Founded: 1938   Members: 23,000
Dues: $20.00 per year (plus $ to local clubs) Contact: Muriel Bryant

Originally a club just for women, ITC clubs around the world now offer training in communication and listening effectiveness to all.

London Club

PO Box 4527, Topeka, KS 66604
Founded: 1975   Members: 150
Dues: $20.00 per year   Contact: Dennis A. Baranski

Criminologists Wanted

Professional and amateur investigative researchers wanted to
assist in the formulation of theories and the submission of data

related to unsolved murder cases of the past and present.

Prerequisites...The gift of intelligence,
Capacity for calculation,
and vigorous instincts.

Originally a group of professionals who met to talk about the mysterious Jack the Ripper Whitechapel murder case, now the London club is open to amateur sleuths. Current investigations include the Kennedy and Lincoln assassinations, the Lizzie Borden case, the Hillsdale Strangler, the Jimmy Hoffa Disappearance, the Judge Crater Disappearance and a handful of others. Groups around the country assist in acting as press bureaus, scouting the papers for leads and information. Communication is achieved through the club paper, *The London Club Journal*. Professions of members include criminologists, physicians, scientists, attorneys, educators, and members of the press.

Lovers of the Stinking Rose

c/o Aris Books, 1621 Fifth Street, Berkeley, CA 94710
Founded: 1982   Members: 3000
Dues: $25.00   Contact: John Harris

Garlic lovers unite! Garlic guru John Harris reports that the practice of giving garlic to warriors did not die in Roman times. The New York Times wrote recently about football coach Joe Kapp of the University of California Bears use of garlic to stimulate his players. "Raw garlic is food for men in the trenches, it does a lot for the glands. Also, we like to breathe on the opponents. Third down is the best time to do it. We spend a lot of time teaching our linemen how to blow in the face and nose." (Unfortunately, all this stink hasn't helped their game.)

Members receive a two-year subscription to *Garlic Times*, the quarterly newsletter and a choice of *The Book of Garlic* or *The Official Garlic Lovers Handbook*. The large "Mail Odor" selection includes a "Plaincloves Button," and the award-winning video cassette, "Garlic is as Good As Ten Mothers."

Man Watchers

8033 Sunset #363, Los Angeles, CA 90046   (213) 278-5304
Founded: 1974   Members: 7500
Dues: Write for details   Contact: Suzy Mallery

If a woman comes up to you on the street and hands you a card that says "Well Worth Watching," she is a member of Man Watchers. The Man Watchers produce "America's Most Watchable Man Competitions," and each year plus they pick the "Ten Top Men in the World." Current projects include a search for "the type of men women really like."

Massachusetts Bay Railroad Enthusiasts

PO Box 136, Ward Hill, MA 01830   (617) 277-2843
Founded: 1934   Members: 650
Dues: $10.00 per year   Contact: William Crawford

One of the largest regional clubs interested in railroads, the club charters special excursion rides on abandoned routes. "Some train freaks want to ride every piece of track in the country," club president Bill Crawford said. Members receive the monthly *Callboy* newsletter.

National Carousel Association

PO Box 307, Frankfort, IN 46041   (317) 654-5807
Founded: 1973   Members: 1000
Dues: $25.00 per year   Contact: Gail Hall

Appreciation, conservation and restoration of hand-carved merry-go-rounds. Publications include *NCA News* and *Merry-Go-Round* magazine.

National Nudist Council

PO Box 112, Newfoundland, NJ 07435   (201) 697-8075
Founded: 1952   Members: 4000
Dues: $15.00 per year   Contact: Astrid E. Keck

Members believe in "the essential wholesomeness of the human body and all its functions: that making the fullest use of sunlight and air by a program of exercise and life in the open air will result in the maximum physical and mental good health." (Where in New Jersey do *these* people come from?)

National Tattoo Association

PO Box 2063, New Hyde Park, NY 11040   (516) 747-6953
Founded: 1974   Members: 600
Dues: Write for details   Contact: Florence Makofske

"Where can one go for a *good* tattoo in our days" is a commonly asked question? The National Tattoo Association will point you to one of their member tattoo artists, who supposedly practice hygienic tattooing practices.

Old Boys Network Turtle Club

Box 1553, Corinth, MS 38834
Founded: 1951   Members: 7500

Dues: Write for details   Contact: Bill Caruth, Chief
Turtle Herder

A social club of "Fun-loving folks who are willing to stick their necks out to
succeed."

Popular Culture Association

Popular Culture Center, Bowling Green University
Bowling Green, OH 43403   (419) 372-3981
Founded: 1967   Members: 3000
Dues: $25.00 per year   Contact: Ray B. Browne

What would you say about a discussion on the social significance of soap operas?
How about a group that discusses television, motion pictures, underground
culture, popular literature, folklore, popular music, even protest music? The
Popular Culture Association has an extensive library of books and records.
Members receive a journal and there is an annual meeting.

Potato Eaters

704 North Carolina Ave., SE, Washington, DC 20003   (202) 544-1558
Founded: 1985   Members: 300
Dues: $20.00 per year   Contact: Tom Hughes

Potato Eaters are members of the Potato Museum who meet at a regular pot luck
Potato Eaters Night, each with a dish made from potatoes. Members share
recipes, and increase their awareness of fine potato cookery. The museum was
founded in 1975 when schoolteacher Tom Hughes, who was living in Belgium,
asked his class about the possible benefits of a potato museum. The children
pointed out the vast history of the potato and its role in keeping whole societies
alive. Hughes moved the museum to Washington a couple of years ago and, today,
three rooms of his home are devoted to potato clocks, potato magic tricks, Mr.
Potato Head, potato-shooting pistols, bleach made from potatoes and lots of
vodka. Hughes has called himself "the voice of the potato," so proclaimed
because "potatoes have lots of eyes but no mouth." Potato Eaters receive the
museum's newsletter, *Peelings,* with recipes and historic uses of this great tuber.

Power Lunch!

PO Box 21280, Washington, DC 20009   (202) 265-EATT
Founded: 1986   Members: 125
Dues: $100.00 per year plus $25.00 per contact   Contact: Sandy Crowe

"Eat Your Way to Success" is Power Lunch!'s slogan. Networking, the 1980's version of matchmaking is re-worked with a new twist for hungry up-and-comers in the Washington, DC area. Power-hungry clients can get the names of experts in the same profession--or in a field of special interest--and then "do lunch." Experts range from jazz musicians, to tax law experts, to someone who can extract venom from snakes. Started by Sandy Crowe, a 28-year-old entrepreneur, Power Lunch! is a substitute for the risky task of striking up a conversation with a stranger. Sandy, who usually grabs a tuna sandwich at her desk for lunch, says that one client called wanting to meet a piano tuner-- sure enough, she was able to serve up one from her extensive database.

Prison Pen Pals
Box 1217, Cincinnati, OH 45201   (606) 491-2713
Founded: 1974   Contact: Lou Torok

Lou Torok, a convict/writer in the early 70s, wrote a plea to the prisoners and guards in Attica to stop the riots, called "A New World Prayer," and later wrote a book for youths called "Straight Talk From Prison." A housewife from Chicago was so moved by Torok's prayer that she started to correspond with him. She wrote, "Do you dare to grow where you are?" Torok said that her letters changed his whole way of thinking. After being paroled in 1972 he started matching prisoners with citizens, to help prisoners redirect their lives. To date, he has linked over one million convicts with the outside world, all-volunteer and non-profit.

Private Islands Unlimited
PO Box 22775, Ft. Lauderdale, FL 33335   (305) 587-2031
Dues: $20.00 per year   Contact: Donald C. Ward

Though there is nearly a zero percent chance of setting up your own independent nation or kingdom, tropical dreamers can have their own private island for as little as $20,000! Donald Ward's library and bookstore dedicated to the ultimate in real estate, including where and how to obtain it, is available to club members.

Railroadians of America
18 Okner Pkwy, Livingston, NJ 07039   (201) 956-8273
Founded: 1939   Members: 500
Dues: $23.00 Per year   Contact: A. R. Ward

A New York area group, interested in the preservation of railroad history. Members receive the *Train Sheet* quarterly.

Roo Rat Society
Whitman College, Walla Walla, WA 99362   (509) 527-5229
Founded: 1963   Members: 215
Dues: Write for details   Contact: James S. Todd

Members catch Roo Rats with their bare hands (wearing gloves is strongly recommended), in an effort to appreciate wildlife in a personal way. The rules of the club insist that the wild adult kangaroo rat be set free after capture. Strict records and rules of conduct are adhered to.

Screaming Eagles Users Group
615 Executive Building
35 East 7th Street, Cleveland, OH 45202   (513) 721-4900
Founded: 1983   Members: 250
Dues: $10.00 per year   Contact: David Yaros

Helps owners of Eagle computers to use them better.

Ships-in-Bottles Association of America
PO Box 550, 1022 Park Pl., Coronado, CA 92118 (619) 435-3555
Founded: 1983   Members: 300
Dues: $12.00   Contact: Don Hubbard

Celebrating not only ships in bottles, but houses and trucks, too, the association participates in international shows (Japan, Germany and Norway have many model builders) and publishes *The Bottle Shipwright* quarterly.

The Society in Dedham for Apprehending Horse Thieves
Dedham, MA
Founded: 1810   Members: 7500
Dues: $10.00 lifetime membership   Contact: Warren Wolloff

What do Mikhail Gorbachev, Pope John Paul II, Ronald Reagan, Racquel Welch and Gen. George Armstrong Custer have in common? You guessed it...they're all members of the SDAHT. The society started with a serious purpose in 1810. The founders declared, at the first meeting, "The great number of horses stolen from amongst us and in our vicinity is truly alarming and calls for the attention of every well-disposing Citizen." The last theft was committed in 1906, but that didn't diminish their enthusiasm. New members are cautioned to "stirrup no trouble unnecessarily, but to gallop in the path of righteousness."

Society of Limerents

R.D. 2, Box 251, Millsboro, DE 19966   (302) 934-7067
Dues: Voluntary   Contact: Randall Tennov

A very loose organization of people who share their personal thoughts and stories on the experience of being in love. Randall Tennov, popularizer of the term, uses these in his newspaper column, "Limerence, Secret Love Madness." The group may grow to be more--but ah, who knows what when love's involved.

Society to Preserve the Engrossing Enjoyment of DXing

7738 E. Hampton Street, Tucson, AZ 85715   (602) 296-4773
Founded: 1971   Members: 1300
Dues: Write for details   Contact: John R. Traveslchold

People who enjoy listening to short-wave radio broadcasts.

Sons of the Whiskey Rebellion

PO Box 509, 525 N. Woodward, Bloomfield Hills, MI, 48013 (313) 646-4300
Founded: 1936   Members: 40
Dues: Write for details   Contact: John H. Norris

"Hail Whiskey!! Down with Taxes!!" are the cries of this club of "gentlemen and rebels," seeking to glorify "one of mankind's greatest boons" and eradicate "one of its greatest scourges." Members must be recommended for and elected to membership. Publishes *Bivouac Notice*.

Tattoo Club of America

823 Sixth Ave., New York, NY 10001   (212) 564-7516
Founded: 1970   Members: 16,000+
Dues: Write for details   Contact: Spider Webb

Members include artists as well as people around the world who have been tattooed. TCA awards Mr. and Miss Tattoo each year.

Taurine Bibliophiles of America

106 S. Walnut, LaCrescent, MN 55947   (507) 895-6640
Founded: 1964   Members: 150
Dues: $15.00 per year   Contact: Ross A. Phelps

Interested in restocking your library of books, videos, posters, or magazines on bullfighting? TBA publishes a bi-monthly newsletter called *La Busca* (The Search), reviewing bullfighting books.

Toastmasters International

PO Box 10400, Santa Ana, CA 92711
Founded: 1924
Dues: $24.00 per year

(714) 542-6793
Members: 125,000
Contact: Terrence J. McCann

The world's largest nonprofit educational organization (with 6000 local clubs) is dedicated to helping others improve their speaking, listening and thinking skills. Notables have included King Vidor who joined Toastmasters so he wouldn't make a fool of himself at the Academy Awards. Toastmasters also conducts the World Championship of Public Speaking each year, drawing the best speakers from all the local clubs.

Voicespondence Club

1711 Bellevue Avenue, D-1214, Richmond, VA 23227
Founded: 1953
Dues: $5.00 per year

Members: 500
Contact: Charles Owen

"Tapes convey our moods and our sincerity far more accurately than most face-to-face contacts do." The Voicespondence Club is a non-profit club linking people by tape. "To various degrees" some of the members "are handicapped, but not on tape!" (40% of members are visually handicapped and 60% are over the age of 58.) Over the years there have been lots of marriages through the tape exchange, although Voicespondence is not a lonelyhearts club. One of the nice things about tape is the "ease of participation ("you don't even have to put on your pants to have a friend drop in for a heart-warming visit".)"Even the cheapest recorder will enable you to make good friends."

The history of the club started really in 1948, when the Russians blockaded Berlin and cut off mail to the city. John Schirmer, an employee in the export division of Webster-Chicago was sent an order by the US Air Force for Wire Recording Equipment that the company manufactured (in those days the voice recorders had a reel of magnetized stainless steel wire, not magnetic tape.) The recording equipment was to be airlifted to Berlin, where John's sister and mother were living. With the wire recorders, he had the idea to send a 15-minute recording for his family. The airlift pilot not only was kind enough to comply, but took the Berliners out to dinner and had them make a recording to send back to John. After that, the wires kept flowing on a regular basis. John expanded on the idea and in 1950, the "Wirespondence Club" was formed, the first of its kind. A couple years later when magnetic tape came in the club was reformed as the "Voicespondence Club."

The club tests and reviews recording equipment and supplies in its quarterly bulletin, and includes a list of all members. For the visually handicapped, a tape of each bulletin is made. A separate corporation was set up to serve the blind, The Tarver Memorial Fund. The funds sells recorders, tapes and other equipment to blind members at less than cost.

World Pen Pals
1690 Como Ave, St. Paul, MN 55108   (612) 647-0191
Founded: 1950   Fees: $2.00 per pen pal

"We are the generation of children who have never known peace. We wish to
speak to you for the millions of boys and girls who do not want to see more war..."
started a letter in 1950 from a class of ninth-graders in Minneapolis to the
President of the United States and the United Nations' delegates. The letter
generated a tremendous response, generating World Pen Pals, a United Way
Agency that today links fifteen thousand students ages 12-20 with their
counterparts in 175 countries and territories around the world.

TRADITIONAL HOBBIES

Ye olde favorite hobbies---stamp and coin collecting, cat and dogs, gardening--but with an unusual twist. Take the Error, Freaks and Oddities Collectors, for example.

STAMPS AND COINS

Active Token Collectors Organization
PO Box 1573, Sioux Falls, SD 57101   (605) 334-6277
Founded: 1982   Members: 650
Dues: $15.00 per year   Contact: William H. Clapper

Collectors of merchant tokens from the United States and Canada.

Amelia Earhart Collectors Club
PO Box 1239, Elgin Tower Bldg., Suite D, 100 E. Chicago St., Elgin, IL 60120
(312) 742-3328
Founded: 1974   Members: 600
Dues: Write for details   Contact: Earl Wellman

Collectors of stamps dealing with Amelia Earhart, the first woman pilot to cross the Atlantic Ocean in 1928, and who disappeared in 1937 while trying to fly solo around the world.

American Society of Polar Philatelists
PO Box 945, Skokie, IL 60077
Founded: 1956   Members: 950
Dues: $10.00 per year   Contact: S. H. Jacobson

Collectors of stamps having to do with the North or South Poles.

American Tax Token Society
PO Box 26523, Lakewood, CO 80226   (303) 985-3508
Founded: 1971   Members: 250
Dues: $5.00 per year   Contact: George VanTrump, Jr.

People who collect tokens, receipts, stamps or anything having to do with the collection of tax....anyone for a spare W-2 or 1040 form?

American Vecturist Association

PO Box 1204, Boston, MA 02104   (617) 277-8111
Founded: 1948   Members: 775
Dues: $12.00 per year   Rev. John M. Coffee

Vecturists are streetcar, bus, car wash and subway fare token collectors. Unitarian clergyman John Coffee has a collection of 10,000 tokens that he's traveled all over the country to collect. His token collection contains ones for a sleigh ride at a California resort, cable car tokens, even car wash tokens. *The Fare Box* is published monthly and the convention is held each August.

American Wooden Money Guild

PO Box 30444, Tucson, AZ 85751
Founded: 1975   Members: 350
Dues: $7.50 lifetime membership   Contact: Matt Weich

These people do take wooden nickels...gladly. "Lignadenarists," as these collectors call themselves, trade wooden coins in the newsletter *Old Woody Views*.

Balloon Post Collectors Club

P. O. Box 25, Deerfield, IL 60015   (312) 948-0522
Founded: 1970   Members: 250
Dues: $8.00 per year   Contact: Stephen Neulander

Collectors of stamps dealing with balloons.

Charles A. Lindbergh Collectors Club

PO Box 1239, Elgin, IL 60121   (312) 742-3328
Founded: 1975   Members: 150
Dues: Write for details   Contact: Emily Brown

Collectors of stamps having to do with the great American pilot. Over 750 first day covers have been issued on Lindbergh.

Civil War Token Society

6733 Post Oak Ln., Montgomery, AL 36117   (205) 277-1529
Founded: 1967   Members: 850
Dues: $7.00 per year   Contact: Cynthia Grellamn

Heavy inflation followed the outbreak of the Civil War, and metallic currency was hoarded so intensely that all coins vanished from circulation. In an effort to meet the need for coins, more than 10,000 varieties of tokens were issued, embossed with the names of all sorts of merchants (even undertakers and taxidermists) and towns--usually these were one-cent coins. The society publishes a quarterly newsletter, has a library, holds auctions and educational programs.

Collectors of Religion on Stamps

208 E. Circle St., Appleton, WI 54911   (414) 734-2417
Fonded: 1943   Members: 700+
Dues: $10.00 per year   Contact: Verna Shackleton

With over 12,000 stamps on subjects from Angels to Israel to the Koran, COROS is the oldest topical stamp society in the U.S. No meetings are held, but the *COROS Chronicle* is published bi-monthly.

Combined Organization of Numismatic Error Collectors of America

Box C, Deadwood, SD 57732
Founded: 1983   Members: 900
Dues: $12.50 per year   Contact: Alan Herbert

Misstrikes, double strikes and other minting errors or oddities make up the collections of these coin collectors. *Errorscope* is published monthly.

Dogs on Stamps Study Unit

3208 Hana Rd., Edison, NJ 08817-2552   (201) 248-1865
Founded: 1979   Members: 275
Dues: $2.00 per year   Contact: Morris Raskin

Three thousand stamps with pictures of pooches--from the Hairless Dog of Peru to Disney's Goofy--the DOSSU collects and catalogues them all. Quarterly journal and annual meeting in conjunction with parent organization, American Topical Association.

Errors, Freaks and Oddities Collectors' Club

PO Box 1125, Falls Church, VA 22041   (703) 820-5449
Founded: 1978   Members: 250
Dues: $10.00 per year   Contact: Daniel S. Pagter

No, no, it's not the sideshow. This is a club of stamp collectors who appreciate the imperfections in life...and in stamps. Usually, EFOs are printing or perforating errors that weren't caught by the post office before being sold. Probably the most famous EFO is a 24-cent U.S. air-mail stamp from 1918, with a picture of a biplane in the center---flying upside-down! Due to its rarity, an eager collector might pay over $150,000 for this misprinted stamp. Other, more common errors, freaks and oddities can be found in the bi-monthly journal.

Fairy Tale-Folklore Study Unit

2509 Buffalo Dr., Arlington, TX 76013
Founded: 1976   Members: 88
Dues: $6.00 per year   Contact: Karen J. Cartier

Fairytales, folklore, mythology, nursery rhymes, legends, children's stories, and Disney are all topics on postage stamps collected by club members. *Once Upon A Time*, is published bimonthly, describing not only available stamps, but often includes the stories to match the stamp.

International Association of Space Philatelists

Box 302, Yonkers, NY 10710   (914) 793-1406
Founded: 1968   Members: 550
Dues: $6.00 per year   Contact: William P. York

Collectors of stamps dealing with outer space.

International Primitive Money Society

PO Box 1510, Redlands, CA 92373
Founded: 1974   Members: 50
Dues: $10.00 per year   Contact: John Lenker

Primitive money collecting is a combination of anthropology, archeology and numismatics. Primitive cultures used animal pelts, stones, metal rings and other curious objects for money. Journal and annual convention.

Love Token Society

1832 N. 77th Ave., Elmwood Park, IL 60635
Founded: 1973   Members: 300
Dues: $10.00 per year   Contact: Lloyd L. Entenmann

These tokens are *definitely* not used on the New York City subway. Love tokens are actual dime-sized coins that were given to loved ones in the 18th and 19th centuries, engraved with a sentimental message, a special date or a drawing and complete with a hole or an attached pin so it can be worn as jewelry. Members receive the bimonthly *Love Letter*.

Luminescent Stamp Club

2921 Oakbrook Hill Rd., Oakbrook, IL 60521
Founded: 1978
Members: 120
Dues: Write for details
Contact: Ray Price

Most stamps in the United States today have a phosphorous coating applied to them so they can be read and canceled by high-speed machines.

Parachute Study Group

623 S. Henderson St., Ft. Worth, TX 76104 — (817) 336-0212
Founded: 1974
Members: 75
Dues: $5.00 per year
Contact: Dr. Charles E. Pugh

If a parachuter with a mailbag drops out of the sky, he's not necessarily a postman from Mars. The Parachute Study Group is made up of stamp collectors interested in stamps on parachuting and skydiving. They sometimes arrange special parachute mail drops to commemorate special first day covers.

Perfins Club

2020 Update:
ACTIVE

10550 Western Avenue, Space 94, Stanton, CA 90680
Founded: 1943
Members: 800
Dues: Write for details
Contact: Mrs. Dorothy Savage

What is a perfin? It's an acronym, meaning "perforated initials" or "perforated insignia." Before the age of postage meters, companies would perforate postage stamps with their initials or designs to keep employees from misusing them. Few institutions use them today, yet collecting perfins is still relatively inexpensive, though the rarest perfin from the 1930 Paris Exposition is worth over $300. The Perfins Club can provide the *U.S. Perfin Catalogue*, a virtual bible on perfins.

Post Mark Collectors Club

2020 Update:
ACTIVE

23381 Greenleaf Blvd., Elkhart, IN 46514
Founded: 1941
Members: 1,000
Dues: $8.00 per year
Contact: Robert J. Milligan

If a PMCC says "Kill it! Kill it!," he or she is merely suggesting that the postmaster should cancel or "kill" the stamp on an envelope, usually with black lines, so that it can't be reused. Postmark collectors the world over come to the postmark museum at Historic Lyme Village (only 20 miles from Sandusky, OH!), with its collection of nearly a million postmarks. The Postmark Collectors Club not only worked to establish a museum, but was influential in changing postal regulations so that anyone can get stamps canceled without mailing an envelope...just go to the local post office and ask. Members come from all over the world except Antarctica.

Scouts on Stamps Society International

7406 Park Drive, Tampa, FL 33610
Founded: 1951
Dues: Write for details

Members: 1900
Contact: James A. Muller

Society of Ration Token Collectors

PO Box 12217, San Antonio, TX 78212
Founded: 1966
Dues: $3.00 per year

Members: 250
Contact: Frank Galindo

Anything you want to know about rationing you can find in this virtual storehouse of knowledge about rationing, including ration tokens from all the hard times in history.

Windmill Study Unit

301 Thornridge Dr., Midland, TX 79703
Founded: 1974
Dues: $8.00 per year

Members: 150
Contact: Jim Lunney

Stamps with pictures of windmills and such.

Zeppelin Collectors Club

PO Box A3843, Chicago, IL 60690
Founded: 1968
Dues: $8.00 per year

Members: 200
Contact: Cheryl Ganz

No, they don't store the airships in their garage or basement. These are collectors of stamps, mail, medals, postcards and books all having to do with the ups and downs of those graceful vehicles.

Zeppelin Collector

PO Box A3843, Chicago, IL 60690
Founded: 1968
Dues: Write for details

Members: 300
Contact: Cherl Ganz

Airship stamps.

Zippy Collectors Club, Inc.
118 W. Sixth Ave., York, PA 71404   (717) 843-0451
Founded: 1972   Members: 150
Dues: $6.00 per year   Contact: Sherwood Suereth, Sr.

Postmarks, stamps, or literature having to do with Zip Code, or Mail Early markings. Of course Zippy, the zip code cartoon is their mascot, and their newsletter is called *ZIP/ME*.

CATS, DOGS AND OTHER PETS

2020 Update: ACTIVE

Akita Club of America
2155 Hackamore Pl., Riverside, CA 92506   (714) 684-8230
Founded: 1960   Members: 500
Dues: $15.00 per year family ($10.00 single)   Contact: Sylvia Thomas

This group seeks to ensure the breeding purity of these guard dogs from Japan and helps owners to care for them. *The Akita Dog* is sent monthly to members.

2020 Update: ACTIVE

American Fancy Rat and Mouse Association
9230 64th St., Riverside, CA 92509   (714) 685-2350
Founded: 1983   Members: 100+
Dues: $10.00 per year   Contact: Karen Hauser

"Rats and mice AS PETS suffer from 'bad press'," reports the AFRMA, which is hoping to put the rodents on a par with dogs and cats as family pets. Little-known rat fact: rats grind their teeth when they're relaxed...it's just like purring. People have had domesticated rats for over 200 years. AFRMA members enter their pet rats into a yearly rat show where they are judged for the best color (there are 28 rat colors including lavender, champagne, silver lilac, and beige), brightest eyes and best disposition. (No, they didn't report that last year's contest was a squeaker....) Fancy rats cost between $2.00 and $5.00 and live for bout 3 years. Rats are very intelligent: they recognize their names quickly, you can teach them to jump through a hoop and they can walk on a tightrope (or a shiprope!.) Each rat has its own personality...some are lazy, most are friendly and don't bite. *Rat and Mouse Tales* newsletter.

American Lhasa Apso Club

2344 Greenwood Ct., Macon, GA 31206
Founded: 1959
Dues: $15.00 per year

(912) 788-0570
Members: 600
Contact: Carol Garrett

Lots o' Lhasa Apso owners ought to opt for this (try repeating that three times quickly!)

Associated Koi Clubs of America

PO Box 1, Midway City, CA 92655
Founded: 1975
Dues: Write for details

Members: 25
Contact: Eddie Fujimoto

Koi are a variety of Japanese carp that can do tricks...Eddie Fujimoto says they're "intelligent" (twice as smart as *beagles*.) Eddie's 150 fish range from two to 28 inches in length, bred in different colors. Owners bring their fish to a koi show, where they are judged on the basis of body shape, color and pattern. Eddie publishes *Koi USA* for club members with tips on how to hold and pet your koi and how to tell a boy koi from a girl.

Bichon Frise Club of America

Route 2, Gulch Lane, Twins Falls, ID 83301
Founded: 1964
Dues: $20.00 per year

(619) 566-6578
Members: 300
Contact: Bernice Richardson

Sets the standards for members and breeders of this French-Belgian breed of small fluffy white dogs with "a merry temperament."

International Cat Association

PO Box 2988, Harlingen, TX 78551
Founded: 1979
Dues: $10.00 per year

(512) 428-8046
Members: 2000
Contact: Georgia Morgan

Cat owners and breeders, who enter cat shows.

International Fancy Guppy Association

8904 Peace Dr., Berkeley, MO 63134
Founded: 1965
Dues: $10.00 per year

Members: 35 local clubs
Contact: William St. Clair

Guppy love.

International Llama Association
PO Box 11530, Bainbridge Island, WA 98110   (206) 842-1614
Founded: 1982   Members: 1000
Dues: $30.00 per year   Contact: Sam Granato

Most of the llama breeders in North America belong, as well as many people who have llamas as pets.

Komondor Club of America
1801 Wassergrass Rd., Hellertown, PA 18055   (215) 838-9983
Founded: 1965   Members: 200
Dues: $22.50 per year   Contact: Richard Heaney

Owners and breeders of the Komondor, a rare Hungarian guard dog.

Papillion Club of America
5707 Hillcrest Drive, Detroit, MI 48236
Founded: 1930   Members: 400
Dues: Write for details   Contact: Mary Jo Loye

These are devotees of this rare breed of dog, which weigh five or six pounds and has ears that look like butterflies. *Pap Talk* is published monthly.

Portuguese Water Dog Club of America
One Greenley Rd., New Canaan, CT 06840   (203) 966-0203
Founded: 1972   Members: 325
Dues: $15.00 per year   Contact: Mrs. Herbert Miller,
Jr

Making a comeback from the brink of extinction, the Portuguese Water Dog was originally a working dog who helped fishermen on the Iberian peninsula.

Pug Dog Club of America
61 Fairfax Ave., Meriden, CT 06450   (203) 237-4600
Founded: 1931   Members: 350
Dues: $10.00 per year   Contact: Polly J. Lamarine

Sacred Cat of Burma Fanciers
5542 Cleveland Rd., Wooster, OH 44691
Founded: 1972   Members: 100

Dues: Write for details   Contact: Julie Collin

Owners and breeders of the Burma Cat.

Silky Terrier Club of America

2303 St. Andrew Rd., Jeffersonville, IN 47130   (812) 283-3982
Founded: 1955   Members: 350
Dues: Write for details   Contact: Beverly Lehnig

The Silky Terrier is a toy breed with long hair, no more than nine inches long, originally from Australia.

World Wide Pet Lovers Society

PO Box 36351, Detroit, MI 48236   (313) 882-2244
Founded: 1983   Members: 5000
Dues: Write for details   Contact: Charles H. Tatham

Dear Mary: I have a large bulldog named Harry....
World Wide Pet Lovers Society is an international pen-pal exchange for pet owners.

GARDENING GROUPS

American Gourd Society

PO Box 274, Mt. Gilead, OH 43338   (419) 946-3302
Founded: 1975   Members: 1700
Dues: $3.00 per year   Contact: John Stevens

Information on raising, eating and curing gourds. Newsletter available.

Cactus and Succulent Society of America

2631 Fairgreen Ave., Arcadia, CA 91006   (818) 447-6180
Founded: 1929   Members: 7000
Dues: $6.00 per year   Contact: Virginia F. Martin

For gardeners and nurserypeople interested in growing cacti.

North American Mycological Association

4245 Redinger Road, Portsmouth, OH 45662   (614) 354-2018

Founded: 1960   Members: 1500
Dues: $15.00 per year   Contact: Harry S. Kingston

"Few mushrooms are actually deadly and few have a genuine gourmet appeal," but these most unusual plants intrigue, with "a long history of distorted fantasies." NAMA conducts field trips in prime collecting areas, with lectures on fungi, holds an annual photo contest and has a toxicology committee on poisonous species. Publishes bimonthly *Mycophile* and the journal *Mcilvainea*.

Seed Savers Exchange
Rt. 3, Box 239, Decorah, IA 52101   (319) 382-3949
Founded: 1975   Members: 600
Dues: $12.00 per year   Contact: Kent Whealy

These backyard gardeners are working to save heirloom and endangered garden seeds from extinction--as large seed companies buy up the smaller family-owned companies, heirloom seeds and seeds specially-adapted to different conditions are being dropped from the lines and are becoming extinct. "Passing on our vegetable heritage," members are offered seeds through the Winter yearbook and Fall Harvest Edition.

NOT QUITE THE COUNTRY FAIR

This wacky almanac's for fun seekers, especially those willing to travel.

The Special Days Club...or...National Clean Off Your Desk Day
Box 71, Clio, MI 48420
When: **January 18**   Contact: A. C. Moeller

January 18th is a day of grave national importance. Recognizing that disorder
threatens the efficiency of business, and yes, the capitalist system, National Clean
Off Your Desk Day has been proclaimed on the third Monday in January.
Sponsors say that the taper-off methods of cleanup are ineffective--only a firm
"cold-turkey" approach will do. With vacuum cleaner, snow shovel, and yes,
friends, even dynamite in hand...go ye now to work and find those treasures that
have been lost for years.

Actually, we lied. There is no Special Days Club that you can join as such.
National Clean Off Your Desk Day, Blame Someone Else Day (First Friday the
13th each year), National Goof-Off Day (March 22), Underdog Day (third Friday
in December), Make-up-your Mind Day (December 31st) and others are special
days made up by Anne Chase Moeller and her family (Anne's dad writes the
perennial *Chase's Guide to Special Days*.) Each person in the family sponsors a
different day to help publicize Dad's book. But go ahead and clean off your desk
anyway. Or goof off, depending on when you read this.

Hat Day Education Committee
Glenmont Elementary School
Route 9W, Glenmont, NY 12077
When: **Third Friday in January**   Contact: Peter Rawitsch

The third Friday in January is "put on your favorite hat day," a day to celebrate
head coverings the world over.

Elk Ridge Brown Baggers
Box 24154, Elk Ridge, MD 21227
When: **Last Wednesday in January**

Sponsors of the "Swap a Brown Bag Lunch Day" on the last Wednesday in
January--finally a chance to taste your friends' lunch. (When I was in school, every
day was "Swap a Brown Bag Lunch Day." Especially spaghetti-and-pea-sandwich
days!)

San Francisco Miracles Foundation

1040 Masonic Ave. #2, San Francisco, CA 94117
When: **End of January**   Contact: Jo Anne M. Hahn

Forgive yourself, forgive your family, forgive your neighbors, forgive your country and ultimately, forgive the world during International Forgiveness Week. This celebration of peace is scheduled the same week as the full moon during the sign of Aquarius (about the end of January.)

World's Largest Rattlesnake Round-up

PO Box 416, Sweetwater, TX 79556   (915) 236-6611
Founded: 1958   Contact: Rick Rhodes
When: **Second weekend in March**   Where: Sweetwater, Texas

Started as an attempt by farmers to rid the area of rattlers that were harming the livestock, the World's Largest Rattlesnake Round-up has rounded up over 90 tons of Western Diamondback Rattlers to date. A fundraiser for the "Sweetwater Jaycees," it's held each year on the second weekend in March. The weekend features: The Rattlesnake Review Parade, Miss Snake Charmer Queen Contest, rattlesnake dances, snake handling demonstrations, snake milking demonstrations, meals of deep-fried rattlesnake with a rattlesnake-meat eating contest (we're assured it's a delicacy), snake hunts and snake awards for the largest rattler and most pounds of rattlesnakes brought in.

Eggs on End; Standing on Ceremony

World Trade Center Plaza, New York, NY
32 Broadway, New York, NY 10003   (212) 269-0320
When: **Beginning of Spring**   Contact: The Lower
Manhattan

                                          Cultural Council

It is said that at the moment of the equinox, when the sun crosses the equator into the Northern hemisphere and day and night are of equal length all over the world--at that precise moment in time--then and only then an egg can be balanced on end!! For a number of years, artist Donna Henes and members of the public have gathered around the large circular fountain in the World Trade Center Plaza at the advent of spring and on cue have balanced eggs on their fat ends. Henes, who has an interest in rituals and ceremonies that mark seasonal rotations, says that the Chinese were the original egg balancers, believing it brings good luck throughout the year to the balancers. Depending on wind conditions, the eggs can stand from a couple of minutes to a couple of hours.

Mule Day

PO Box 66, Columbia, TN 38402   (615) 381-9557
When: **Early April**   Contact: Tom Bowman

It's held in Columbia, a crossroads of mule dealing where street sales of mules were so common that the first Monday in April, Mule Day, was known throughout the US as "the day when mule is king." The Mule Day celebration is now held the first weekend in April. The main events of this fundraiser are the mule shows for the prettiest mules and a dozen races and games played on the backs of the mules. Other events include a liar contest for the best farfetched fib, a mule-pulling contest (the noble beasts pull heavy rocks), the Mule Day Parade, the pancake breakfast and the traditional Mule Sale.

Cimarron Territory Celebration

Chamber of Commerce, PO Box 878, Beaver, OK 73932   (405) 625-4726
                                                 Contact: Nancy Calhoun
When: **Mid-April**   Where: Beaver, Oklahoma

Beaver has the de-**stink**-tion of being the cow chip throwing capital of the world. Yessir, home of the annual World Championship Cow Chip Throwing Contest. Their Organic Olympics is replete with a rules book and a logo of a cow chip with arms, legs and crown, standing on top of a pile of dung--so he can see that the people of Beaver really take their...manure...seriously!

The New York Rat Race

New York Road Runners Club
140 East 63rd Street, New York, NY 10021   (212) 319-8760
Founded: 1987   Contact: NY Road Runners
Club
When: **April 15th**   Where: Wall Street, NYC

Celebrating the end of tax season, financial-district runners are required to run this 4 kilometer race in *suit and tie, while holding their briefcase!* Starting at New York's South Street Seaport and winding through the caverns of Wall Street, all of the top finishers received a bottle of champagne and a tin of caviar upon completion. Yuppies on the run!

Mosquitofest

PO Box 932, Stuttgart, AR 72160   (501) 673-1602
When: **Five days in mid-April**   Contact: Sherry Welch

Fish fries, bake sales, a mosquito run and a mosquito-calling contest are just some of the events during this festival, when the town of Stuttgart is abuzz. Blood-sucking is one event not listed.

National Whistlers Convention

PO Box 758, Louisburg, NC 27549   (919) 496-2521
Contact: Allen de Hart
When: **Weekend at the end of April**   Where: Louisburg, N.C.

Professional and amateur whistlers give lectures, seminars and performances of classical and contemporary musical pieces during this festival.

Paris Fish Fry

Paris, TN 38242   (901) 642-1884
Contact: John R. Dunlap, Jr.
When: **End of April**   Where: Paris, TN

The World's Biggest Fish Fry.

Hell Hole Swamp Festival

PO Box 125, Jamestown, SC 29453   (803) 257-2430
Founded: Contact: Elbert L. Howard
When: **Early May**   Where: Jamestown, SC

A town festival that includes a parade right through the local swamp, dubbed "The Hell Hole."

International Chicken Flying Meet

Farm Information Hq., PO Box 330, Rio Grande OH 45674   (614) 491-2225
Founded: Contact: Mary L. Cusick
When: **Mid-May**   Where: Rio Grande, Ohio

Lots of great poultry events, like a prize for the rooster that can crow the loudest or the chicken that can fly the farthest (the record is more that 300 feet.)

Gee Haw Whimmy Diddle World Championship

Southern Highland Handicraft Guild
PO Box 9545, Asheville, NC 28815
Founded: 1980   Contact: Robert W. Gray
When: **First or second weekend of May**   Where: Asheville, NC

"Solve the Whimmy Diddle Riddle and you could be a World Champion"

"What is a Whimmy Diddle, and what is the Whimmy Diddle Riddle?" you may
ask. Well, a whimmy diddle is a mountain folk toy made from laurel wood that
looks like a stick with notches in it and a little propeller attached to the end.
Solving the riddle is to figure out how, when another stick is rubbed across the
notches, the whimmy diddle makes a "gee" or a "haw" sound. The championship
includes a prize for the most unusual whimmy diddle (it must also work) and a
competition for the best "gee-hawer." One winner was a working whimmy diddle
that measured almost ten feet long. Even if you forget *your* whimmy-diddle, there's
lively clogging, singing mountain songs and a Whimmy Diddle dance and concert.

National Hollerin' Contest

PO Box 332, Dunn, NC 28334

Admission: $3.00

When: **Middle of June**

(919) 892-4133

Contact: Ermon Godwin, Jr.

Where: Spivey's Corner, N.C.

Been hearing a fearful racket emanating from Spivey's Corner, North Carolina?
"Helping to revive the almost lost art of Hollerin'," the National Hollerin' Contest
is held the third Saturday of June each year in rural Spivey's Corner, the Hollerin'
Capital of the Universe. Farmers would holler to each other early in the morning
or late in the afternoon, as they were on their way to and from the fields. Many
times a farmer would holler and listen for his neighbor's own unique holler. This
would often happen with several neighbors finally joining in, each one recognized
by his own style of hollerin'. With the advent of tractors and automobiles, the
hollerin' stopped...until revived 18 years ago. Ladies have their own hollerin'
contest, too, and there are conch shell and fox horn blowing sessions, and
whistling contests too.

Old Maids Day Club

224 N. Jefferson St., Allentown, PA 18102

Founded: 1948

Contact: Judith A. Toiomecsek

When: **The first Wednesday in June**

Honoring all old maids and never-married women over the age of 35, with fun
and humor. Roses and daisies are the symbols of the day.

America's Great Teddy Bear Rally

Zoological Society

34th Street and Girard Avenue, Philadelphia, PA 19104   (215) 243-1100

When: **Two days in late June**   Contact: Deborah Derrickson

Kids'll enjoy the talent shows, favorite ancient bears contest, paw reading, best largest and smallest bear, best-dressed bear and bear look-alike contests, too. If your bear is under the weather, take your ailing friend to the Teddy Bear Clinic, where he can be diagnosed, and remedies can be prescribed for eyeball dislocation, thinning fur, seam-splits, or clumped stuffing disorder. "This year, Dr. Sigbear Freud will be consulting for those whose problems run just a bit deeper."

Different Colored Eyes Day
10708 Hawkins Drive, Southampton, PA 18966
When: **July 12**   Contact: Jeanne Fetch

July 12th is the day to recognize and salute people with two different-colored eyes.

Lumberjack World Championships
Hayward, WI 54843
Founded: 1957   Contact: Tom Kelly
When: **Late July**   Where: Hayward, WI

The "Olympics of the Forest" is watched by thousands of spectators, as well as being televised. "Paul Bunyan" types compete for prizes in contests like the speed climb, where contestants climb a 100-foot fir pole and slide back down. Lumberjacks with giant axes cut through 14-inch white pine logs and the most exciting event is the logroll, where two competing "birlers," as they're called climb onto a floating log and try to spin their opponent off balance into the water.

World Championship Bathtub Race
Box 565, Nanaimo, BC Canada V9R 5L5   (614) 753-RACE
Founded: 1967   Contact: Kay Hudspeth
When: **End of July**

This is no ordinary bathtub race...no, the Loyal Nanaimo Bathtub Society, runs this race with a strict code of rules...for example, each tub must weigh at least 350 lbs.....dry. No, the tubs themselves don't float--they are mounted into a boat. The entire rim of the tub must show above the boat and the motor must be mounted on the tub--plus, most importantly--the skipper must sit in the tub (showercaps are not required, though.) At the first race in 1967, "The Bathtub Racing Capital of the World," saw 212 tubs at the starting line. Eighty sunk---one headed for the bottom of the harbor only 30 seconds after the gun, thus becoming the first winner of the coveted 'Silver Plunger' award. When the tubs arrive on the shores of Vancouver after the 34-mile race, the skipper must leap from his tub and run up the beach to ring a bell (not an easy task after sitting in their tubs for three hours.)

The Bathtub Race Festival Week is a time of many special events in Nanaimo. Of course, the main event is the bathtub race from Nanaimo to nearby Vancouver, but other events include the bathtub parade, the World Championship Bathtub Bubble Gum Blowing Contest --- complete with banana-flavored gum. Then there's the Tug-of-war of the Malls, the Egg Throwing Contest, a children's Watermelon Eating Contest, and a Tricycle Race. Each year, a Canadian "Bathtub" dollar is minted to celebrate the event. The first one issued in 1969 is now worth $50.

Friends of Calamari

India Joze Restaurant
1001 Center Street (Next to Squid Row),
Santa Cruz, CA 95060   (408) 421-3554
Founded: 1979   Contact: Tom Ellison
When: **August**

This squid squad felt its beloved and tasty sea creature had an undeserved poor reputation, "The only way squid used to be eaten in this area was if someone, under cover of night, would put on a trench coat and slither down to the docks for a mess of fried squid." India Joze restaurant, in an effort to educate the West Coast about squid started the Calamari Festival in 1979 with the theme "From Bait to Plate." August is now Squid Month, with over 80 calamari dishes on the menu at India Joze. Festival highlights include a squid parade, the Calamari Chorus and a squid art contest--the winner is a provocative art piece made out of squid. (Fortunately, the artists generally prefer to use plastic squid--last year's winner was a squid high-heeled shoe.)

National Peace Day Campaign

93 Pilgrim Rd., Concord, MA 01742   (617) 369-3751
Founded: 1980
When: **August 1**   Contact: Marie M. Strain

The first peace day was August 1, 1980, the Sunday nearest to the anniversary of the bombing of Hiroshima. The Peace Day Campaign is a grassroots organization helping people promote peace via Peace Day Celebrations throughout the country. They pushed for the first Sunday in August to be designated as a "National Day of Peace."

American Publishing/National Jigsaw Puzzle Championship

Hallmark, NJPC, PO Box 747, Athens, OH 45701   (614) 592-4981
Founded: 1982   Contact: Donna Atkins
When: **Weekend in Mid-August**   Where: Athens, Ohio
Entry Fee: $15.00 singles, $25.00 doubles

Over 1000 puzzlers compete against the clock, in the nation's only jigsaw puzzle contest. Teams of two work on 1000-piece eye strainers and individuals can enter with a 500-piece jigsaw puzzle, all competing for cash prizes of more than $13,000. Other puzzle events include the sprints (individuals working on small-- 75-piece--puzzles to find who's the fastest.) And there are the double-doubles, where teams of two work on two small puzzles whose pieces have been mixed and dumped together in one pile. An exhibit of puzzle art is on display at the same time.

Miscellaneous Sun Tanning Contest, Miss Crustacean Pageant & Hermit Crab Races

City Hall, Ocean City, NJ 08226   (609) 399-6111
When: **Middle and End of August**   Contact: Mark Solfer

Just three of the events on the Boardwalk at Ocean City each summer.

Miscellaneous Sunning Tanning Contest: (Held the end of August)
Over 100 contestants enter, competing in categories such as the best left-arm tan (for the driver with their elbow out the window), the best T-shirt tan (for construction workers), the best back-of-the-neck tan, and the best sock tan. Babies with tans can compete in the baby parade. Joggers have an advantage in the "best tanned soles of feet" category. The Count Dracula award goes to the overall palest person. Liz Taylor would have a hard time winning the "palest ring finger" category, but Telly Savalas might find it easy to walk away with the prize in the "golden dome category." The strangest tans are found in the "best design" category. Contestants wear adhesive tape on their skin for weeks at a time, and then sit out in the sun to create unusual tan designs on their flesh.

Official song: "This is my sun tan, my only sun tan" (Sung to "You are My Sunshine, My only Sunshine")

Miss Crustacean Pageant and Hermit Crab Races (Held middle of August)
Started as a publicity ploy, this beauty pageant for crabs is now a regular event at Ocean City. Crabs compete for the coveted "Cucumber Rind Cup." The winning crab stalks down a flowered-decked runway with the "Here it comes, Miss Crustacean" theme playing in the background. Crustacean experts wonder if the contest should be called the "Miss Crustacean Pageant" in as much as it's impossible to tell the sex of these spiny creatures.

Following the beauty show, the thrilling, spine-chilling Hermit Crab Races are held. Over 150 crabs going by the names of "Harvey Wallbanger" and "Mozzarella" to name a few, race (usually into each other) trying to make it to the championship heat. Winners are dubbed "King of Klutz, Grand Champion."

Great American Duck Race
PO Box 8, Deming, NM 88031
Founded: 1980

When: **Weekend in Late August**

(505) 546-2674
Contact: Ed Waggoner,
Chief Quaker
Where: Deming, NM

Waddlers compete against each other in a contest of speed, agility and patience. Duck owners plead with and prod their feathered friends down a 17-foot long track, sprinting to victory. The weekend is complete with a Duck Queen Ball, horseshoe tournament, parade and tortilla toss.

Toad Suck Daze
PO Box 969, Conway, AR 72032
Contact: John Ward
When: **End of August**

(501) 327-6621

Where: Conway, Arkansas

Town residents differ on the origin of the name of this festival---the popular story is that a visitor who stopped near the town said that residents of the area sucked on jugs of moonshine until they "swole up like toads." Events include toad-jumping competitions, baby races, tobacco-spitting, and cow-chip throwing contests.

International Town Criers' Championships
Collins' Bank
Historic Properties, Halifax, NS, Canada, B3J 1S9   (902) 429-0563
Founded: Contact: David B. Webster
When: **Mid-September**   Where: Halifax, Nova Scotia

Town criers from around the world come to Halifax competing with their own individual song-styles. This is one of the only events in the world for the dying art of Town Crying.

Mule Skinners Festival
PO Box 2627, Ruidoso, NM 88345
When: **Middle of September**

(505) 257-5888
Contact: Melvin Means

Mule races and contests in Ruidoso. It ends on a high note with the mule auction.

Cabbage Patch Scarecrow Contest
Peddler's Village, Bucks County
PO Box 218, Lahaska, PA 18931
When: **Last weekend in September**

(215) 297-8733
Contact: Carla B. Coutts

Held the last weekend in September, this is an annual contest to design and create a "bigger-than-life" scarecrow. Many entrants spend the whole year collecting the pieces and parts to make their scarecrows. Visitors to Peddler's Village pick the winners in the categories of most unusual and original scarecrow, and the best traditional scarecrow.

Ask A Stupid Question Day

Flint Journal, 200 E. 1st St., Flint, MI 48502

When: **September 30**   Contact: David Larzelere

"To encourage curious people to overcome their timidity and ask that "stupid" question."

World's Wristwrestling Championship

Argus-Courier

830 Petaluma Blvd., N., Petaluma, CA 94952(707) 762-4541

When: **October**   Contact: Bill Soberanes

Known as the "Wrist Wrestling Capitol of the World," Petaluma holds contests for men and women in classes ranging from featherweight to heavyweight.

Whole Enchilada Fiesta

PO Drawer CLC, Las Cruces, NM 88004   (505) 526-0385

Contact: Sam Craft

When: **Beginning of October**   Where: Las Cruces, New Mexico

The climax of this festival is the building of the world's largest enchilada--it's seven feet in diameter and sits on a steel plate. Then it takes a two-story crane to lower it into a gigantic pot.

Hello Day International

Box 993, Omaha, NE 68101

When: **November 21**

On November 21, World Hello Day, say hello to ten strangers. Heads of state from 85 nations have endorsed this activity for promoting world peace.

Giant Tinkertoy Extravaganza

Franklin Institute
20th and the Parkway, Philadelphia, PA 19103   (215) 448-1200
Founded: 1977   Contact: Robin Lynch
When: **Thanksgiving**   Where: Franklin Institute,
Phila.

Something special happens each year at Thanksgiving, inside the domed hall of the Franklin Institute. Thousands of giant Tinkertoy pieces are placed at the foot of the statue of Ben Franklin. Under the watchful eye of Ben, these spokes and spools are constructed into bridges, buildings, airplanes, and abstract sculptures by builders of all ages.

Tinkertoys were invented by a tombstone cutter from Illinois and were first available in 1914. The extravaganza has over 15,000 participants, and is held the three days following Thanksgiving. The Franklin Institute is one of the nation's first science museums, dedicated to "learning by doing." Admission to the Tinkertoy Extravaganza is included with the regular museum entry.

Chitlin' Strut

Town Council, PO Box 484, Salley, SC 29137   (803) 258-3485
Founded: 1966   Contact: Brenda Walker
When: **Late November**   Where: Salley, SC

"Fust yuh gits yuh self a set of chitlines bout three yards long, " reads the Annual Chitlin' Strut Souvenir Recipe, "I knos a lady over in Alabama whut laks em topped off wif whipped cream; dats what she say." Held the first Saturday after Thanksgiving, the Strut began as a fundraiser for the small town of Sulley, South Carolina. At a recent Strut, more than 10,000 pounds of chitlins (strips of fried, breaded hog intestines) were "inhaled" along with bar-be-que from 50 hogs and 1,500 chickens by some 35,000 visitors. But the Chitlin' Strut competition is the main attraction. It was described by one local reporter as "a kind of a dance. It looks like a clogger on Valium." There is also a hog calling contest and the official Chitlin' Strut parade and the country music show.

RETURN TO SENDER...ADDRESS UNKNOWN

Club detectors...can you help us find these lost groups, meeting in secrecy somewhere in this vast country?

American Society for the Conservation of Gravity
Contact: Darwin Crum

"The United States, with only six percent of the world's population, uses 59 percent of its gravity" and "a single moon rocket launching uses more gravity in a few moments than the entire world used during *all* the 18th century," according to the American Society for the Conservation of Gravity. Darwin Crum, ASCG's chairman, is doing what he can to conserve and protect what remains of "our most precious terrestrial resource." He's even tried contacting President Reagan and petitioning him to reduce the size of the ton to 500 pounds. Members receive a "desktop gravity status indicator, which provides an at-a-glance check of gravity in the immediate area." The membership package also includes a scratch-and-sniff patch duplicating the "sweet smell" of a manned space capsule after 18 gravity-free days of flight. Crum says that ASCG scientists are researching gravity alternatives, such as "synthetic gravity, or new gravity mines." Crum is even contemplating black-hole towing as a last-ditch effort.

American Walking Society
Founded: 1980

Barf Bag Collectors Association
Providence, RI
Contact: Dan Hillman

Pan Am, Delta, Swiss Air, even Air India...if your seat pocket is missing the ubiquitous bag with the airline insignia, a barf bag collector may have sat there on the flight in. Dan Hillman has over 250 bags--from the first bag issued by Pan Am on their clipper flights 50 years ago to the brown no-frills People Express Bag (soon to be a *real* collectors' item.) Hillman says the bag most frequently used in the industry is the hot-pink Air Mexico bag...he could only guess why.

Bobs International

St. Paul, MN
Contact: Bob Idso

A club celebrating the Bobs of the world.

Challenger 7 Fund

Contact: Maurice Magly

A nationwide project to construct a new space shuttle for NASA, funded by public contributions.

Gay and Lesbian History on Stamps

Founded: 1982

Impotents Anonymous

Chevy Chase, MD
Contact: Eileen MacKenzie

The problem of impotency hits 10 million men, yet until I.A. started, each one was alone. In our society that idolizes virility, the emotional pain can be devastating.

International Society for a New Atlantis

Founded: 1983

Man will return to the sea! International Society for a New Atlantis was interested in worldwide colonization of the seas. They conducted "research" on the feasibility of living in the sea, as a way of solving problems of mineral resources, water, plants and overpopulation.

National Snurfing Association

Snurfing is the sport of snowskiing on a skateboard-sized board.

Shrine O' Stuff

Livingston, NJ
Contact: Richard Szabo

First there was SpaghettiOs and Jell-O, but to Richard Szabo and Richard Crater collecting O's was O! so much fun. The Shrine O' Stuff is their collection of 900 things that have O's in the brand name. The shrine is located in Crater family's 1950s bomb shelter. To qualify for inclusion, the "O" can be surrounded by dashes, as in the "Back-O-Door shoe rack, or can be followed by an apostrophe replacing the "F" as in Bag O' Fruit Artificial Fruit. The two lifelong friends started their collection with a toy called Bag O' Bees which buzzed. After realizing that Bit-O-Honey candy, Wint-O-Green Life Savers and Land-O-Lake butter were just the tip of the iceberg, they built their collection like Balls O' Fire Fluorescent fish bait. "It's pop culture, something that's around you in everyday life," said Richard Szabo. While their Shrine O' Stuff is not an honest-O-goodness club, they do accept new entries to the shrine. Recent acquisitions include the Drip-O-Lator teapot and the Bunn Pour-O-Matic coffeepot.

Society to Hunt Crocodiles in the New York Sewers
New York, NY

We've heard that there is a group in New York that hunts the elusive albino "sewer crocodile"---any leads?

Society for the Promulgation and Encouragement of Amazon Conduct and Attitude
Contact: Velvet Rhodes

Men were made to serve women, she said. "Men are mutants...imperfect beings who can only find true happiness when they are worshiping and serving women." Velvet Rhodes at 175 pounds is "Amazon Supreme." (In Greek mythology, the Amazons were male-hating female warriors who took themselves so seriously that they cut off a breast in order to operate their bows more efficiently.) Rhodes says that there is nothing wrong with slapping a guy around a bit when he gets out of line. "All men secretly want to be ruled by women," she said. "After all, the natural order is a matriarchal society." I want men in the kitchen where they belong. I want them doing my washing, making my bed, sweeping my floors. Men are tremendous domestics. They aren't built for the rigors of corporate life. Look how many of them die of heart attacks and peptic ulcers. I want men to kiss their women's feet on command," she growled. "And I want them to like it. Men have brainwashed women for centuries...made them slaves. It is time for women to stand up and slap men down to their proper place." 60% of the group member are men... of 1,500 members worldwide, 900 are men. Men who join are put through a four-stage training program, beginning with the lowest level and ending with "chevalier"--a man who has learned to accept the "Twelve Basic Amazonian Principles." Offices in New York, and Chicago.

Sue Club

Girls and boys named Sue unite! Further information appreciated.

World Organization to Restore Male Supremacy...or....WORMS
Contact: Bob Fenton

These WORMS say that there are "just too many groups for the advancement of
women." Founder Bob Fenton adds, "and who are they advancing against? Men,
that's who." The WORMS creed states that "males are supreme and our objective
is to make one woman a day SQUIRM." Fenton had the idea for the group for
years, but it wasn't until the nomination of Geraldine Ferraro for the Vice
Presidency and when the Jaycees had to admit women, that he invested his time
and money in getting the group started. Members get a Certificate of Lifetime
Membership ($5.95), plus a wallet-sized membership card, WORMS pin and a
bumper sticker. When asked about the acronym, WORMS, Fenton said, "you
know, when women get disgusted with men, when they've reached the limits of
their endurance, they'll say: 'Why, you...you worm you!"

GONE BUT NOT FORGOTTEN

Too wonderful to overlook, too inactive to put anywhere else, these clubs have served their purpose admirably. (They've brought back red M & M's and heralded the departure of Howard Cosell--a fair trade, no?)

100 Tons of Fun

This was a sports event open to people weighing in at over 200 pounds (with relay races, leapfrog and the like.) Unfortunately, this event is not run anymore-- probably for obvious reasons.

American Cricket Growers Association
Founded: 1969

Wholesale distributors and growers of crickets who conduct the National Cricket Race, and maintain a "Cricket Hall of Fame."

American Tarantula Society
Founded: 1979

Dale Lund folded his 500-member organization after he got sick and tired of answering questions about what tarantulas eat and how one can tell their sex. Apparently, Lund's tarantulas named Alice Brown and Sar liked the time to themselves, though.

American Tentative Society
Founded: 1970

Dedicated to the view that all knowledge is tentative--after ten years of operating, they couldn't fix on any policy, members or activities.

Buffoons of America
Founded: 1981

An association of amateur pranksters, whose motto was: "Buffoons are just happy clowns." They elected the King Buffoon of the year.

Citizens for a Quieter City
Founded: 1966

Helping to create awareness of the noise problem, this New York City-based group helped stimulate interest in noise abatement projects, helped get legislation passed and promoted "Quiet-Week."

Cuspidor Hitters Association Worldwide...or...C.H.A.W.

Tobacco chewers unite!!

Enough is Enough Club
Founded: 1980

"Get Howard Cossell off Monday Night Football!!!" they yelled and won. Johnny Carson used to say that Cossell was "a legend in his own mind." Group members minded his "Constant unnecessary chatter" and his abrasiveness. They started their campaign with a boycott of sponsors' products, explaining the reason to clerks and shopowners. Then there were the letters of complaint to advertisers and a "Boot Howard" bumper sticker. Well, it worked; as of the 1985 football season, he was off the air!

Flying Psychologists
Founded: 1960

The group died last year when only three shrinks could come to terms with their interest in flying (could it be a repressed fear?)

Golden Onion Dome Club
Founded: 1980

The people of Winooski, Vermont wanted to build a transparent dome over their fine town. Residents of Winooski, with its harsh winters, thought that an energy-saving dome covering the town's 1.3 square miles would be a good idea. But like most good ideas, it failed after naysayers brought up little problems, like who was going to clean it, or what happens if a plane crashed into it or what happened if a 50-inch snowstorm hit?

Ice Cream Connoisseurs Club
Founded: 1983   Contact: Robert B. Heller

Ice cream lovers would meet at parties and ice cream tastings, deciding if Ben & Jerry's or Hagen Daz, or Baskin-Robbins made the grade.

International Dull Men's Club
Founded: 1980

Promoting a sense of pride and brotherhood among dull men. "Be out of it and proud of it" and resist trendiness whenever possible, said club president Joseph L. Troise. One club member said "Dull men drive Chevies and drink Budweiser. They would never let Perrier touch their lips." Their goal was to plunge the entire country back into the early 1950s (Authors note: so *that's* who elected Reagan!) The club launched a dull Hall of Fame, inducting dull stars like Ozzie Nelson, Robert Young of "Father Knows Best," economist Milton Friedman and Walter Mondale.

Jewish Penicillin Connoisseurs Association
Founded: 1985

Nothing kills the sniffles like a hot bowl of chicken soup. The magic of the broth is known world over, but only in the homes of Jewish mothers does it reach world-class proportions, baffling even chemists at the Salk Institute. The Jewish Penicillin Connoisseurs Association was a short-lived group, billed as "a consortium of Jewish mothers, grandmothers and related perpetrators of 'old wives' tales.'" Too bad it's disbanded, though--because once and for all the truth would be known-- my grandmother's chicken soup is really the best.

Milkbottles Only Organization (MOO)

MOO was a group of avid milk bottle collectors.

Mistresses Anonymous

Help for women who were involved with married men. Members received *The Triangle Tabloid*.

New Games Foundation
Founded: 1974

Inventor Nancy Miller would hold two- or three-day workshops where adults could try new games that promoted trust, communication and "new possibilities for fun."

North American Man-Boy Love Association

We are purposely going to leave this one blank...it's your guess!

Official E.T. Fan Club

When the film E.T. was at the height of its popularity, kids would send letters filled with crayoned pictures of the Extra-Terrestrial one and Elliot. Sometimes the envelopes were quite colorful, too--addressed only to "E.T. in Hollywood" Even so, many made their way to the official E.T. Fan Club in Illinois.

Overeaters Victorious

They believed in "dieting with Jesus." Members were urged to read God's Answer to Fat by Francis Hunter and More of Jesus, Less of Me by Joan Cavanaugh. Ms. Cavanaugh says, "Only buy foods that Jesus, or John or Peter would buy. God gives us the good stuff. I can't imagine Jesus Christ coming out of the supermarket with twelve bags of potato chips, one for each apostle."

Parents of Punkers
Founded: 1981

Though no longer in existence, Parents of Punkers has to rate as one of the most unusual organizations of all time. Serena Dank was a counselor who knew the "Punk Rock" world like no other adult ever has. She was able to bring young teenagers back together with parents, save these kids from certain drug deaths and provide probably the only adult, responsible contact they had.

Serena, a white, middle-class, unassuming woman, worked with violent Hispanic female gangs in Los Angeles in the 1970s. Through this, she was introduced to one gang member who was a "punk." This young girl became close to Serena and took her into the underworld subculture of the punks. Serena vowed to learn everything she could about the punk rock scene. "I was leading a double life," she said, leaving her suburban home in the station wagon and going to the clubs and hangouts. At this time, about 1980, no one really understood what it was all about. The radical costumes, the violence, and the music were escapes for young teens with poor home lives. The scene served to further separate them from their families.

Serena decided in 1981 to place a small ad in the *Los Angeles Times* for Parents of Punkers. Within 48 hours, over 200 parents had contacted her. The need and success of the organization were overwhelming, and Serena gave up her entire life for it. She was interviewed on local and national media, including the Donahue show and *People* magazine. She would get calls from kids and parents at all hours of the day and night. She would work with the kids in her home and have weekly working sessions with the parents. Her young children knew more about the punk world than most psychologists did. Finally, it had to end. There were death threats on her message machine from unstable kids, warning that she and her children would die in 48 hours. But the real deciding factor was the breakup of her marriage. "It probably wouldn't have worked anyway," she said, "but the work just quickened the breakup." We honor Serena Dank and her devotion to people who are in trouble.

People's Transit Inc.

Help for hitchhikers was a toll-free call away when People's Transit was around. Thumbers could find out directions or advice 24-hours a day.

Pet Switchboard

Owners of lost pets would phone the toll-free Pet Hotline, to report their pet missing. When someone found the dog or cat, they would call the hotline and a match was made.

Rosalea's Hotel's Volunteer Nobility
Founded: 1966

The townspeople of Harper, Kansas didn't know what they were missing when they forced Rosalea's Hotel out of business. What Roselaea Hostetler operated was probably the most eccentric hotel in the United States. Visitors to her seven-room flaming-red inn were greeted with incense burning in a lobby decorated with a green shag rug and tinfoil wallpaper. Guests could choose between the Lily Tomlin shrine room with posters and pictures from Tomlin's greatest characters, or the "Mom's Apple Pie" Room, equipped with a steamer trunk filled with wigs and lingerie and a sign reading "Fulfill your fantasies in the privacy of your own room." Of course all hotel guests were invited to use the Jesus Bathroom. Her fans (The Volunteer Nobility), mostly hippies, feminists, artists and gays loved her "oasis in the Bible Belt," but the people of the town hated her. To them, Rosalea was the devil in disguise--so a baseball bat waited in the lobby to greet the most "vocal" neighbors.

Society for Connoisseurs of Murder

Detective and mystery lovers---fictional or factual.

Society for Indecency to Naked Animals

This society was started as a hoax by comedian Alan Abel. The purpose was to promote the idea that cows, pigs and other animals should wear underwear to preserve their modesty.

Society for Lost Causes
Founded: 1981

Founder Joel Shreck said, "We realized that almost everything that ever succeeded in the world began at one time as a lost cause for someone, whether it was the automobile or the rocket ship or the bicycle." The group had three purposes: to recognize lost causes that should be saved, to recognize successes that should be lost and to encourage those who gave their best, only to fall flat on their face. Well, now that the Society for Lost Causes is a lost cause, we say "nice try!"

Society for the Restoration and Preservation of Red M & M's
Founded: 1982

It seems that they may have succeeded after years of valiant effort. Red M&M's are back! They were taken out after the 1976 red dye health scare. "The rest of the colors are pretty dull," says Hethmon. "We need red in there to liven up the mixture." For $2.97 members received five sheets of official stationery, one official wallet-sized membership card, and four issues of *The Red M & M Newsletter*. The group seems to have disbanded though, since through the miracles of modern science, and the persistence of hundreds of letter-writing M&M lovers, someone has created another way of making a red M&M. (How 'bout straightening out the Middle East, guys?)

Son of a Witch

Members are men who are "proven lineal or collateral male descendants of witches or person accused, tried, convicted or executed as witches."

Students to Save Baltic & Mediterranean Avenues
Formed: 1973

Atlantic City would have never been the same, if it weren't for this group. They, in conjunction with the Monopoly Players though the United States, caused the Atlantic City Commission to hold a hearing on the proposed name change of Baltic and Mediterranean Avenues. The arguments were so convincing that the bill was dropped.

Tricycle Racing Club of America

No, this was not a society for toddlers---in fact, most tricycle racers were senior citizens, sprinting on large three-wheelers.

www.ingramcontent.com/pod-product-compliance
Lightning Source LLC
Chambersburg PA
CBHW031051250726
48655CB00004B/1388